A PASSION FOR JUSTICE

To Gertie
With best wish
John
Jany 2015

A PASSION FOR JUSTICE

Social Ethics in the Celtic Tradition

Dr Johnston McMaster

Irish School of Ecumenics,
Trinity College Dublin, Belfast

DUNEDIN

Publication of this book has been assisted by the generosity of
The Collum Cille Trust, Edinburgh.

Published by
Dunedin Academic Press Ltd
Hudson House
8 Albany Street
Edinburgh EH1 3QB
Scotland

ISBN 978–1-906716–04–2

Typeset by Makar Publishing Production
Printed in Great Britain by Cromwell Press

Dedication

For Lilian, a wonderful sister.
In living you were 'health to the ailing' (Columba),
in dying you showed us faith as courage,
giving us the gift of vulnerability and hope.

Contents

List of Illustrations

Acknowledgements: Figures 1.1, 1.2 and 2.1 are reproduced by permission from Richter, M. (2005) *Medieval Ireland* (Gill & Macmillan, Dublin). Figure 6.1 is reproduced with kind permission from Ó'Ríordáin, J. J. (2003) *Early Irish Saints* (Columba Press, Dublin).

Preface

As Ireland enters into a new phase of peacebuilding with the hope, at last, for a new and shared future, the story of early Irish or Celtic faith communities provides insights, models and inspiration for a new Irish story. Documents and sources provide us with a profile of people, often struggling to live faithfully and ethically in their social world. How did they do it and how did the Christian faith motivate and shape their faithful response?

In every age faith and ethics are inseparable. The approach to contemporary religious education has recognised this, whether religious or theological education with young people or adults. How we live in the world, at the heart of community is crucial. It is of particular relevance in this twenty-first-century moment of opportunity in Ireland, a *Kairos* moment, God-given and filled with the possibility of transformation and change. We are now lured and beckoned towards *Shalom* and it requires ethical responses.

A Passion for Justice will explore this early Irish or Celtic Story of people and personalities, their stories part history, part myth, in Celtic perspective both powerful means of recognising truthful ethics. It will be important to recognise the context for their social ethics and then explore the lives of some of these saints and their socio-ethical praxis. From this we will identify key Celtic socio-ethical themes and attempt to connect these with contemporary challenges to build an ethical community, inclusive of human and environmental relationships. The chapters on social ethics, in characteristic Celtic style, have a triune structure. Each chapter begins with an overview of the contemporary ethical issue, followed by an exploration of biblical perspectives. The chapters then develop insights from the early Irish and Celtic tradition using early poetry and writings. The focus on the Irish Celtic experience is not intended to exclude other Celtic regions, but to show within an Irish context, and in the contemporary context of an Irish peace process, that there is a rich Irish Celtic ethical tradition with contemporary resonance.

The final chapter explores the spirituality of Celtic ethics, the spiritual resources that inspired, motivated and shaped ethical praxis. The theo-poetics, theo-myths and theo-ethics of an early Celtic Christian heritage can echo across the centuries and fire the imagination and commitment for a new moment in Irish history. As explorers of history we can become history makers. Out of a shared past we can build a just peace and a shared future. In connecting the social ethics of the Irish Celtic tradition, we are, in the words of the medieval mystic Eckhart, 'Back in the house you never left.'

This book had its origins some years ago in an exploratory meeting in Armagh hosted by Rev. Dr Wilbert Forker. Wilbert shared his dream of an educational legacy in the Celtic tradition. The publication of this book has realised something of Wilbert's dream and I am grateful to him for his inspiration and patience. My thanks also to Sr Brighde Vallely O.P., former lecturer at St Mary's University College Belfast, and Rev. Robert Brown, former lecturer at Stranmillis University College Belfast, for their encouragement during the writing process. As religious educationalists they saw the need for such a text.

Colleagues on the Education for Reconciliation team of the Irish School of Ecumenics Belfast have helped in very practical ways. Karen Nicholson has word-processed most of the chapters with help from Arlene Poole. Both, but especially Karen, have transposed what often resembled my ogham script into a legible text! My grateful thanks to them. I am grateful also to my colleague Dr Cathy Higgins for her critical perspective and preparation of Key Points and Test Questions.

The writing process was delayed in the beginning by the illness and untimely death of my sister. In one of my last conversations with her I promised to dedicate this book to her. I hope that what I have written on an earlier page is a fitting tribute to her memory and continuing presence in life's 'thin places'.

Johnston McMaster

July 2008

Foreword

by President McAleese

UACHTARÁN NA hÉIREANN
PRESIDENT OF IRELAND

Writing one hundred years after that almost primordial event in modern Irish history, the Famine, and a lull of fifty years before the coming into being of the Celtic Tiger, the poet Patrick Kavanagh re-imagined the meaning of the Great Hunger in his poem of the same name, not merely as a physical hunger but as a spiritual hunger which was choking the potential of the young country where 'life dried in the veins of these women and men'. Almost seventy years later, it remains a siren reminder of a human need felt by many, for completion not just at the quotidian, material level, but at a more fundamental and transcendent spiritual level also.

A Passion for Justice addresses this need head-on. It forms a thorough, wide-ranging study of those elements of the Celtic tradition, which, sharpened by the lens of Christianity, give us what Dr McMaster terms the Celtic Social Ethics – of hospitality, forgiveness, compassion, gender equality, environmental care, justice and peace building. Context permeates every corner of this fascinating book: having located each ethic squarely in its original context, and traced its evolution through history, Dr McMaster states clearly the relevance of each ethic to the present day. He takes the ethic of hospitality, for example, from its treatment in Biblical texts, in Celtic times, and in monastic times, right through to the present day and its applicability to current issues such as immigration.

It is testament to the calibre of the author that he has condensed such vast tracts of thought and diverse sources into such an eminently readable, relevant text. Moreover, Dr McMaster has chosen to publish this book at a highly opportune time. For the first time, a combination of peace, prosperity and education has afforded this generation of Irish men and women the possibility of determining their country's future afresh, of being less in thrall to the pull of history, more cognisant of its capacity to stifle, more confident in the writing of their own chapter. It is a kind of rare zero-hour – Dr McMaster refers to a *Kairos* moment – when the decisions we make in today's opportunity-laden moment will sow seeds that will be reaped for generations ahead.

CONTEXT FOR SOCIAL ETHICS

1   Socio-Political Roots

Today's brand name is Celtic. We are familiar with Celtic Twilight and Celtic Tiger, Celtic Spirituality and Celtic jewellery, Celtic tenors, Celtic Christmas, Celtic seaweed baths, not to forget Glasgow Celtic and Boston Celtics. In a newspaper feature the Irish journalist Fintan O'Toole claimed that Celtic Ireland is all bogus.[1] 'There never was a Celtic invasion of Ireland or Britain.' Celtic identity was invented in 1707 when it was first suggested that Celtic languages spread to Britain and Ireland through migration. For various reasons this argument had great appeal, especially in nineteenth-century Ireland, not least with the rise of cultural nationalism and the so-called scientific racism debates of the same era. The danger and legacy of these nineteenth-century imagined identities are all too obvious.

O'Toole's claim is that our ancestors were not Celts, they were copycats. This is a reference to the Iron Age material culture evident in findings from northern Europe as far east as Prague. The culture is described as La Tene in Switzerland, characterised by highly decorative art, abstract and fantastic. La Tene culture belongs to a period from 600 to 100 BCE. According to Frank Delaney: 'the term "La Tene" defines the essential vision of the Celts and their civilisation, marks their major cultural presence in Europe, when their attitude, personality, style, came of age.'[2]

Whether or not the people of La Tene culture described themselves as Celtic or not may be debated, but an extensive and distinctive culture did exist with considerable influence on much of Europe. We do not know if a European Celtic consciousness existed and there are still major problems in defining Celts and Celticness. Ethnic boundaries are fluid and blurred and language is an imprecise identity marker. What we do know of a people generally comes from their neighbours. Archaeology provides us with La Tene and this cultural phase represents 'the *Floruit* of Celtic civilisation'.[3]

Such art has been unearthed in Ireland but it is limited. The oldest La Tene object was a gold buffer torque found at Knock, Co. Roscommon. A more established presence in Ireland is indicated by a decorated bronze scabbard found in a Co. Antrim bog at Lisnacrogher. Barry Raftery claims that: 'These objects are unquestionably the products of local workshops.'[4] It is the 'local manufacture' argument that convinces O'Toole. 'What did happen in the Iron Age is that an emergent aristocracy began to adopt the international style they knew from trade and other contacts. Local craftworkers produced their own versions of Celtic chic – a bit like us copying Gucci or Prada. It was a way for the knobs to distinguish themselves from the yobs'.[5] From this perspective La Tene style art in Ireland was not an ethnic identity marker but a status symbol, a sign of wealth and power.

Raftery, though, is not completely dismissive. These finds are evidence of craftworkers of 'the highest accomplishment, thoroughly in command of all the intricacies of La Tene technology and art'. Significantly he adds: 'It is difficult not to suppose that included in their number were master-craftsmen from abroad who played a part in the introduction of these complex innovations'.[6] Undoubtedly there were Irish La Tene craft skills and it may have necessitated a European La Tene cultural presence, but in no large invasive numbers. Those who did arrive here perhaps left the European mainland just before the second century BCE. It is only on this small scale that we can speak of Celtic immigrants and we have no idea about the numerical relationship between such immigrants and settled population. 'All we know is that the Celtic element was not originally indigenous to Ireland'.[7] We cannot go beyond this and need to have a healthy scepticism about the romanticism of the nineteenth century. All is interpretation and there was little foundation to nineteenth-century claims, especially in relation to nationalism and racism. We are often dealing with invention and propaganda. When and how Ireland became Celtic is a 'persistent conundrum'.[8]

1.1   Political Roots

The first people, nomadic hunters, arrived in Ireland around 10,000 years ago. The island on the edge of the western seaboard was probably the last place in western Europe to be inhabited. Prehistory remains in the far distant mists of time. Like the different layers of soil and rock visible on a cliff face, Ireland's population is multi-layered. There is no pure Irish race, or pure any race for that matter. We have no monochrome ethnicity or racial purity or ethno-cultural homogeneity. We are a hybrid people among whom the term 'native' is a misnomer. Immigration we have always had and still have. The Iron Age itself, when La Tene art or a local version of it became evident in Ireland, was a genetically mixed era. Marianne Elliott asserts that: 'Prehistoric Ireland was a considerable racial mix'.[9]

This is important for the sense of historical and political roots. The ideas of Celt and Celticism have been made definitive of authentic Irishness and have been at the heart of nineteenth- and twentieth-century Irish nationalism. This has created an in-group, out-group, an exclusive and excluding identity with serious consequences for modern Irish history and Irish lives. There is no historical continuity through a common gene pool. 'There was no single, original Gaelic or Irish race, just as there were no discernable natives in the sense of an original people than whom all others and their descendents are less truly Irish'.[10]

In contemporary Ireland where we are trying to embed a peace process and the ethics of peacebuilding, ridding ourselves of an ideological Celtic myth, especially of racial

1.1   Ireland 800 C.E. provinces and principal sites.

purity, is imperative. Acknowledging the failure of violence to resolve problems, both state and paramilitary, and crafting a more inclusive identity characterised by diversity, including the latest wave of immigrants, will require a realistic and critical appraisal of history. We may need to acknowledge that Celtic is a nineteenth-century invention and that no people in Ireland BCE or in the centuries following described themselves as Celtic, neither racially nor culturally. Those who accepted Christianity did not speak of the Celtic church either.

This does not necessarily mean that we should drop Celtic as a shorthand description, albeit a modern one for a broad shared cultural tradition. There are linguistic, musical, poetic, spiritual and artistic connections between Ireland, Scotland, Manx, Wales, Cornwall and Brittany. It is the racial and ethnic claims that are dangerous as well as misleading and delusional. The shared common threads, cultural, spiritual and linguistic, each with their own diversity, can use the umbrella Celtic. It is shorthand for a particular self-consciousness and distinctiveness as in Nordic and as such can be celebrated. It is in this shorthand way that Celtic is used in this book.

The hybrid people who lived on this island were never invaded by the Romans. Britain was occupied and colonised but not Ireland. Invasion was considered and a small landing force was gathered near modern-day Stranraer. Agricola believed that no more than a single legion would be required for the conquest of Ireland. Ireland's population was around half a million. Agricola was diverted by the troublesome Caledonians. Roman occupation of Scotland was a more pressing problem. Somewhere north of the Perthshire Highlands Agricola put the Caledonians to the rout. Agricola was recalled after the battle of Mons Grampians. Lowland Scotland was occupied by the Romans, 'but the Highland tribes reclaimed their freedom and were never penetrated by the Roman legions'.[11]

Ireland remained free from Roman presence but not altogether from Roman influence. The two islands have always been neighbours and trading did not cease because the Romans were over there but not here. Roman coins have been found in Ireland suggesting two-way traffic. The slave trade operated in both directions. Patrick, later famous for his contribution to Irish Christianity, arrived first in Ireland as a Romano-British slave. Yet Ireland did not have a centralised Roman administrative system as did Britain and much of Europe. Ireland's political system was decentralised.

The basic unit of administration was the *Tuath*, meaning tribe as well as territory inhabited. There were as many as 100–150 *Tuatha*. Each *Tuath* had a king, Rí, who was wedded to a goddess to ensure the welfare of the kingdom. This also contained the idea of fertility. The king's responsibility was to rule the people in times of peace and to be the military leader in times of war. He presided over the annual assembly but he himself was never above the law. Every king had a special judge, *Brithem Ria*, 'whose duty it was to decide cases in which the king's rights were involved'.[12]

In this ancient world there were three levels or degrees of kingship. The king of the *Tuath* was bound by personal allegiance to a superior king, who in turn was bound to the provincial king. This involved tribute and help in war to the superior king but did not allow the superior king to have authority over the territory or people of the subordinate.

Ireland did not have a geopolitical centre but two locations did have power over grazing land, Tara and Cashel. In practical terms Ireland was divided by a line roughly from Dublin to Galway. The northern half was known as *Leth Coinn* or Conn's Side, and the southern as *Leth Moga* or Mug Nuadet's Side. Both Conn and Mug were mythical figures.

In prehistoric times Ireland had five provinces. These were Ulaid, Lagin, Mumu, Connachta and Mide. Today we recognise four of the provinces as Ulster, Leinster, Munster and Connacht. The ancient fifth was Meath with its centre at Tara. The division of five kingdoms gave us the word *coiced* or fifth, from which we have 'province'.

'In the fifth century we merge from myth and legend into the world of history,'[13] and at this point we are dealing with four provinces. The idea of a high king, Ard Rí, has no basis in history. From the ninth century some powerful kings did try to impose a single, powerful kingship on Ireland. Brian Boru did so in 1002, but even if that did establish a high kingship it only lasted until the Norman invasion in 1172. Ireland's political state from the beginning of history to the eleventh or twelfth centuries was decentralised. As the Roman administrative model provided the diocesan model for the British church, so the decentralised Irish political model provided the administrative shape for the Irish church. This was true until the eleventh century when a more centralised, diocesan model was introduced by ecclesial-political reforms.

1.2   Social Strata and Legal System

Early Irish society was highly stratified. Writing and therefore history came with the Christian monks. They did not confine their writing to sacred texts and scriptures, but also copied down the cycles of myths and legends. It is from one of the great Irish myths that we have a profile of the social structure of pre-historical society.

The Ulster Cycle provides the epic, *The Cattle Raid of Cooley, Táin Bó Cúailnge*, one of the great pieces of European literature. The 'Earliest preserved manuscript dates from around 1100, although it is generally assumed that older written versions, which are now lost, went back as far as the seventh century.'[14] The Ulster Cycle is a large corpus of heroic tales based on the *Ulaidh*, the ancient people of Ulster. The *Táin* is part of the Cycle. It is a military-political myth without historical basis, except that the external details, weaponry and dress, reflect a real-life period. The hero is Cúchulainn, a young warrior of amazing strength, who single-handedly it seems defeats Queen Méabh of Connacht. 'The great slaughter on the plain of Muirtheimlne' is all part of the battle over the stealing of the brown bull of Cooley. Cattle raiding was a typical practice of warrior kings in this period. Cattle was wealth and power and the Ulstermen had been raided by their Connacht neighbours.[15]

There are four basic themes in the story:

- rivalry between Fearghus and Conchobar;
- struggle between the Ulaid and Connachta peoples;
- contest between the bulls;
- heroic exploits of Cúchulainn.

The rivalry has to do with the Ulster kingship and reflects ancient rituals. Méabh may be the female personification of Tara sovereignty and symbol of Connacht power. The bulls have a mythic background and may provide evidence of a special bull cult. Cúchulainn may be a sacred personification of war and a cult figure of some group. The Ulstermen may have enjoyed telling and developing the story as a foil to Connacht's expansionism. This is not history but powerful myth and the external details reflect life and culture in prehistoric times.

The society described in the *Táin* is stratified. There are kings, noblemen and officials. The warrior hero thrives in a militarised and conflictual society. Heroes are born and battles reveal their status. Cúchulainn in Conchobar's court was how young men were educated and initiated into war. The warrior had a strict code of honour and fought from a two-wheeled chariot often in single combat. The head of an opponent was a battle trophy to be displayed. Feasting was part of culture at court and every court had musicians and poets. The poet was also the historian and reciter of genealogy. He did not fight in physical battle but often composed poetry consisting of defamation and maledictions. All of this is reflected in the *Táin* and provides a window on pre-historic society.

When writing was introduced, the Irish legal tracts provided windows into post-fifth century society. Irish society was hierarchically structured, the three degrees of kingship illustrating the top of the social pyramid. Though the kings had power they did not make or maintain law. Law was the people's responsibility. Legal scholars settled legal cases and by the eighth century the king was not above the law. There was the practice of fasting against the king and thereby forcing him to acknowledge and pay reparation for wrongs. 'If he allowed the person on hunger strike to die, he had to pay compensation to the injured kin.'[16] Such fasting was not only possible against the king but also the defendant could be anyone. Fasting was from sunset to sunrise and if the defendant disregarded the fast and refused to pay he lost his honour. In an honour-shame society this was serious. Compensation was estimated according to damage done and according to the rank of the injured party. Honour-price of the victim determined the fine.[17] Justice, especially in its restorative mode was part of the Irish legal system in historic times.

The Irish legal system had two sources. There was law inherited from the pre-Christian past. It may even be claimed that the legal code, originating in ancient history, pre-dated the arrival of any Celtic people in Ireland. There are issues addressed which are not part of any Celtic tribal culture and life. The second source is in Christian law making. At this stage in development the church took over an inherited legal system and drew on its own laws to enrich it. This was now Christian law for Christian people, reflecting a church with some power and within a Christendom model, the roots of which go back to the fourth century and Constantine's Edict of Milan. When Irish law is first recorded it has been heavily influenced by Christianity. The earliest law texts are seventh century.

The largest collection of law is *Senchas Már* meaning the Great Tradition. It dates from the eighth century and its source is possibly in Armagh. Legal issues dealt with are: pledges, fosterage, kindred, clientship, relations of lord and dependant, marriage, personal injuries, public liability, theft, title to real estate, law of neighbourhood, which has to do with trespass and liability, honour-price and the contractual obligations of clergy and laity.

There is also a Munster collection *Bretha Nemed*, focusing on poets and learned classes and the relationship of clergy to society.

Much of the above is described as *Brehon Law* and was the law of Ireland from the earliest historical period to the Anglo-Norman invasion of the twelfth century. It is *Brehon Law* which provided for the hunger strike and the principle of fasting against a superior in order to enforce a claim against the superior. Three responses were possible: to concede

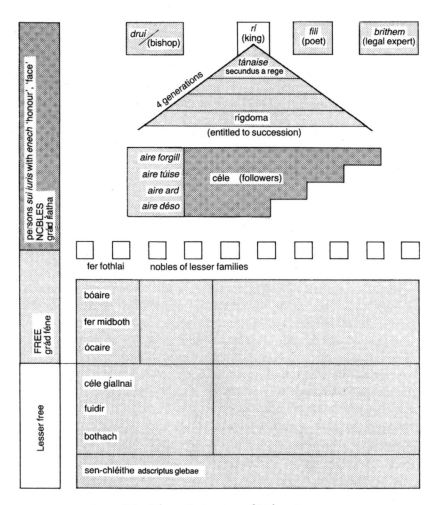

1.2   Schematic structure of Irish society.

the claim, begin a counter-fast, or let the hunger striker fast to death. The purpose of this had to do with land but there was an irony in the law. If the hunger striker died during the fast the superior could be charged with the capital crime of murder.

At the top of the judicial structure was the *Brithem* or judge, the paid interpreter of law and the one who was the arbitrator in cases of justice. Such a legal system was in place when Christianity first came to Ireland, probably in the fourth century. Certainly this was the legal system encountered by Patrick when he arrived sometime in the fifth century.

In the following centuries the church reworked the legal system in the light of its own developing canon law. Key to this in Ireland was Ruben of Dairinis near Lismore. Ruben died in 725 CE and his canon law collection was known as the *Hibernensis*. It has been described as a remarkable piece of work, drawn up outside a Roman environment, and 'a comprehensive legal framework for all aspects of Christian life'.[18] Clergy, it seems, were often the lawyers.

Within the political unit of the *Tuath* there were further sub-divisions. The different levels each had their own honour-price. They were nobility, freemen, lesser freemen and serfs. A free person was a legal person in his own right and owned land and was obliged to offer for military service in conflict situations. The noblemen had a retinue of lower-class free persons. A serf became such on failure to pay an honour-price and therefore 'sold' himself to his master. Serfs could also be prisoners brought from battle.

Druids were important, on a par with poets and judges or legal experts and would undertake training lasting seven to twelve years.

The *Tuath* was the political unit and the community to which one belonged and within which there was protection and safety. The communitarian nature of the unit was also emphasised by communal responsibility for individual rights through enforcing the honour-price.[19] Economically the *Tuath* was also self-sufficient.

1.3   Demographics

It is wrong to see Ireland at this time as a densely populated island. It was not and there were more trees than people.

> Ireland instead had between a quarter and a half million people settled along its coasts, rivers, lakeshores, and her uplands. They lived in fortified homesteads or small clusters of huts, and to survive they farmed and herded. Even their warrior leaders were farmers.[20]

This rural community was largely involved with cattle. Wealth and social position were measured by cattle and the honour-price was paid in cattle or female slaves. It is thought that only 5% of cultivated land was used for crops.[21]

Early Ireland was a kinship society, a network of family relationships. Kin determined personal identity. 'Kinless men were landless outlaws.'[22] Kinship or family was the foundation model for social organisation. The extended family was the basic landholding legal unit. The *FINE*, as the extended family was known, owned the kin-groups land. The *FINE* protected any of its members from becoming clients of a wealthier person and was liable for defaulted rents. It was also a farming co-operative protecting and supporting its members. The kinship model was essentially a community model with a community ethic. No Roman model existed in Ireland and when Christianity took root the monks and nuns turned to the model they knew and structured the monastic framework within the community political structure. Communities were organised on a communitarian basis whether ecclesial or political and both were really concentric circles. Kinship provided the socio-economic structure and legal rights. Kinship offered an ethical basis for community and at the heart of the community model was often a passion for justice.

Key Points from Chapter 1

❏ There was never a Celtic invasion of Ireland or Britain.

❏ Evidence of La Tene cultural influence in Ireland from archaeological finds of highly decorative art may indicate small-scale Celtic immigration to Ireland from Europe before the second century BCE.

❏ Celtic element was not originally indigenous to Ireland.

❏ No pure Irish race existed. No original Irish people, no racial purity, Celtic is a nineteenth-century invention connected to development of Irish nationalism.

❏ Ireland was never part of Roman Empire, therefore did not have centralised administrative system; the Irish political system was decentralised.

❏ The decentralised Irish political model provided the administrative shape for the Irish church until the eleventh century, when a centralised, diocesan model was introduced.

❏ The Táin is a military political myth about the Ulster hero Cúchulainn's defeat of Connacht's Queen Méabh when she and her army attempted to steal the brown bull of Cooley.

❏ The myth reflects life and culture in prehistoric times; a stratified, communitarian, militaristic and conflictual kinship society based on the Tuath that operated an honour-shame code.

❏ Irish legal tracts described as Brehon Law shed light on post-fifth century society and were operative until the twelfth century. Law was the people's responsibility. Restorative justice was part of the legal system.

❏ Earliest law texts were recorded in the seventh century and they reflect Christian influence i.e. Ruben of Dairinis. The largest collection of law dating from eighth century is Senchas Már.

❏ Brehon Law was in place when Christianity came to Ireland in fourth century.

Test Questions

❏ Explain the following Irish terms: Tuath, Rí, Brithem Ria, Coiced, Táin Bó Cuailnge, Táin, Bretha Nemed, Hibernensis and Fine.

❏ Comment on the claim that at the heart of early Irish society there was a passion for justice. Justify your answer.

2   Religio-Historical Roots

2.1   Pre-Christian Ireland

Pre-Christian Ireland was religious. It was so religious that Frank Delaney can claim that his Irish ancestors 'took to Christianity with ease, adroitness and piety'. The voyage from oaken grove to communion with Christ may have taken several thousand years, but when it came it 'offered everything the Celts already had – and more'. Delaney is enthusiastic and almost ecstatic. 'Finally, just as Celtic civilisation reached its apogee, the Celts encountered this Son of God. And – glory be! – he, it was found, was human like themselves and he surrounded himself with real people, the saints.'[1] According to this the faith was not new, the impulses and symbols of pre-Christian religion were confirmed in Christianity.

Certainly when Christianity came to Ireland it took root, unlike elsewhere, without bloodshed. There were no early martyrs for the new faith which might suggest an easy journey, even a relatively smooth acceptance by local culture. Perhaps those who first heard it felt that they had always known it! Or it could be that pre-Christian ritual, symbols and imagery long survived the introduction of the Christian faith. Old habits or practices die hard!

In the Cúchulainn myth the custom of collecting the heads of slain warriors as war trophies is evident. There are Irish churches where stone heads are part of the decorative masonry. At Killeshin in Co. Laois the west doorway has a single head. The better known St Brendan's Cathedral at Clonfert in Co. Galway has twenty heads in the richly decorative west doorway. On Boa Island in Lough Erne, Co. Fermanagh there is a back-to-back, Janus-faced figure. Ireland has a number of stone heads and they are among the most significant in Britain and Ireland. They appear to be both pre-Christian and Christian and in many cases there is little agreement or understanding of their meaning.

The god Lugh was known in Europe, Britain and Ireland and appears frequently in place names. There is little other evidence of gods' crossing over. In the myths of origin we encounter 'the tribes of the goddess Danu'. After a mythical battle of Moytura, Lugh arrived in Ireland, and because he possessed 'all the arts' he was accepted as leader. In this battle all the gods assemble to reclaim Ireland from the older gods. After the battle Ireland is the sole possession of the gods of the *Tuatha Dé Danann*.

Danu is the mother-goddess referred to in the Mythological Cycle, a collective term describing those stories in Irish literature reflecting the activities of other-world characterers.[2] The *Tuatha Dé Danann* literally means 'peoples of the goddess Danu'. That this goddess was worshipped in Europe is reflected in several names such as the Danube. In Ireland, though, Danu is associated with the land rather than the rivers. Two mountain tops in Co. Kerry are known as 'the Two Paps of Anu'. An early text calls Ireland 'the land of Anu'.[3]

The main deity was Daghdha. The Daghdha was characterised by hugeness, generosity and a voracious appetitie.[4] Above all, he was known as 'the good god', not in any moral sense, but 'good for everything' – a leading magician, a redoubtable warrior, an artisan – all powerful, omniscient'.[5]

It is not possible to summarise a system of pre-historical belief and nothing can be called 'theology' in any modern sense of the term. Yet it is clear that from the mythology these early people lived in a sacral world, a world of gods, spirit and the supernatural. Nora Chadwick draws attention to 'the naturalness with which men, women and the gods meet and pass in and out of the natural and the supernatural spheres. In many circumstances there does not appear to have been any barrier'.[6]

The year itself moves around the rhythm of four seasons, a spiritual rhythm. The year began on 1 November with the festival of Samhain. At this festival all the barriers between humans and the other-world were down.

Imbolc was next on 1 February and was a fertility ritual associated with the lactation of ewes. A goddess Brigid was associated with this pre-Christian festival and the Christian church incorporated the festival and the goddess into a Christian St Brigid's Day.

Beltane was the May Day festival on 1 May with fertility ritual playing a significant part. Fires were lit and cattle were driven between them with people dancing in a sunrise direction.

On 1 August Lughnasadh connected with the god Lugh. This was a harvest festival but again stock-rearing emphasised the cattle currency of early Irish society.

The other-world intersects with this world. 'The Ireland of the tales comprises two worlds, 'real' and 'other' but the time between them is not well demarcated'.[7] The 'other' is an idealised version of the real one, its location unknown, sometimes to the west or over the sea. In the Irish other world the joys of life are endless, hunting, feasting and love making. It is a place of beauty. It 'contains little that is ugly. There is no sin and no punishment. There are few monsters, nothing to cause alarm, not even extremes of climate. There is no serious warfare, no lasting strife … The heathen Irish erected a spirituality, a spiritual loveliness which comes close to an ideal spiritual existence'.[8] It was into this spiritual and ethical climate that Christianity took root. Perhaps the new faith was not so new and not so strange.

2.2 Early Christian Ireland

The popular story is that Patrick brought Christianity to Ireland in 432 CE. There is no historical basis for the date or for Patrick as Apostle of the Irish. Patrick was in Ireland, arriving sometime after 432 CE but was not the original missionary or apostle, nor did he single-handedly convert the whole of the island. His activity was confined to the northern half. Christianity was in Ireland perhaps a century before Patrick. It may well have had three sources.

Christian Slaves from Britain

Slave trade was a vital part of the economy and raiding parties operated in both directions across the Irish Sea. Patrick himself first came to Ireland after being captured by an Irish raiding party to Britain.

Christianity arrived in Britain first. There are no records but Tertullian writing in 200 CE claims that there are places in Britain which 'have yielded to Christ'. Origen in 240 CE alludes to the Christian faith as a unifying force among the Britons. Early martyrdoms for the faith appear to have taken place in Britain between 250 and 260 CE.[9] Three British bishops are recorded as attending the Church Council at Arles in 314 CE, and also at the Synod of Rimini in 359 CE. It is probable that some of the slaves brought to Ireland were Christian and were the first to introduce the Christian story.

Trading Routes

Trading was another channel by which the faith story entered the island. Ireland had trade routes with mainland Europe and perhaps even North Africa. West Cork was the Irish recipient of a lucrative wine trade. The skull of a Barbary ape found at Navan Fort, Armagh, suggests an Irish African route before the fifth century. North Africa at that time was strongly Christian. In the first century the faith had travelled from Jerusalem to Rome by trading routes and by traders. The same kind of channel was undoubtedly open to Ireland.

Refugees from Gaul

Refugees fleeing from oppression and persecution are not new. It was the cause of population movement from Gaul and Britain in the fourth and fifth centuries. The earlier movement was probably from Gaul, where the Christian faith had taken root in the second century. The church in Lyons was sufficiently strong by 177 CE to attract persecution, with its bishop being among its martyrs. Between 250 CE and the Edict of Milan in 313 CE dioceses were established in Gaul, based as elsewhere on Roman imperial administrative divisions. Fourteen bishops represented these dioceses at the Council of Arles in 314 CE.

Much of this territory was invaded by barbarians at the beginning of the fifth century creating a flow of refugees, some of whom may have arrived in Ireland with their Christian faith. This may be described as an unplanned infiltration of the faith rather than a missionary strategy. In all probability it was another channel for faith into pre-Christian Ireland and is part of the context for the more strategic event of 431 CE.

The one authentic date we do have for Christian faith in Ireland is 431 CE. Prosper of Aquitaine was a leading opponent of Pelagius, possibly an Irish-born lay theologian who was causing problems in Rome to the unity of the church. Prosper was also the informant of Pope Celestine. Celestine sent Germanus, bishop of Auxerre, to Britain where Pelagian views were considered to be corrupting the British church. A certain Palladius had suggested this course of action to Celestine. He may have been the same Palladius, who two years later in 431 CE – so Prosper tells us – was sent to Ireland. 'Pope Celestine ordained Palladius and sent him as first Bishop to the Irish who believe in Christ.'

In other words there were already Christian believers in Ireland and Palladius was sent as a bishop, not primarily an evangelist but overseer and nurturer. Did Pope Celestine fear that the small Irish Christian community was also contaminated by the so-called Pelagian Heresy? There is no record of where Palladius landed. Strangely there is no authentic record of Palladius or his Irish episcope. Yet:

> Despite the fact that Palladius disappeared almost without trace from the historical record, in Ireland and in his native Auxerre, his formative influence on the earliest Irish Christianity cannot be denied. There can be little doubt that the tentative first steps in organising the first Irish Christian communities were made by him and his companions.[10]

He was not to become the apostle to the Irish or be remembered in any significant way in Irish Christian history. He disappeared as quickly as he arrived 'subsumed in the all-devouring Patrick legend.'[11] Or, maybe, he was later a victim of Armagh's power politics where propagandists rubbished him to elevate Patrick and advance Armagh's claim to primacy in Ireland.

Patrick was not the 'Apostle of the Irish'. That too is an exaggerated claim. His significant contribution was in the northern half of the island and the only authentic documents we have on Patrick are his letter to the soldiers of Coroticus and his Confession. They are both remarkable documents providing down-to-earth insights into a very human and humble servant of God who incredibly returned to Ireland having earlier been a victim of slavery. Yet he returned to spend the rest of his life there enabling transformation to take place among the very people who had ill-treated him.[12]

Patrick also came as a bishop from the British church as his confession makes clear. Leaders of the British church opposed him and sought to discredit him to the end of his life. Yet he came to the northern half of Ireland with a twofold task. He came to pastorally care for Christians already present in the region and to proclaim the gospel to any non-Christian Irish who would listen. It is likely that in coming from the British church Patrick brought the diocesan system of church organisation with him. He certainly set up local churches under the care of bishops, priests and deacons. But this system was

2.1   The most important Irish monasteries.

based on the Roman administrative system, while Ireland had a decentralised system of governance, politically shaped by 100–150 sub-kingdoms. As Ireland was a 'totally rural island, the normal church organisation found in Britain and continental Europe could not be applied'.[13]

We know very little about the church Patrick founded or nurtured during his lifetime. Information is very fragmentary, but we do know that in the sixth and seventh centuries monasteries began to develop in Ireland and became the centres of Christian life and church government.

The Monastic or Community Model of Church

Because of the lack of Roman influence and structure 'the way was open for the Irish church to evolve in its unique fashion'.[14] The monastic model was more suited to Ireland's rural and decentralised socio-political life.

The origins for monasticism lay elsewhere and they say something about the external relationships that influenced Ireland. The monastic tradition came from Egypt via Gaul, Wales and Whithorn in Galloway, Scotland. Two of the important persons in the Egyptian desert tradition were Anthony and Pachomius. Around 285 CE Anthony went off into the solitude of the desert and for twenty years lived in total isolation. But many followed him to the desert and about 305 CE he re-emerged from his solitude to teach and direct life in the community. The model of living together in a religious life was taken further by Pachomius. By the time he died in 346 CE he had founded nine monasteries for men and two convents for women. The monastic model spread to many places not least to Gaul through Martin of Tours and then through Martin's pupil Ninian to Whithorn and to Wales. If Patrick had introduced a diocesan system it was, in little over a generation after him, overtaken by monasticism. It was at Whithorn that the founders of northern monasticism were educated. These were Enda of Aran, Tighernach of Clones, Eoghan of Ardstraw and Finnian of Moville. The influence of the desert tradition lives on not only in Irish place names like Desertmartin, combining both desert and Martin, but also in the location of communities in wild places. Ireland had no deserts but it did have wild, isolated, off-shore islands like Skellig Michael.

These monasteries were characterised by study, prayer and work. Built inside ring forts the important buildings were the church, kitchen, dining room, scriptorium and guest-house. They were open communities, interacting with local people, providing education for children and engaged with the rural community. Some like Clonard, Glendalough, Moville and Bangor were the early universities of Ireland. Life was characterised by austerity, prayer (private contemplation and communal), the hours of prayer, manual work and study. Each monastery had a rule of life; no two in Ireland appear to have been the same. The monasteries were centres of prayer and worship and if we are to judge by Adamnan's *Life of St Columba*, describing life on Iona, and the Bangor Antiphonary and Stowe Missal, then the Eucharist was central to the worship of Irish monks. There was intense exegetical work on the scriptures and a remarkable learning output. Scholar-monks produced 'hymns, religious poems, prayers, martyrologies, sermons, liturgical material, hagiographical works, calendars, annals and chronicles, letters, voyage and vision tales, prophesies, Latin grammars and treatises of a scientific nature'.[15]

The monasteries were also characterised by leadership in the hands of the abbot and not a bishop. Bishops were 'retained for their sacerdotal and sacramental functions but seemingly shorn of real authority'.[16]

By the late sixth century wanderlust had become the characteristic of a number of monks. Voluntary exile from the shores of Ireland was a living martyrdom, in some cases to spread the gospel, in others to take Irish forms of monastic life to the centre of the Christian world. Columcille, or Columba, was one of the first to leave behind his high status in Irish society and travel to Iona to found a monastery which became a strategic base to evangelise the Picts of Scotland and the Saxons of northern Britain. Fursa travelled from eastern Ireland to northern Gaul to establish monasteries. Perhaps the best known of the Irish pilgrims for the sake of Christ was Columbanus, who left Bangor with twelve monks, including Gaul, and established monasteries throughout central Europe, ending his days at Bobbio in northern Italy. In 613 CE he wrote to the Pope: 'We Irish who live at the ends of the Earth are followers of Saints Peter and Paul and all those who wrote the Scriptures under the direction of the Holy Spirit. We teach nothing beyond the truth revealed in the gospels and by the Apostles.'[17] Into the seventh century these Irish pilgrims journeyed to Britain and mainland Europe bringing culture, learning and gospel to places as far away as Kiev.

In relation to the Irish story and the building of the monastic model of church, the heroes are not Pallidius nor Patrick. 'Perhaps we should look rather to the great monastic founders of the sixth century as missionaries who effectively built a new and different kind of church and who may well have evangelised the people of the Tuatha,'[18] (the sub-kingdoms).

The monastic model lasted until the twelfth century. During those centuries it was not always heroic. The image of the golden age of Irish Christianity needs to be tempered. This was not a church independent from Rome but always in critical communion with the Bishop of Rome. Power could and did corrupt. In the eighth century a new office appears in the Irish monastic church, 'Royal Abbot'. This reflects growing abuses of power as some monasteries became rich and were caught up in 'dynastic struggles of the warrior aristocracies'.[19] Monastic violence coincided with the adoption of princely tithes and the loss of celibacy with the perpetuation of dynastic power. Columba's great foundation at Durrow was caught up in violence in 776 CE and Clonmacnoise, Armagh, Glendalough and Kildare were regularly attacked and burnt: 'tribal violence and dynastic power struggles ... came close to destroying Christianity in Ireland from the tenth century onwards'.[20]

Situations like this called for reform and there were various reform movements. The most notable was the Celi De in the eighth century. Sometimes known as the Culdees (750–900 CE), which means 'serving companions of God', this movement was founded by Mael Ruain of Tallaght in 750 CE. It was a return to old monastic ideals, discipline and obedience; choral duties were reintroduced, as was care for the sick, poor and travellers. Personal asceticism was renewed, which led to the rocky foundation of Skellig Michael off the Kerry coast. Most important was the 'Rule of the Celi De' which tried to define the functions of the bishop, priest and benefactor of the monastery. The Eucharist was also returned to a central place. It was a renewal movement but was limited in halting the decay of the monastic system. A major political trauma blocked the growth of the monastic movement and ultimately prevented its survival. The political trauma was the Viking invasions. By the time the Vikings had done their destructive work and begun to assimilate into Irish culture and life, including building Ireland's first towns and urban areas, the Celi De reform was exhausted. Irish Christianity was about to move beyond the monastic era.

2.3   The Twelfth-Century Irish Church: Romanisation and Anglicanisation

Not all had been lost of the Celi De reform. In 921 CE Gothfrith, the king of Norse Dublin, attacked Armagh. Significantly 'he spared from destruction the prayer houses with their communities of Celi De, and the houses of the sick, and also the monastery except for a few buildings which were burnt through carelessness'.[21] Even a pagan Norse king recognised the value of the Celi De monastic heart and treated it with respect. But great changes were taking place, changes that few churches in medieval Christendom had to undergo. It began early in the twelfth century with a major attempt at church reform and the twelfth century ended with a loss of political independence for Ireland and lordship over the country claimed by English kings.

'Gregorian reforms' was the title given to the twelfth-century reform movement from Pope Gregory and an assertion of papal authority. Reform began outside Ireland with the role of two Italian archbishops of Canterbury, Lanfranc and Anselm. The Norse had converted to Christianity and in their newly built towns they established episcopal sees. A Non-Irish episcopate looked to Canterbury for consecration and allegiance. In 1074 CE Lanfranc consecrated the first Norse–Irish bishop. Six more consecrations followed, four for Dublin, one each for Waterford and Limerick. 'These Norse–Irish bishops swore canonical submission to Canterbury and that in a form which acknowledged Canterbury's primacy over Ireland.'[22] Lanfranc and later Anselm were now involved in Ireland and from time to time they sent letters of rebuke. From surviving letters we have some idea of their concerns. Lanfranc wanted to get rid of certain evils – defective marriage law and sexual ethic, maladministration of the sacraments, excessive manipulation of bishops and simony.[23] Anselm listed two faults. These were marriage practices, saying famously: 'It is said that men exchange their wives as freely and publicly as a man might change his horse.'[24] His other concern was the consecration of bishops without their having a defined territory for pastoral care, i.e. the Roman-based diocesan system.

The impetus for reform had begun and in Ireland it was initially led by Munster. In 1101 CE a council was held at Cashel. Three important things happened. Cashel was a king's seat but it was handed over to the church without any lay involvement or conditions. It was to become an archbishop's seat. Furthermore a conciliar programme of reform was begun. And third, the bishop of Munster presided over the council, not only as chief bishop but also as papal legate with the authority of the Pope. This was a different direction for the Irish church. Cashel's decrees dealt with simony, clergy quality, freedom of the church, clerical celibacy, clerical privilege and marriage law.

Ten years later another council was held at Ráth Breasail in 1111 CE. This council set about restructuring Irish episcopacy. Gilbert, the bishop of Limerick, was now papal legate as well as president of the council. In the earlier system every little community had a bishop under the monastic abbot. Lanfranc had complained about it; too many bishops, too little power. Also the Irish church was not diocesan and these many bishops had no jurisdictional power. This was further compounded by the fact that many abbots were lay persons. Episcopal power was being undermined. So Gilbert produced a 'diagrammatic representation of the hierarchical pyramid' ... At the apex sits Christ whilst beneath him are his vicar the Pope, flanked by Noah, Christ's Old Testament prefiguration and the emperor, head of the hierarchy of the lay world.'[25] This was very clearly a hierarchical and patriarchal system. The bishop had power, not the abbot. Ráth Breasail aimed to carry on the reforms of ten years earlier enforcing good conduct on the whole church and what was really new; it saw the establishment of territorial dioceses. What the Pope had ruled for England in the sixth century was now to be the model for twelfth-century Ireland: two provinces, Armagh and Cashel, with twelve dioceses each.

Key to reform was Malachy, native of Armagh and bishop. He developed a close personal relationship with Bernard of Clairvaux, the great Cistercian. Bernard considered Malachy's task immense: 'he had been sent not to men, but to beasts ... shameless in their morals ... so unclean in their life ... In the churches was heard neither the voice of a preacher nor of a singer.'[26] Bernard also described Malachy's activity. 'Barbarous laws disappeared, Roman laws were introduced ... the sacraments were daily solemnised, and confessions were made ...'[27] The most significant activity of Malachy was to introduce continental monasticism to Ireland. Augustinians and Cistercians were introduced. Mellifont became the first Cistercian foundation and a centre for reform. On his way to Rome for papal approval for reform structures, Malachy died at Clairvaux, but he had set the pace for reform and there was no going back. The council of Kells–Mellifont in 1152 – presided over by the papal legate Cardinal John Paparo – adopted a new and more extensive diocesan system. The Norse–Irish dioceses were integrated, the link with Canterbury cut, Armagh was affirmed as the primal see, four provinces were established each with their archbishop: Armagh, Cashel, Tuam and Dublin. There were then thirty-eight dioceses in Ireland, and these have more or less remained to the present in the Catholic and Church of Ireland structures. Ireland was now in line with Rome and the process of Romanisation was advanced. The early monastic church was disappearing.

By the mid-twelfth century Ireland was a volatile country, which was now open to the wider politics of Christendom. Ireland lost its political independence and was ruled by foreigners. English kings became lords of Ireland. It is a complex story, quite different from the popular ideological version. Dermot MacMurragh, a deposed Irish king, went to Wales to enlist Norman help in recovering his throne. He returned with Richard, earl of Pembroke, Strongbow and regained his power but in the process threatened the independent politics of Ireland. The Normans liked power and saw an Irish future, so much so that the Anglo-Norman king Henry II arrived in 1171 to control his own people. Henry took oaths of loyalty from leading Irish rulers. He was concerned about the Irish episcopate and required Bishop Christian from Mellifont to preside over a national council at Cashel in 1172.

Henry was in Ireland because of the Pope's gift. In 1155 Pope Adrian IV 'granted and donated Ireland' to Henry, the papacy having concluded that the religious well-being of

Ireland demanded its political subjugation to English kings. The key phrase in relation to Henry was 'and the people of that land should receive you honourably and reverence you as lord'.[28]

That is precisely what happened at Cashel. The Irish bishops without question accepted Henry and Henry's position was validated by the Pope. Now 'all the laws and customs which are observed in the realm of England should be observed in Ireland'.[29] As time went on, not only did the papal validation hold good but the proportion of English bishops in Ireland increased. By the end of the thirteenth century more than half were English. What emerged in Ireland was an English parliament, better a colonial parliament on a smaller scale to the English one. Also the church was increasingly shaped by English models. The partial conquest of the Anglo-Normans created two nations in Ireland, Gaelic and English. The twin process of Romanisation and Anglicisation changed the politics and ecclesiology of Ireland. It is worth noting that until the sixteenth-century Reformation the papacy never reconsidered its validation of the English claim to sovereignty in Ireland. But whether the Irish church would remain so passive was another question.

KEY POINTS FROM CHAPTER 2

❑ Pre-Christian Ireland responded positively to the Christian mission. Pre-Christian rituals, symbols and imagery co-existed alongside the new faith.

❑ The Celtic world did not distinguish between sacred and secular; people lived in a world of gods and the natural and supernatural co-existed, overlapped and intersected.

❑ Christianity was in Britain from at least 200 CE and was in Ireland perhaps a century before Patrick, who arrived sometime after 432 CE.

❑ Christianity may have been initially brought to Ireland by British men/women captured during raids and enslaved, also possibly via trading routes with Europe or North Africa, or by Christian refuges fleeing persecution in Gaul.

❑ Palladius was sent as bishop to Irish Christians in 431 CE

❑ Patrick's mission as bishop in Ireland from the British church was concentrated in the northern half and the only authentic Patrician documents are the Letter to the soldiers of Coroticus and his Confession.

❑ Patrick probably established the diocesan system of bishops, priests and deacons, in Ireland. Little is known about the church he founded and pastored.

❑ In the sixth and seventh centuries monasteries became centres of Christian life and church government in Ireland. This suited the rural, decentralised socio-political lifestyle and replaced the diocesan system.

❑ The monastic tradition had its roots in Egypt and arrived at Whithorn via Gaul, where Enda, Tighernach, Eoghan and Finnian encountered it.

❑ By late sixth-century Irish monks had left Ireland to establish monasteries and the monastic way of life in Scotland, Britain and Europe. Columba and Columbanus were among the best known.

❏ Power struggles and violence between monasteries resulted in cells for reform, the most notable being the Celi De in the eighth century. Ultimately the Viking invasion and assimilation put an end to the monastic movement by the twelfth century.

❏ A major attempt at church reform began early in the twelfth century initiated by Pope Gregory and supported by the Norse, who had converted to Christianity and acknowledged Canterbury's primacy over Ireland.

❏ Two significant church councils at Cashel (1101) and Ráth Breasail (1111) strengthened papal authority and episcopal power, which was hierarchical and patriarchal.

❏ The Council of Kells–Mellifont (1151) affirmed Armagh as the primal see and set up four provinces each with an archbishop, along with thirty-eight dioceses. Ireland was now in line with Rome.

❏ By the late twelfth century Ireland had lost political independence as English kings became lords of Ireland. This political subjugation was confirmed by Pope Adrian IV who donated Ireland to the Anglo-Norman King Henry II in 1155, believing it would enhance the religious well-being of Ireland.

Test Questions

❏ Outline the contributions of monastic communities to Irish society.

❏ Comment on the claim that 'the twin process of Romanisation and Anglicanisation changed the politics and ecclesiology of Ireland'.

Saints
and
Social Ethics

3   Patrick the Apostle: Kyrie Eleison

Patrick is something of a national legend in Ireland. Therein lies the problem, distinguishing legend from fact and there is little of the latter. Two of his own writings have survived, his Confession and Letter to the soldiers of Coroticus, and these are the only reliable sources of information. Though the information is limited, the documents are unique. 'His is an account unparalled in the history of the West of one man's experience as a captive beyond the frontiers of the Empire.'[1] There is simply no other person from this time who had such an experience and lived to tell it in written form. 'Patrick's missionary career, and the fact that he left an account of it, mark him out as a figure of unique importance in European history.'[2]

Patrick gives very little detail about himself in these writings. They are not autobiographies, strictly speaking but a defence of his missionary activity against criticism and an angry call for justice against a brutal British prince.

Biographies have survived from the second half of the seventh century. One is by Muirchú, an Armagh cleric and the other by Tíreachán, a bishop. Both seem to have used a common source, now lost, but written by a Louth abbot, Ultán. The material contains legends drawing on 'materials relating to native mythical figures … and on native rituals such as lighting of fires'.[3] Muirchú has Patrick arriving at Arklow and then travelling north to Slemish, Co. Antrim. The legend of the Easter fire at Tara is also included. Muirchú introduces Saul and Downpatrick to the Patrician stories and has Patrick buried at the latter. The writing is political, reflecting a power struggle for ecclesial primacy at the time. It is in support of the late seventh-century claim that Armagh should be pre-eminent in the Irish church.

Much of this is legend without historical reliability, as is Tíreachán's account. It is shorter and less colourful. Patrick is located in north Connacht. In the Tara story Laoghaire refuses conversion and Patrick is located at Croaghpatrick, Co. Mayo on his famous retreat. Perhaps Muirchú and Tíreachán created a trend, because over the following centuries Patrick continued to loom large in folk legend, such as the tradition of his banishing a monster into Lough Derg, Co. Donegal. The legends also include banishing snakes from Ireland and using the shamrock to illustrate the doctrine of the Trinity. That people have literally believed these stories, and some still do, speaks loudly for the power of legend and legend making, and of the churches' general failure to educate.

Patrick himself gives us few and often vague details of his life. He was a Romano-British citizen, probably born in the late fourth century. His grandfather was Potitus a priest and his father Calpornius, a deacon and an important local magistrate or collector of imperial taxes. His family appear to have belonged to the Roman upper class, residing on a reasonably wealthy estate. When a teenager he committed an unnamed sin, so serious that it almost destroyed his ministry decades later in Ireland when a friend made at least an outline of the story public. We have no idea what this 'sin' was but at the time there were three serious post-baptismal sins: sexual immorality, idolatry and murder. Our unhealthy preoccupation with sexuality will probably suggest that first, but murder is a likely explanation. All Patrick says in his Confession is that he 'hinted to my dearest friend about something I had done one day – indeed in one hour – in my youth …'4 Had the young Patrick taken to himself the power of God over life and death? Twentieth-century war, violence and genocide removed the power of life and death completely from God. It is now no longer in God's hands, a reality with which we live. Perhaps Patrick, like Moses centuries before, had encountered injustice and in anger killed someone. Whatever Patrick's great 'sin' was, he had carried its guilt from his fifteenth year and his subsequent traumatic life provided him with little space for reflection.

Patarick's birthplace, Bannavem Taburniae, is now an unknown location. Various locations have been suggested, but if Patrick was captured by Irish pirates and taken into slavery it must have been fairly close to the coast. At sixteen he was kidnapped and taken to slavery in Ireland where he herded, probably pigs, for six years. Patrick himself does not identify the location of his slavery years. Gradually he experienced a spiritual awakening and eventually he escaped from Ireland, making his way back to his family. Later in response to a vision in which he heard the voice of Victor, the voice of the Irish, he returned to Ireland and engaged in extensive missionary work. Geographical detail seems to have been unimportant to Patrick and we do not know the exact extent of his missionary activity. It was not the whole of Ireland but probably confined to Ulster and north Connacht. He experienced many difficulties, which included threats, kidnapping, robbery, violence, and had to pay protection money.

The reason for writing his Confession towards the end of his life was to defend himself against criticism that was internal to the church and threatened to destroy his mission in Ireland. Patrick found himself having to deal with three harsh criticisms.

There was the sin committed when he was fifteen, and when he was forty-five it was made public by a close friend.

The Confession makes several references to money and the difficult question as to how Patrick's work in Ireland was financed. The criticism includes the misappropriation of money. But Patrick claims that he refused gifts (C37), that he returned gifts and ornaments (C49) and that he never charged for ordination (C50). Patrick never tells us how he was financed but it is clear that he was spending money, giving presents to kings (C52) and having to pay protection money (C53). But he still does not disclose how his ministry was financed.

The third criticism is against his beliefs. His orthodoxy and authority were called into question. In response Patrick cites a creed, a reflection of the Apostles Creed (C4). He also cites his call to ministry in Ireland, modelled on Samuel's call in the Hebrew scriptures (C23–25). Ultimately, he asserts, it is God who has called and appointed him, whatever humans may think (C13). So Patrick defended and justified his orthodoxy and ministry in the face of very public criticisms.

Three significant themes emerge from Patrick's writings with ethical implications.

3.1   Patrick's Experience of God

At sixteen Patrick was taken into slavery in Ireland, along with thousands of others. He confessed to being ignorant of the true God (C1), but while being out in the woods and mountains in hail, rain and snow he learned to pray, up to one hundred times in daytime and again at night. These were obviously short prayers, perhaps 'one liners' but through this experience love and reverence towards God grew and faith increased (C16). In what way did Patrick experience God?

God of the Elements

In later Celtic prayers and theological reflection God of the Elements becomes an important focus. There was always a nature element, a creation dimension central to Celtic theology and spirituality. Patrick's use of shamrock as a window on God is pure legend but it had a nature dimension. Nevertheless, Patrick's early encounter with God was in the woods and on the mountain. That is where he herded his pigs while exposed to the Irish elements of hail, rain and snow. It was in this context that his God-consciousness was raised and he became aware of the mystery and nearness of God. 'He met the green fields and rainy skies of Ireland before he met its people. There is a sense in which he felt his way into the Christian faith through long and painful contact with the elements.'[5]

Perhaps later Patrick became familiar with the Benedicite and with the spirit of this ancient hymn of creation. All nature joins in the chorus of praise to God the creator of the elements and of all that lives. Belonging as he did to a third-generation Christian family, he had some memory of faith, even though his adolescent years had taken him on a journey of abandonment of faith, possibly atheism. Whatever memory he had of the Christian story, it was the elements that brought to life his God-consciousness. Reflection undoubtedly played its part as he struggled to come to terms with his traumatic experience. Under the sky, close to the Earth, living with the natural elements became the point of his engagement and relationship with God. Something of divine disclosure was experienced through the natural elements. Relating to the God of the Elements has ethical implications for the relationship with the elements themselves. The experience of God and the care of nature are indivisible. Early Irish spirituality was strongly elemental and nature-centred.

God as Trinity

Wherever the woods and mountains were located in which faith came to life for Patrick, he is not likely to have had any awareness of God as Trinity. That came later through his more formal Christian formation and theological education. Patrick did, however, live at a time when theological controversies were widespread and efforts were being made to define theological orthodoxy. That this was taking place in the context of early Christendom – the marriage of state power and faith, throne and altar – is not insignificant. The Nicene and Chalcedonian formulations happened in this context and introduced the concept of heresy to Christian discourse as well as defining orthodoxy. The end of Christendom was reached in the twentieth century and just how much 'orthodox' Christianity has served the Kingdom or Reign of God needs serious discussion. In Patrick's time the Trinity had become the key metaphor for God. The classical theological explanations of these early centuries may not make much sense to twenty-first century people of faith.

Patrick received the imagery and metaphor, and early in his Confession he cited a summary of faith. At this point, probably towards the latter part of the fifth century, he was at least familiar with the earlier Apostles Creed and Patrick's confession of faith echoes this creedal statement.

It is Trinitarian in its structure (C4) expressing awareness of the dynamics of God the Father creator, the Son Jesus Christ and the gift of the Holy Spirit. All of this is in the context of 'the great grace which the Lord saw fit to give me in the land of my captivity' and which calls for the 'return of thanks to God' and the desire to 'glorify and bear witness to his wonderful works' (C3). Not surprisingly the confession of faith ends with doxology: 'This is who we confess and adore, One God in Trinity of sacred name' (C4).

Faith is not intellectual assent to propositions or formulations. It is essentially experience and begins and ends in doxology. Patrick's confession is reflected faith, and theology is reflection on experience. His faith as reflection and faith as doxology arises from his experience of God, his growing and developing God-consciousness. The God of the Elements experienced in the woods and on the mountains is the creative source of all that is. Patrick's God-consciousness would have included consciousness and experience of God as elemental mystery, other and beyond. Yet at the same time there was the sense of God in God's nearness, the Father 'without a source, from him everything else takes its beginning … the one who keeps hold of all things' (C4). For Patrick this is the God of great grace, other yet near, mystery and gracious, beyond yet loving (Father). Patrick's experience of God was deeply relational and also an experience of sacred community.

The God of the Elements for Patrick is truly disclosed by Jesus. The Christ event takes him to the heart of God and the divine–human relationship. The Spirit, in the form of the gift of God's presence and activity in life and the world, opens up the possibility of divine–human relationship, creates and sustains the community of believing people and fills life with hope of sharing God's ultimate purpose for all life and creation.

Patrick's experience of God in Trinity is an experience of community, the sacred community of life shared with humanity and creation. Again faith as doxology to the 'One

God in Trinity of sacred name' is a commitment to the ethics of community – human and elemental – and highlights the ethics of relationality.

God as Liberator

In the Letter to the soldiers of Coroticus we hear the voice of pain. Many of Patrick's new converts to Christian faith have been murdered by Coroticus and his homicidal pirates or they have been taken off into captivity as slaves. Patrick's anger in the Letter is tangible. There is the strongest possible protest to Coroticus and his soldiers and there is also in Patrick's voice of pain a cry for God's help and retribution.

Such a cry is possible because of Patrick's experience of God. It is not at heart a cry for human vengeance. Motives can be mixed and ambivalent in our human fallibility and weakness. But ultimately the cry of pain is rooted in the moral sense of justice and the consciousness of God's justice. In the Hebrew scriptures the God of Exodus is the God who sees, hears and knows the cries of people in political and economic oppression inflicted by the imperial power of Egypt. Exodus is for ancient Israel the paradigm for justice and liberation. The God of justice is the God of liberation who is engaged with human collaboration (Moses and Aaron) in bringing about freedom from all that dehumanises and oppresses and building communities of justice, fairness and abundant life and well-being. 'The cry of the slave ... is always and everywhere the cry for liberation.'[6] Patrick's voice of pain arises from his solidarity with those killed and enslaved and from his relationship with the Trinitarian God of community and justice. His profoundly intimate God-consciousness is of a God who cares and who is engaged for justice in the world and who liberates. After all at the heart of the Jesus story is a cross, symbol of injustice and violence and at the same time a window into the suffering of God in the face of violence, injustice and innocent suffering. In the Letter to soldiers of Coroticus Patrick's voice of pain is one of hope and committed action with God for liberation. His God-shaped ethical consciousness, rooted in his experience of God, becomes an ethic of liberation praxis.

God as Violent!

'I am Patrick. I am a sinner: the most unsophisticated of people; the least among all the Christians; and, to many, the most contemptible' (C1). So Patrick begins his Confession, often understood as an expression of great humility. It may well be and it may reflect the kind of self-effacing person Patrick was. Overall, though, the Confession gives an impression of someone with an inferiority complex. Sometimes Patrick appears to be putting himself down and in the face of his critics needs to improve his self-esteem. God's great grace may indeed have lifted him like a stone and 'in his mercy raised me up' (C12). There are occasions in his defensiveness, when one would like to hear Patrick express that a little more and really believe it!

There is a more disturbing emphasis in his Confession. With thousands of others he was taken into captivity in Ireland and then adds in his Confession: 'This occurred according to our merits for we had pulled back from God; we did not keep his commandments ... And so the Lord poured upon us the heat of his anger and dispersed us among many peoples' (C1). Later he reflects again on his experience: 'that before I was punished I was like a stone lying in the deepest mire' (C12). He sees his capture and enslavement in a foreign land as God's punishment, the heat of divine anger. This is not a fact of experience but Patrick's interpretation of his experience of captivity. It is important to make that distinction since people of faith frequently confuse fact and interpretation. He was taken into captivity and in later reflection interpreted the traumatic fact as divine punishment for neglecting God in his adolescence. Is this a worthy image of God? Or is O'Loughlin correct to suggest that 'there is a very particular need for those who believe in God to explain how bad things that happen to good people can be seen within the plan of a loving God'.[7]

Patrick had no shortage of biblical precedent for this view of a punishing God.[8] Israel was scattered among the nations or crushed by neighbouring nations or empires as God's punishment for covenantal infidelity. The view still persists that suffering is the result of sin and that God's punishment is to purify people, correct them and lead them to renewed faithfulness. Plague, famine and the AIDS pandemic have been interpreted in this way.

Apart from portraying God as a God of violence and terror, this theology diminishes personal and social ethical responsibility for identifying causes of suffering and solutions. Patrick interprets his experience as God's punishment instead of identifying greed and violence as primary causes. Ignoring the socio-economic and political causes avoids developing strategies and commitments to change, especially systems and structures.

3.1 Patrick and Columba from Kildare Cathedral.

The image is basically of a violent God and 'is ultimately destructive of a true appreciation of the Christian view of God as infinite love ...'.[9] It is an image of God as punitive, a violent, terrorising God who can destroy people and creation at will in response to human disobedience. It is the kind of theology that translates into punitive justice systems and produces the non-thinking, undemanding and cheap response, 'lock them up and throw away the key'. It not only portrays God at times as the divine abuser but legitimises abuse of people through physical, sexual, psychological and verbal violence. Patrick's image of God at this point is unethical and is probably a projection of human violence on to God.

3.2   Protesting Evil

The Letter to the soldiers of Coroticus reflects a disturbing and difficult time for those living in Britain. The Roman imperial control was breaking down, soldiers were being recalled to deal with the collapse of the Empire at its heart. Angles, Saxons, Jutes and Frisians were constantly raiding Britain, while Picts and Irish made life difficult from the north and west. Raiding parties were commonplace and many were taken as prisoners of war or as slaves. Such raids also took place to Ireland and in one such raid many of Patrick's recently baptised Christians were killed or taken from Ireland into slavery, itself a brutal and dehumanising experience. The Letter protests against Coroticus and his soldiers, and it includes a cry for God's retribution.

In the face of serious injustice, genocide and ill treatment the cry for retribution is understandable. It is a sign that moral sensibility is alive and well. Anger in the face of injustice, even hatred for the abusers and their actions, is a just and ethical response. It is when like is returned with like, violence is met by violence and evil is returned with evil, that ethics is diminished and such actions in response become immoral. The cry for retribution is, nevertheless, the cry for justice and liberation.

Patrick protests evil in the strongest possible terms. Coroticus and his soldiers are 'father-killer and the brother-killer ... raging wolves' (L5). They are like 'someone who hands over the "members of Christ" to a whore house' (L14). The latter is a strong image describing a prostitute as a 'she wolf' devouring parts of Christ's body (C10). Coroticus is behaving like the apostate he is.[10]

Patrick's language mirrors the Psalms of Lament in the Hebrew scriptures. Here too are strong cries of protest, at times savage urgency in the honesty of expression and the cry for justice and divine action. The strength of the language sometimes disturbs us, no doubt in our self-made comfort zones. The cry to 'dash the heads of little ones against the rocks' (Psalm 137) may well horrify us as a literal response to the enemy and rightly so. But we may have experienced little of the community trauma and total collapse of all the institutions and symbols of meaning experienced by the southern kingdom of Judah at the hands of the Babylonian superpower. It is impossible to sing the Lord's song by the rivers of Babylon (exile). Patrick has some sense of such loss as he protests the genocide and captivity of Irish Christians.

The Letter is a decree for excommunication and at the same time a prayer to God for divine justice and liberation.

The actions of Coroticus are condemned as sacrilege. The image of the God of life has been wiped out or destroyed by someone who claims to be part of the Christian community. The basic right to life has been denied while others are dehumanised and treated as sub-human or, worse, non-entities – objects of commercial gain.

Passivity is not possible in the face of such inhumanity. Silence is not an option in view of the evil of genocide and the abuse of life and freedom. It is a particular evil when carried out by people making faith claims and, worse, legitimising murder, 'collateral damage' or personal or structural abuse of the innocent by co-opting God.

The strength of Patrick's protest and language used is obvious and an ethical impera-tive. Patrick is committed to justice and such a commitment leads him to protest evil. The strength of his justice commitment and compassion is also encountered in the stirring lament towards the end of the Letter for the victims of murder and those victims still alive but whom he fears he many never see again. 'So with sadness and grief I cry out ... And so my dearest friends, I grieve, grieve deeply, for you ...' (L16–18). The cry for justice, the protest against evil is born in the shared pain and solidarity with life's victims.

3.3   On the Edge of History

The end of the world has always held a fascination for many people. Every generation has produced its predictions and so far everyone has been wrong. Patrick appears to have held a particular world view, or perhaps other-world view. He seems to have been motivated and energised by a belief that he was a missionary to the ends of the Earth, the edge of the world, and that when his ministry was complete the end of time and history would come. He saw himself living in the last times with the end imminent.

Patrick paraphrases Matthew 24: 14 and writes that 'the kingdom will be preached throughout the whole world, as a testimony to all nations before the end of the world'. Patrick and his helpers were now witness to the fact that the 'gospel has been preached out to beyond where any man lives' (C34). It is God who in the last days has heard him (C34).

Three hundred years before Patrick the Greek philosopher Strabo described Ireland as a 'frozen land at the edge of the earth'.[11] Ireland was perceived as the last stop, the 'back of beyond'. Patrick seems to have shared this geographical perspective and to have interpreted the Matthean text literally, that he was in the last days of human history. Once the gospel had been preached to the furthest limits, Ireland, then the end would come. 'He is the one who is preaching in the very last place on Earth to the very last nation to hear the message.'[12] His end hope is expressed in his credo: 'And we look forward to this coming, in the time that is soon to be ...' (C4).

Did Patrick share with the early Christians the conviction that they lived in the last days and soon Christ would come again? If this was the expectation of the early Chris-tians it was clearly not realised. The letter of II Peter recognises this hope unfulfilled and attempts to reinterpret the delayed End. This theology of the End-times is known as es-chatology, the theology of the End and is often expressed in 'he will come again'. If Patrick was a literalist in relation to the Matthean and other texts from the Christian scriptures, then he too was disappointed as were the early Irish Christians. The other-worldly hope was not realised, history did not end and a literal eschatology disappointed. But there may be an understanding of eschatology beyond literalism and a theology of End more ethically realistic than the end of history. Christian faith and hope may be pointing to something transformative at the edge of history rather than at the chronological end. We have no way of knowing for sure but Patrick may not have been a literalist in his interpretation of sacred texts.

Patrick was writing during the break-up of the Roman Empire, a time of crisis and trauma. A world order was coming to an end. It was the dissolution of a world super-power, the collapse of a domination system that led Augustine to write his famous 'City of God'. The very world order was coming to an end but for Augustine there was something more ultimate than the political and economic superpower and its collapse. The City of God remained, and the vision of a new Jerusalem offered the hope of transformation and a new beginning.

Rome itself was sacked and the Germanic tribes were on the rampage. The known civilisation was collapsing and many were tempted to despair and wonder how life could continue. Ireland was a long way from Rome but the political tsunami had crashed into the shores of the other island. A whole era in history was ending, a deeply unsettling and traumatic moment. What could faith say in such circumstances?

Eschatology has something to say to historical crises. It is an end of the era theology in which the God of the future comes to us in the here and now in its entire catastrophe. To live in the eschatological horizon is to live in active partnership with God in openness to the future and socio-political transformation. It is to live in active, open anticipation of the coming of the New Creation, which means thinking and acting in the world, the world that is ending, from a distinctive standpoint. It means living from the 'other end', shaped by God's ultimate vision of a new heaven and earth, a new Jerusalem, a new crea-tion. Eschatology means the human partnership with God in living the *not yet, already* in the present. Eschatology is commitment to God's future in the here and now, a com-mitment that is liberating and anticipating. 'To live in anticipation means letting one's present be determined by the expected future of God's kingdom and God's righteousness and justice.'[13]

This approach to eschatology is not only liberating but also ethically motivating and enhancing. An other-worldly eschatology diminishes ethical commitment. One of the bestselling religious books of the twentieth century was Hal Lindsey's *The Late Great Planet Earth*. It was a doomsday scenario book painting in God's blueprint or divine plan for the destruction of the Earth in the last days. From an ethical perspective this other-worldly view generated irresponsibility. Why care for planet Earth and the mending of creation if it is all destined for destruction? This-worldly eschatology, partnering God's not yet in the now, is active for social justice for humankind and ecological justice for the Earth. God's future breaking into the present commits us to social ethics and the transformation of the catastrophic moments in history.

Whether Patrick's end-time theology was understood by him in this way we cannot tell. He did live on the edge of history, in an 'end' moment. Perhaps his cry for justice in the Letter to the Soldiers of Coroticus was a this-worldly eschatology, rooted in God's vision of justice at the heart of the New Creation. It certainly was Patrick being ethically responsible.

A this-worldly eschatological dimension is crucial to faith struggling to live ethically on the edge of history. 'Christian ethics are eschatological ethics. What we do now for people in need we do filled with the power of hope, and lit by the expectation of God's coming day.'[14]

KEY POINTS FROM CHAPTER 3

❏ Two of Patrick's own writings have survived – his Confession and Letter to the Soldiers of Coroticus – and these are the only reliable sources of information on him.

❏ Confession is the first written account of slavery beyond the boundaries of the Roman Empire in the West.

❏ His writings are a defence of his missionary activity against critique from within the church system.

❏ Patrick has to account for a serious sin committed in his youth, defend his use of money and justify his orthodoxy.

❏ Muirchú's and Tireachán's biographies of Patrick, dated the second half of seventh century, are extant. The former account is political, reflecting a power struggle for ecclesial supremacy, and it states the case for Armagh. Both accounts lack historical reliability.

❏ Patrick experienced something of God through the natural elements, in keeping with early Irish spirituality that was nature-centred and therefore respectful of nature.

❏ Patrick's faith is Trinitarian in structure: he reflects on his experience of the God of the Elements, who is also disclosed in Jesus and the divine–human relationship is sustained by God's spirit. His experience of God was both relational and communitarian.

❏ The Letter to the soldiers of Coroticus is a lament, a protest at their inhumane and murderous acts against Patrick's Christian community, and a cry for God's help and retribution, and for committed action with God for liberation.

❏ Patrick interprets his experience of captivity and enslavement along with others as divine retribution for past failings and for neglecting God in his youth. He falls into the trap of portraying God as a God of violence and the cause of suffering and retribution. This God image is unethical and detracts from the socio-economic, political roots of suffering.

❏ The strength of Patrick's protest against Coroticus underlines his ethical perspective and commitment to life and justice in the face of evil and inhumanity.

❏ Patrick's eschatology reveals an openness to work in active partnership with God to make real God's kingdom on Earth and bring about the necessary socio-political transformation.

TEST QUESTIONS

- ❏ What information can be gleamed about Patrick's life from his Confession?
- ❏ How ethical was Patrick? Support your answer with reference to his writings.

4   Brigid of Kildare: The Flame of Justice

Brigid is one of the three patron saints of Ireland and one of the most popular and loved. This is all the more remarkable given that there is very little historical data. She is almost legendary or mythological. The problem is that there was an earlier Celtic goddess called Brigid of huge significance in Ireland, and the cult of the goddess and that of the Christian have been merged. Perhaps that is the fascination with Brigid, that her life is so interwoven with early myth and Irish folklore. In Brigid we have a synthesis of pre-Christian religion and Christianity. The earliest Life of Brigid, written by the Christian monk Cogitosus, has achieved this synthesis through the use of miracle stories and imagery such as fire, light and water. Such a synthesis is built into the Lives of the early Celtic saints and is part of the literary genre known as hagiography.

4.1   Why Hagiography?

The word itself is a combination of two Greek words, *hagios* meaning holy and *graphos* meaning writing. This key genre in early Christian Ireland was essentially about the holiness of Celtic saints. It was in vogue from the seventh to thirteenth centuries and hundreds of Lives were produced. Sadly only about 150 Lives have survived. The earliest extant life is that of the Welsh bishop Samson. The earliest Irish life comes from the second half of the seventh century and was the Life of Brigid by Cogitosus. The motivation for writing these Lives is varied.[1]

Propaganda Purposes

Ecclesial politics it seems have always existed, and they are an inevitable dynamic influencing the hagiographic. There were alliances and rivalries, which is why the Book of Armagh has Patrick and Brigid meeting in unity of mind and heart. There is no historical basis to the story, not least because they lived in different eras. At a time when ecclesial politics was engaged in a battle for episcopal supremacy of Ireland, Cogitosus' Life may well have been written to establish the claim of Kildare over Armagh.

Economic Realities

Money is always a factor and monasteries needed financial resources often in the form of sponsorship. The economic well-being of the monastery depended on its standing in the monasteries 'league table'. Relics and shrines were a seventh-century development and it mattered that the monastery had a Life of the saint to 'accompany, explain and enhance the relics'.[2]

Tourism Industry

Lives and relics increased the trade in pilgrimages and this became a major financial factor between the eighth and tenth centuries. Monetary tribute was paid and the many pilgrims were a source of monastic wealth. The hagiography, therefore, enhanced the saint's unique holiness and spiritual power. The greater the miracles the greater the number of pilgrims, the greater the tourist trade the greater the local income.

It is not being overly cynical to see the hagiographers as being engaged in 'spin', nor does this undermine the faith dimension. It is the realism that faith is sociological as well as spiritual and that saints, hagiographers and theologians are always human influenced by political and economic realities. In this context the hagiographers wrote out of theological conviction.

Model of Holiness

When Cogitosus wrote his Life of Brigid or Adamnan his Life of Columba, they wrote to portray their saint as a model and example of holiness. They believed that ultimately Brigid or Columba 'had something important to teach people about holiness, prayer, service, and ultimately union with God'.[3] They wanted people to encounter living mentors and soul friends. They did write in the context of propaganda, economics and tourism, and they also knew the reality of local community politics, the all-too-real human limitations, vulnerability and struggle of life in the midst of disease and tribal conflicts. The Celtic saints were real people who had been there and though dead were present to accompany and journey alongside.

The hagiographers were not writing history or biography. They were offering theological reflections on what it means to live a holy life in the context of socio-economic and inter-personal realities. In writing their Lives they drew on a number of sources.

Early Mythology

A core component of the Lives is mythic. Stories of pagan Celtic heroes were borrowed and woven into the Life of the saint. This is why it is difficult to distinguish the goddess Brigid from the Christian Brigid. Cogitosus has synthesised the pre-Christian mythology with Christian story. It is remarkable, from our perspective to recognise that the early Celtic monks had no difficulty writing down the earlier myths and legends of Irish folklore, or combining these with Christian gospel stories to present their saint as a model and example of holiness. The language of mythology was not strange to them. We have been conditioned to reject mythology as fairy tales and untrue. Apart from failing

4.1 Brigid's Cross at Solas Bhride, Kildare

to understand the power of fairy tales, this is a one-dimensional approach to truth. Truth is much more than historical, literal or factual. There is always more than meets the eye, realities that cannot be perceived or experienced by the intellect. The language of symbols, poetry and metaphor is needed to describe mystery and to disclose deep inner realities.

Mythology is a powerful medium of truth, speaking to us at a level deeper than flat literature. It has been described as 'poetic rationality',[4] a way of making sense or explaining what is beyond the rationalism of literalism or a one-dimensional use of language. The hagiographers enthusiastically embraced mythology and the twenty-first century Western world urgently needs to rediscover its power and profundity.

Faithful Ancients

The hagiographers undoubtedly tapped into an oral tradition. Memory has always been handed on by storytelling and storytelling 'was a favourite entertainment among the Celts …'[5] The *fili*, or poet, was much in demand on a long winter's night from Samain to Beltain. The oral tradition had stories of Brigid, and a hagiographer also drew on older stories of saints. Stories were borrowed and adapted to 'fit' the Life in question. Adamnan and Bede refer in their writings to these 'learned and faithful ancients'.[6]

Jesus Stories

The key source for shaping the Life of a saint was the Christian scriptures and especially the gospels. On occasions they drew on stories from the Hebrew scriptures such as the call of Samuel echoed in the call of Patrick or Abraham and Solomon, all alluded to in the Life of Brendan. The main source, however, was the Jesus story. When Cogitosus has Brigid turn water into beer there is a connection with the Johannine story of water into wine at the Cana wedding feast. Beer had more appeal in an Irish context! Stories of healing also allude to healing stories of Jesus. What the hagiographer is really trying to underline is that holiness has to do with being a living symbol or image of Christ. Long before Thomas A. Kempis wrote his classic *The Imitation of Christ*, Celtic hagiographers were making the point; *Imago Christi* is the heart of being Christian. Holiness is ongoing transformation by Jesus into Christ-likeness. 'The Celtic saints' Lives reflect each saint's spiritual kinship with Jesus: how all of them, by uniting their hearts and minds with his, were changed profoundly by Jesus and his story.'[7] Such transformation and holiness were open to all and expressed through healing wounded lives, feeding the hungry, living in solidarity with the poor and creating friendship through peaceful relationships and gender equality. On the surface hagiography appears to tell fantastic stories about a saint, but in the theopoetics and mythology are a profound social ethics, an *Imago Christi*.

4.2   In the Shadow of a Goddess

When Christianity came to Ireland it encountered a strong goddess tradition. Already established was a powerful cult of the goddess Brigid. The name literally means 'the exalted one', and exalted she was as a triple goddess of poetry, prophecy and fertility. She was adored by poets, wordsmiths and medical practitioners and may well have been identical with the goddess Minerva, as Caesar believed: 'She was mother-goddess par excellence, a seasonal deity, and she presided over the important purification feast of Imbolc.'[8]

The goddess Brigid may well have been an immigrant to Ireland. She was worshipped in Britain under the name of Brigante by a tribe who controlled the Pennine Hills called the Brigantes. She was their principle goddess and 'off-shoots of them settled in south-eastern Ireland in or about the first century CE. It was probably through such settlement that the cult of this goddess came to Ireland'.[9] The Irish adoption of the name was Brigid, while on the continent of Europe, where there is also evidence of her cult, the name was Briga. It is this goddess who is often indistinguishable from the Christian saint. We are never sure when we are dealing with goddess, saint or folklore figure. 'The figure of Brigit moves imperceptibly from the theatre of myth to that of history.'[10]

The ninth-century Irish glossary, *Cormac's Glossary*, describes Brigid as a poetess and the daughter of Daghdha. She had two sisters with the same name, a Celtic tendency to triplicate deities. Daghdha is the 'good God'. As well as being the goddess of poets she is associated with agricultural fertility. Another Irish document, the *Lebor Gabala*, states that the poetess daughter of Daghdha had two oxen. Brigid was the goddess of domestic animals, and this connects to the spring festival or feast of Imbolc. This feast 'was a direct reference to the birth of young animals in the spring.'[11] Brigid was also said to 'breathe life into the mouth of the dead winter'.[12]

There is a classic Irish saga known as the 'Battle of Moytura' in which Brigid takes over the role of Danu, the mythical ancestress of the 'People of the Goddess Danu'. This was one of the earliest names given to the Irish. In the saga Brigid is the wife of leader of the Fomorians, the enemy of the People. Brigid is a mediator in a power struggle. Her son Ruadán is taught weaponry by the People, his maternal kin, and then goes over to his paternal kin, wounding the sacred smith of the People, who although weak kills Ruadán. Brigid weeps and laments for the loss of loyalty and life. The myth expresses the change in social organisation in Ireland through Ruadán's use of his maternal kin to established patriarchal forms of social organisation in Ireland. The goddess has lost power in Ireland and has been replaced by the male god. Brigid can move between these two worlds in the myth, and again the myth 'provides us with vital clues as to the changes about to take place in Irish culture with the advent of patriarchal forms of organisation'.[13]

In Cogitosus' Life and other Lives of the Christian saint, there are links with the earlier Irish goddess. Brigid of Kildare moves easily from goddess to saint. The goddess and the saint each have flames coming from their head. 'The images of milk, fire, sun, serpents are common stories of St Brigid, while the themes of compassion, generosity, hospitality, spinning, weaving, smithwork, healing and agriculture run throughout her various Lives.'[14] The Christian saint lives in the shadow of the goddess.

The earliest text on the Christian Brigid is Ultán's Hymn, a seventh-century composition and perhaps one of the earliest hymns in the Irish language. The Hymn uses a variety of metaphors to describe Brigid.

> Brigid, woman ever excellent, golden, radiant flame,
> Lead us to the eternal kingdom, the brilliant dazzling sun.[15]

Here pre-Christian and Christian motifs overlap, especially the fire image or symbolism, which is found in Cogitosus' Life, too. Brigid is also described in the Hymn as 'the mother of Jesus', which is given other variants such as 'Mary of the Gaels', 'foster-mother of Christ' and 'Mary's midwife'.

The best-known and earliest Life of Brigid is by Cogitosus, written within 150 years of her death. He was a monk of the Kildare monastery; other than that we have no information on him. Cogitosus tells us that her father was Dubtach and her mother Broicseach, and 'from her childhood she was dedicated to goodness. Chosen by God ...'[16]

An 'Irish Life of Brigit' has been dated from 774 CE to early ninth century and is a series of miracles by the Christian saint. It informs us that Brigid's mother was a slave woman and that she was brought up in the house of a druid. This Life also tells the story of her consecration as a bishop by Mel.[17]

Brigid is historically associated with the foundation of a monastery at Kildare. Her main symbol is that of the oak, hence Cill Dara (Kildare), church of the oak. The site may have been originally a druidic site. Pre-Christian Kildare was already known as the 'City of Brigid', again the goddess connection. It is also possible that an early religious site, Dun Ailinne, a major Iron Age site comparable with Emhain Macha in religious significance,

4.2 Brigid of Kildare with the flame of justice

influenced the establishment of Kildare. Ritual burning or fire was associated with Dun Ailinne and the fire at Dun Ailinne may have been transported to Kildare when the former lost its importance following abandonment after 695 CE. Maybe Christian Brigid set up Kildare as a religious rival to Dun Ailinne.

Historical data is very scarce and what is most clear is that Brigid's life moves between mythology and spirituality. In identifying themes from the Life by Cogitosus and others we are dealing with theomythical material, no less profound for all that, perhaps even more so, and above all expressing holiness in terms of a significant social ethics.

4.3   Brigid's Social Ethics

Active Compassion for the Poor

Kildare is reputed to have been known as the 'City of the Poor'. If we are to judge by the Life by Cogitosus, it is a reputation well deserved. Compassion is a major theme in the Life with twenty-three of thirty-two chapters in Cogitosus' hagiography dealing with Brigid's concern for friends and strangers, the marginalised and guests, including lepers – a widespread disease in Ireland at the time: 'One day, when a certain person came asking for salt, just as other poor and destitute people in countless numbers were accustomed to come to her seeking their needs, the most Blessed Brigid supplied an ample amount.'[18] The poor and strangers were drawn from every quarter 'by the reputation of her great deeds and the excess of her generosity'.[19] Kildare was also described as 'the safest place of refuge among all the towns of the whole land of the Irish, with all their fugitives'.[20]

The transformation of water into the best beer story is in response to lepers.[21] These were social outcasts, the most avoided and dreaded people in sixth-century Ireland. Compassion is the key virtue in Brigid's life as she responds to the poor, the fugitives and the untouchables. Not only do they reflect the Jesus story and his preferential option for the poor and marginalised, but they are also a reminder that religious worship and prayer and social justice are indivisible. Spirituality is inseparable from active solidarity with the poor, the nobodies, the abused and the marginalised.

Concern with Animal Welfare

Cogitosus has a number of animal stories. Brigid is frequently portrayed as practising prayer: in one story she is in a trance, 'her soul in celestial meditation'. She put a large quantity of bacon down beside her dog and a month later found it intact! The dog emerges as a hero![22] In another story a hunted wild boar joins her herd. She blessed it and it served her tamely and humbly.[23]

Wolves act as swineherds for her, a wild fox is produced to take the place of a king's pet and saves the life of a poor man who killed the king's fox, and wild ducks came to her. Indeed 'Brigid felt a tenderness for some ducks'.[24]

Brigid, according to Cogitosus, had a close relationship with animals. This animal kinship is a familiar theme in the Lives of all Celtic saints. Wild animals become friends. Again the theomythical point Cogitosus is making is about the importance of compassion towards all life, human and animate. The story of the wild fox combines both the man sentenced to execution and the fox as recipients of Brigid's compassion. She is concerned for the welfare and well-being of all life.

An anthropocentric view of life assumes that humans are in every way superior to all other forms of life and that animals only exist to serve the needs and pleasures of humans. This world view frequently leads to abuse of animals and cruelty, justified by human superiority and the right to dominate. Cogitosus' theomythical stories are the reminder that humans are not at the centre of the world or at the top of the bioladder, and that they have ethical responsibilities to care for the animal world. The praxis of spirituality is about friendship and partnership with all creation.

Living Beyond Patriarchy

There is no evidence that any hagiographer was a woman, even though there were communities of women and double communities, both of which were places of learning. Brigid is a significant leader in the early Celtic communities. But there is no surviving document that has been signed off *by a woman*. Even though large numbers of women committed themselves to the monastic life, the surviving Lives are mostly male. Given that the Lives were written later – Brigid's Life by Cogitosus about 100–150 years later – the lack of women may reflect the growing patriarchy in the Irish church as well as beyond Ireland. 'Patriarchal attitudes which negated the value of women's lives and leadership came to dominate much of the Western church, and this too contributed to the scarcity of stories about female saints.'[25] Patriarchy, the marginalisation of women and the ethic of gender equality will be more fully developed in two later chapters.

The Lives do portray Brigid in a struggle with patriarchy. 'Issues of sexual politics raised their head several times in Brigid's relationship with the male saints Patrick and Brendan.'[26] There is no historical basis for their ever meeting one another, yet the hagiographers have them meet 'outside' history and are making a significant point. Reflected in the stories are struggles, not only over primacy and therefore ecclesial politics but also over gender struggles and therefore useful insights into sexual politics and the sexual dynamics of the time.

After one of his voyages when sea monsters attacked his boat, Brendan discovered that invocation of his name and that of Patrick had no effect but the naming of Brigid did subdue the monsters. He arrived to meet Brigid and immediately told her to make confession. Brigid responded by telling him to make his confession first! Brendan responded by suggesting that the sea monsters were right to honour her! In another version of the story Brigid hangs her cloak on a sunbeam but when Brendan tries to do the same his cloak falls in the mud. The hagiographer obviously wanted Brendan to look foolish and Brigid to appear superior. The story reflects sexual politics and Brigid's unwillingness to submit to patriarchy.

The other remarkable story about Brigid is that of her ordination as bishop. Cogitosus does not tell the story but the Irish Life of Brigid does. Both Cogitosus and the Irish Life tell the story of MacCaille, a pupil of bishop Mel, placing the veil on Brigid's head and how she held the ash beam that supported the altar. The wood was not consumed by fire. What happened next has been denied or repressed, reflecting again the power of patriarchy.

> The bishop, being intoxicated with the grace of God there, did not know what he was reciting from his book, for he consecrated Brigid with the orders of a bishop. 'Only this Virgin in the whole of Ireland will hold episcopal ordination', said Mel. While she was being consecrated a fiery column ascended from her head.[27]

An intoxicated bishop, not aware of what he was doing and limiting episcopal ordination to Brigid only, indicates an uneasiness with the practice.

Historically there is nothing to indicate that Brigid or any other woman at this time could or would have become a bishop. Brigid as bishop is very difficult to reconcile with what we know of women in the Irish church or elsewhere, and of the early second-century suppression of women as leaders of the church, already indicated in the Pastoral Letters of the Christian scriptures. Yet the story is intentional, and: 'Brigid's hagiographer meant for Mel to bungle the ordination ... What better illustration of the complex, contradicting ideas about gender interaction flourishing among the early Irish.'[28]

Again the stories reflect gender dynamics and sexual politics, and Brigid through her theomythical Lives is engaged in a struggle to live beyond patriarchy. Cogitosus does not relate the story of her episcopal ordination but he does tell of the male hermit who 'might rule the church with her in episcopal dignity' (whose episcopal dignity?). Significantly he also writes of 'Their episcopal and feminine see ...'[29]

Gender equality has always been difficult to achieve in the church and society. Patriarchy is an institutional ethos and is a structural injustice. Whatever other peace factors are required, world peace also depends on peace between the sexes and a justice ethic demands living beyond patriarchy.

The flame of justice, symbolised by the fiery column ascending from Brigid's head following her episcopal ordination, is both a sign of Brigid's solidarity with the poor and her struggle to overcome patriarchy.

Anamchara

The hagiographers were aware that the role of the anamchara, or soul friend, was central to spirituality in the Irish/Celtic tradition, so they sought to present these saints as real spiritual mentors and soul friends. When Cogitosus wrote his Life of Brigid, she was long dead but in a real sense was very much alive in the theomyth and could accompany another in their struggle to live faithfully and ethically in the world. Hagiographers portray her as being consulted by many lay people and spiritual leaders. She is consulted by Finnian of Clonard, Brendan of Clonfert and Kevin of Glendalough, even though in reality they never met and were not of the exact same era. The point is the power of Brigid as pastor, confessor, mentor and soul friend.

Another story tells of her encounter with a young cleric from a community in Ferns, 'a foster-son of Brigid who used to come to her with wishes'. Being a foster-son in the Celtic tradition meant that he had spent some of his younger life with Brigid, who had responsibility for his educational and spiritual formation. On this visit she asked him if he had a soul friend. He replied in the affirmative, but the truth was he had died. 'For your soul friend has died, and anyone without a soul friend is like a body without a head.'[30]

The tradition of anamchara/soul friend is closely associated with the Celtic tradition, and Brigid in particular. She was a wise soul friend who was a mentor, guide and companion to many on their life journey. The soul friend was considered indispensable. The young Ferns cleric was told: 'Eat no more until you get a soul friend.'[31]

A life journey is a spiritual one. It is a journey of faith seeking understanding, a pilgrimage in living theology. Every life story has sacred and mysterious dimensions and it is not a story that can be woven in isolation or alone. Understanding the dimensions, making sense out of life commitments, and life praxis, unravelling ambiguity and struggle with loss and suffering, requires a body with a head, a wise, open, perceptive and often wounded soul friend. Such was Brigid, and the soul friend is a strong insight from her Lives and from the Celtic tradition.

Key Points from Chapter 4

❏ Earliest life of Brigid by Cogitosus synthesises pre-Christian religion and Christianity through the use of miracle stories and nature imagery.

❏ Cogitosus sought in his life of Brigid to underline her holiness and use her as an example for others seeking union with God. The account also sought to promote Kildare as an ecclesiastical centre and attract pilgrims to improve economic income.

❏ Cogitosus draws on the stories of pagan Celtic heroes, i.e., the goddess Brigid as well as gospel stories to reflect theologically on the holiness of Brigid's life. He wants to show that her spiritual journey is an imitation of Christ by following his example.

❏ Historical data on Brigid is scarce and relies heavily on the interweaving of pagan myth and Christian spirituality. Reflection on the stories and poems available reveals an emphasis on social ethics in the presentation of Brigid.

❏ Brigid's primary concern is to alleviate the suffering of the poor and protect the most vulnerable and outcasts.

❏ Brigid's connection to animals and concern to nurture all living creatures is also underlined.

❏ Brigid is also presented as challenging patriarchy in church and the social and political arena in an effort to establish gender equality.

❏ Brigid's belief in the value and importance of soul friends on life's journey to mentor, guide and act as companion is also reinforced.

Test Questions

❏ Outline the role and importance of hagiographers in the Celtic world.

❏ What does Cogitosus reveal about his understanding of holiness in his Life of Brigid? Illustrate with reference to his text.

5 Columba: The Ambivalent Peacemaker

Tradition has it that Columba[1] lies buried in Downpatrick along with Ireland's other two patron saints, Patrick and Brigid. The truth may be long since past finding out! The problem with many of the early Celtic Christian traditions is in discerning when legend ends and history begins. The Celtic art of storytelling wasted no time with any of its heroes. Columba was no exception. He can even claim an annunciation story. Adamnan, in his Life of Columba, describes the signs and wonders which foretold his birth. An angel appeared to Columba's mother Eithne in a dream telling her she would bear a son of great beauty who would be remembered among the Lord's prophets.[2]

Abbot Buite, who founded Monasterboice, said on his deathbed that: 'A child illustrious before God and man will be born in the night tonight, and he shall come here before thirty years from this night.'[3]

There are echoes of the Christmas annunciation in Matthew and Luke, and it may well be that the real point is not in any literalistic dimension to such stories but in the rich poetic symbolism. The Hebrew and Celtic minds had greater appreciation of poetic symbolism and metaphor than Western moderns conditioned by rationalism and literalism.

Columba's storytellers were writing much later and part of their purpose was to proclaim his royal blood as much as his spiritual mission. This person was related to the kings of Tara, and royal blood ran in his veins. Only literalistic moderns have hang-ups about legends!

5.1 Columba's Story

Columba was born in 521 CE at Gartan in Donegal. The traditional date is 5 December and an ancient piece of Hebridean folklore held Thursday, presumably his actual birthday, to be the day of kind Columcille.

His mother Eithne belonged to a royal Leinster family, while his father, Fedlimidh or Phelim, was the great-grandson of the famous Niall of the Nine Hostages, from the northern Uí Néill dynasty. Niall had come to political power with his late fourth-century capture of the northern capital, Eamhain Macha (modern-day Navan Fort near Armagh). Columba's grandmother Erca was a daughter of King Erc and sister of Fergus Mor, who led the conquest of Argyll at the end of the fifth century. Columba, therefore, not only had royal blood in his veins from both sides of his family but he was also born into the circle of political power which may account for his political orientation. Who knows, had he not become a Celtic monk, evangelist and Christian educator, he may well have been a king or chieftain.

His baptism is said to have taken place at Temple Douglas, between Letterkenny and Gartan. Baptised by Cruithnechan, a person who prepared boys for the newly formed monastic schools, he was given the name Columba, meaning a dove. The story has it that he would often wander away from other children to the quiet church where he would reflect and pray. 'Has our little Colum come today from the church?', the children used to say. So Columba became known as Columcille – Columba of the church (cille).[4]

Fostering was an integral part of the Celtic social system.[5] At a very young age a child was fostered for educational purposes with payment often made in the currency of the day, namely cattle. Cruithnechan the priest was chosen to foster Columba, suggesting that the young boy was intended by his family for the church. With Christianity still relatively new in Ireland, a few generations earlier Columba might have been fostered by a druid, the highly honoured bard, poet and storyteller.

His education included training as a bard or poet by Gemman and this education was to stay with him, not only in the poetry he wrote but also in his advocacy role on behalf of the bards at the Druim Cett Convention in 575 CE.

A childhood story illustrates the memory training, which was part of bardic preparation. Columba and his foster-father visited the bishop, and Cruithnechan was asked to celebrate the festival. His memory failed him when it came to Psalm 100, but his young pupil came to the rescue even though he had only learned the alphabet.[6]

One story suggests that Columba may have been offered kingship. 'He was eligible to the Kingship of Eriu according to family, and it was offered to him, if he himself had not abandoned it to God.' An alternative translation reads: 'would be offered' rather than 'was', with the suggestion that kingship was not offered because he had chosen the church.[7] However the text is read, Columba appears to have had a strong sense of vocation. The royal power that might have been his was abandoned to God. Though his faith-calling was to shape his life, he was ever the politician engaging the power politics of his day for both good and ill.

Probably as a teenager, Columba was sent to the monastic school of Moville, part of modern-day Newtownards. Moville was founded as a school in 540 CE by Finnian, whose own education had been shaped at Whithorn. Under Finnian Columba was 'learning the wisdom of Holy Writ' and he became a deacon. Scripture study was not the totality of the curriculum. Classics, philosophy, literature, science (as understood at the time) and Latin were all taught subjects. Columba spoke and wrote in both Latin and Irish and appears to have been quite a scholar. Study in the monastic school, the university of the day, provided opportunity to obtain the Seven Degrees of Wisdom. The first was awarded on reading all 150 Psalms in Latin and the seventh degree was that of doctor or professor of literature.

From Moville Columba moved to Leinster, where his bardic training took place under Gemman, described as a 'Christian bard'. The study of Irish literature and rhetoric were now part of Columba's education. After bardic training Columba moved to one of the great monastic schools at Clonard in Meath. Clonard had been founded in 520 CE by another Finnian who, instead of going on pilgrimage to Rome, founded Clonard to renew sound faith in Ireland. Clonard became quite a 'campus' with up to 3,000 students and has been referred to as a 'city'.

At Clonard Columba was in the company of eleven other outstanding students, described as having their 'heads full of dreams'. They became known as the Twelve Apostles of Ireland and were not mere dreamers. Ciarán of Clonmacnoise, Brendan the Voyager, Brendan of Birr, Mobhi of Glasnevin, Cainnech of Aghaboe and Comgall of Bangor were the greatest of the Celtic monastic founders.

At Clonard Columba was ordained priest and eventually left for Glasnevin. After a short stay there Columba returned to Ulster, and in 545 CE he founded his first monastery at the Place of the Oaks, Derry. He was so fond of the Oaks that he would not allow any to be cut down to make way for his church. If they fell through natural decay, they were either used to light a fire on the arrival of strangers or they were given to the neighbouring poor. The Celtic option for the poor was further expressed through the feeding of up to a hundred poor every day in the Derry monastery.

Though Columba founded other monasteries at places like Durrow and Kells, Derry had a special place in his heart. As he lay dying and was making his last will, he is reputed to have said: 'My soul to Derry'. Other words expressing the depth of feeling and attachment to Derry have been attributed to him, or more likely put into his mouth by later poets. Yet they must express something of what he felt:

> Were all the tribute of Scotia mine,
> From its midland to its borders,
> I would give all for one little cell
> In my beautiful Derry.
> For its peace and for its purity,
> For the white angels that go
> In crowds from one end to the other.
> I love my beautiful Derry
> For its quietness and its purity,
> For heaven's angels that come and go,
> Under every leaf of the oaks,
> I love my beautiful Derry.
> My Derry, my fair oak-grove,

> My dear little cell and dwelling,
> Oh God in the heavens above!
> Let him who profanes it be cursed.
> Beloved are Durrow and Derry,
> Beloved is Raphoe and pure,
> Beloved the fertile Drumhone,
> Beloved are Swords and Kells.
> But sweeter and fairer to me
> The salt sea where the sea-gulls cry
> When I come to Derry from far,
> It is sweeter and dearer to me,
>   Sweeter to me.[8]

Behind the exile on Iona lies a story of crisis in Columba's life. It could be described as a mid-life crisis because he was about forty-two years of age when it happened.

When on a pilgrimage to Rome, Finnian of Moville is said to have brought a very beautiful copy of the Psalms back to Moville and placed it in the church there. Another version claims it was Jerome's translation of the Scriptures, which would have been the first of this translation to arrive in Ireland.

Columba was very impressed by the manuscript but knew Finnian well enough to know that permission to copy would not be forthcoming. So when the Daily Office was complete, Columba would slip into the church and begin to copy, probably the Psalms. On the last night Finnian sent for the Scriptures and Columba's cover was blown. Finnian was extremely angry and claimed the copy as rightful owner.

Columba appealed to Diarmit, the high king, and with Finnian set out for Tara. The case was presented and Diarmit gave his now-famous judgement:

> To every cow her calf, to every book its transcript
> Therefore the copy you have made, O Columcille,
> Belongs to Finnian.[9]

An angry outburst and retort followed from Columba; 'It is a wrong judgement and you shall be punished for it.' One thing led to another and tribal politics began to dominate. Columba after all was of royal blood and tribal power politics came into play. The northern Uí Néills to whom Columba belonged were roused against Diarmit. Political gain was to be had and a great battle ensued.

The theology of prayer should be noted since Columba aimed his prayer against the druidical rites of the enemy: 'My Druid – may he be on my side! – Is the Son of God, and Truth and Purity.'[10]

Christ is the superior druid on Columba's side. Meanwhile Finnian prayed for victory for Diarmit, but when he saw the greater effectiveness of Columba's prayers he stopped on the grounds of damage limitation; a speedy Columba victory would lessen the casualties!

Nowhere is prayer more abused and the name of God misused than in a conflict or war situation.

The battle of Culdrevney (north of Sligo) was a disaster for Columba. His side won but as many as 3,000 lost their lives. The crisis was far from over. The fallout and the consequences were far-reaching. A synod was called at Teltown in Meath, and it accused Columba of having caused the death of 3,000 people. The synod excommunicated him in his absence. When he arrived, Brendan of Birr rose, bowed and kissed him. The rest of the synod members were none too happy, but Brendan pleaded Columba's cause. He succeeded and the synod revoked the sentence of excommunication. Even then Columba stopped short of penitence, still choosing to blame Diarmit's judgement. 'It was not I who caused it', he kept saying, 'it is hard for a man unjustly provoked to restrain his heart and sacrifice justice.' Better the victim mentality than accept responsibility!

The synod commanded Columba to convert as many to Christianity as had lost their lives in the battle. Columba left Teltown ill at ease with himself. In deep remorse he turned to his soul-friend Molaise and was advised to accept the verdict so he exiled himself from Ireland. Whether his exile was voluntary or the direct outcome of the battle and the synod, Columba did not leave Ireland forever. Adamnan suggested that he returned to Ireland on ten occasions. In 563 he left, perhaps with the intention of never returning to his beloved Derry. At forty-two years of age he left Derry, and on 12 May 563 CE he arrived on Iona. Undoubtedly he left Derry in deep remorse, willing enough, perhaps to fulfil the synod's sentence and Molaise's advice. But the politician was still active and he was also motivated by the need to liberate the Dal Riada Scots from the Pictish King Brude and secure their independence in western Scotland. There was also the motive of evangelisation. The non-Christian Picts needed conversion. His visit the following year to King Brude in Inverness was political and evangelistic. It was also strategic since to have the king with you would open up the highlands and islands to the Christian mission of Iona. Under Columba and his successors Iona became the great centre of mission and evangelisation for much of Scotland and Northumbria. From Culdrevney to Iona was more than a physical journey for Columba. The warring politician never ceased to be the politician, but he became more of a prophetic peacemaker as well as evangelist and educator.

5.2   The Druim Cett Convention

From Iona Columba launched his mission to the Picts. It is claimed he worked for nine years among the Picts. The Pictish mission did not succeed in all it set out to do. Despite the meeting with King Brude, the king did not convert to Christianity even though political relations between the Pictish kingdom and Scottish Dal Riada were relaxed. Brude may well have had his own agenda since good relations with Dal Riada might provide an ally against the strength of the Northumbrians. No churches or monastic foundations appear to have been established in Brude's capital. The significant missionary activity seems to have been immediately north of Dal Riada and in Strathtay. They were not insignificant achievements, but perhaps fell short of what Columba hoped for.

When Columba arrived on Iona, Connall was king of Scottish Dal Riada. Relaxed political relationships had been negotiated with Brude in Inverness, but Scottish Dal Riada was an Irish dependency. Nine years after Columba's arrival on Iona, Connall died and the way was open for independence or home rule.

Eogan was in line to the throne but Columba had other ideas. Claiming that a dream came to him on three consecutive nights, Columba returned from the island of Himba to Iona and crowned not Eogan but Eogan's brother Aidan as king.

The incident shows how powerful the role of Columba had become in Scottish Dal Riada. He overthrew the natural right of succession, bypassed the rightful heir to the throne and crowned Eogan's younger brother Aidan. It is tempting to be cynical about the dream story and divine intervention! On the other hand Columba may have recognised greater leadership qualities in Aidan. He did have a better military record and, if a home-rule campaign was on the horizon, good-quality leadership would be required to achieve an independent Dal Riada.

Columba's power was again evident in that he did a new thing. He summoned Aidan to Iona for the coronation, which was really a consecration. Tradition has it that the stone on which the crowning took place was the black Stone of Iona, the Stone of Destiny. The story goes that it was removed from Iona to the Scottish mainland and then on to England. It is claimed to be the stone on which successive British monarchs were still crowned. Only in November 1996 was it returned with great ceremony to Scotland, evoking not a little Scottish pride. Whatever the truth about the stone, and it might be difficult to convince a Scot otherwise, the act of consecration on Iona was a powerful political act. Columba delivered a thundering charge and sounded like 'a grand Old Testament theocrat'. Aidan was anointed, but the power behind the throne was Columba. The message was clear to King Brude and the Irish king. Aidan's consecration was a political statement, a declaration of independence. The year was 574 CE. Did Columba know of the forthcoming Convention of Druim Cett in Ireland? Did his action in part precipitate it?

The Druim Cett Convention took place in 575 at modern Limavady and it was a National Assembly of Irish kings and clergy. To this great occasion of church and state came Columba, returning to Ireland from exile. He also brought Aidan with him. Whatever else was on the agenda, home rule for Dal Riada was, and Columba seemed intent on negotiating and achieving it.

His arrival at Druim Cett must have been impressive. Columba still had many friends in Ireland and these joined him on arrival. This was his first visit home since the exile in 563. One poem speaks of forty priests, twenty bishops, fifty deacons and thirty students, all singing Psalms.[11] And that was only the ecclesiastical retinue. To be sure Aidan did not travel without his attendants. If, as a story suggests, they were delayed by a storm and almost shipwrecked, the late arrival at Druim Cett must have been spectacular. Here was no exile returning, but a church dignitary, leader and peace negotiator, sponsor and

guarantor for the king of Scottish Dal Riada. When the Irish king Aedh was told Columba
had arrived, he was so disturbed that he threatened death on any assembly member who
showed Columba respect. There is no record of what Aedh said or thought when his
son Domhnall welcomed Columba, kissed him and gave him his seat! That no doubt
undermined Aedh's authority, but Columba's approach had already created insecurity in
Aedh. Never mind the ecclesiastical and regal retinue from Scotland, with Derry only
up the road from Druim Cett, the Columba 'supporters club' no doubt enthusiastically
joined their hero *en route*!

There were three key items on the Druim Cett agenda, and Columba was a main player
in all three.[12] He negotiated accommodation in all three, not without compromise, all
of which is worthy of note in sixth- or twenty-first-century Ireland. There is a sense in
which Druim Cett was a sixth-century peace process.

Columba Negotiated the Release of Scannlan

Scannlan was the son of the king of Ossory and was a prisoner of Aedh the king of Irish
Dal Riada. According to the story Scannlan had been given by his father to Aedh as
hostage with Columba acting as surety for his release after a year. Aedh refused to release
Scannlan and built a small hut around him, put nine chains on him, fed him only salt
food with very little drink and placed fifty guards around the little hut. Scannlan was
unjustly imprisoned and harshly ill treated, yet Aedh was refusing to release him. Not
surprisingly Aedh became disturbed when Columba approached Druim Cett!

Columba demanded the release of Scannlan but Aedh still refused saying that the prisoner would die in his hut. According to Adamnan's story the only real comfort Columba
gave Scannlan was that he would outlive Aedh. Another story suggested that Scannlan
was eventually released.

The issue in the story is a justice one and Columba is involved in seeking justice for
Scannlan. Aedh's action is unjust, but Columba is prepared to confront the king with the
moral demands of justice. Evangelism and justice are not in separate compartments, nor
are they either/or issues. The evangelistic proclamation of Jesus is Lord is always a protest
against all social, economic and political injustice.

Columba Negotiated the Preservation of the Bards

The bards were the successors of the druids. The bardic tradition, therefore, was an old
institution in Celtic society. They were among the top strata of the Celtic social system.
They were a professional class highly qualified by skill and wisdom. The bards were the
poets, storytellers, eulogists, genealogists, historians and satirists. They were feared for
the last skill. In a few lines a prince's or a king's reputation would be demolished, perhaps
deservedly so.

The bards were powerful people and their role was open to abuse. Blackmail could be
a weapon against a Celtic prince or chieftain. Large fees could be charged. They developed a reputation for having a 'cauldron of greed'. Numbers became large and it is said

that on three occasions: 'the people of Ireland rose up against them and insisted on their suppression. But they were saved each time by the intervention of the men of Ulster.'[13] The last of the three occasions was in fact at Druim Cett.

Columba himself had been trained as a bard and had some empathy with them. At Druim Cett, the political establishment and the church wanted to suppress them. As satirists were they getting too close to reality for the establishment?

With regard to finance Columba argued that God had bought thrice fifty psalms of praise from David. Throw out the bards, he argued, and Ireland would be deprived of a wealth of folklore, which would never be replaced. The compromise situation was to reduce their numbers and carefully regulate their activity. They were to work and be given the means of support.

When the agreement was reached, it is said that 1,200 bards entered the convention and sang songs of praise to Columba. At this point Columba covered his head with his cowl to protect himself from the demons of pride.

The negotiated preservation of the bards not only saved a rich cultural heritage but also preserved the role of the satirists, which meant the retention of the critical voice. Those in power rarely, if ever, like criticism. Power has the tendency to preserve itself. With the retention of the bards Columba won a victory for the freedom of speech, especially the speech of those who could expose corruption and hypocrisy and articulate an alternative arrangement of power and relationships.

Columba Negotiated Political Accommodation

This was a major agenda item and the one for which he had brought Aidan the new king of Scottish Dal Riada to the Druim Cett. For the latter Ireland was the mother country. Scottish Dal Riada was under obligation to pay taxes to Aedh and Irish Dal Riada. Adamnan described the convention as a 'conference of Kings'. Columba has been portrayed as political advisor to Aidan, but his role seemed to have been more prominent and pro-active. Scottish Dal Riada was a province of Irish Dal Riada, which meant having taxes and military obligations or support for any project the Irish king decided to pursue.

Columba had ensured Aidan's kingship, thus putting a strong person on the throne. Druim Cett was about negotiated independence or home rule for this Scottish kingdom. In this, Columba succeeded with another compromise solution. Scottish Dal Riada was freed from all payment of taxes to Aedh, but was obliged to support any land war involving Aedh. There was no obligation to assist in any sea or maritime expedition. Aidan was now independent and home rule was secured for the Irish colony. The spin-off politically and militarily was that King Brude of the Pictish kingdom now also recognised the independence of Scottish Dal Riada. Aidan took this to mean expansion of his own kingdom and a number of conquests followed, including the Isle of Man. It has been claimed that Aidan's 'military might together with Columba's political sagacity laid a foundation on which ultimately the Kingdom of Scotland was built'.[14]

That was no small achievement, and again it was Columba's negotiation skills that found accommodation between kingdoms with potential for conflict. Again compromise was needed, as it always is. There were no absolute winners in 575 CE, and there have been no absolute winners in the modern Irish conflict. Negotiation, compromise and accommodation are the key words from the Druim Cett Convention. They remain key words for the resolution of any contemporary conflict.

Evangelist, Christian educator, diplomat and peace negotiator, these were the characteristics of Columba. He held them together as a whole. Not for him was there any great divorce between evangelism and justice, faith and politics.

As for relationships between all the peoples on the island of Ireland, some legendary words put in the mouth of Columba may still speak to those with ears to hear in contemporary Ireland:

> There are three pets that Colmcille had, a cat and a wren and a fly. And he understood the speech of each of these creatures ...
>
> And it happened that the wren ate the fly and the cat ate the wren. And Colmcille spoke by the spirit of prophesy, and he said it was thus people should do in a later time: the strong of them should not eat the weak, that is to say, should take his wealth and gear from him and should show him neither right nor justice. And Colmcille said that while the God of Erin was thus, the power of foreigners should be over them, and whenever right and justice were kept by them, they should themselves have power again ... 'When the Gaels do justice and right among themselves', said Colmcille, 'I make great joy ...'[15]

5.3   Peace and Unfeigned Charity

These are literally the last words Columba is reputed to have spoken. It was just before midnight as 8 June 597 CE drew to its close. Columba had just been to the Sunday evening prayer vigil. He returned to his hut with his servant Diarmit and gave him one last message for the Iona monks.

> These, O my children, are the last words I
> address to you – that you be at peace and
> have unfeigned charity among yourselves,
> and if you thus follow the example of the
> Holy Fathers, God, the Comforter of the
> good, will be your helper.[16]

After speaking his final words, Columba lay in silence until the bell rang for midnight prayer. Dying as he was, he went to the church. The key notes in the story, as it is told, are light and radiance. Columba's final vision was of the delight and joy in the community beyond. With that joyful vision he peacefully slept away. It was 9 June 597 CE.

It is said that Columba was eventually buried with Patrick and Brigid in Downpatrick.

A piece of old verse has it:

> His grace in Hii (Iona) without stain,
> And his soul in Derry;
> And his body under the flagstone
> Under which are Brigid and Patrick.[17]

Wherever his final resting place, and Downpatrick has no historical basis, it is Columba's last words that live on and speak across the centuries. There is no authentic community in any age without peace and love. They are relational values, and Columba, true to the Celtic tradition, was thoroughly relational. That in turn was firmly rooted in the primary gospel metaphor of the kingdom.

The kingdom of God was the core idea and vision for Jesus. The Hebrew prophets before him and he himself never offered any precise definition of the kingdom. They painted various word pictures none of which by themselves could exhaust the meaning. Instead the metaphors, similes and parables provided windows through which to see something of what God's kingdom or gracious activity in the world meant. Clues and signs are what the prophets and Jesus offered.

Whatever else the kingdom is about, there are enough windows, clues and signs to suggest that the kingdom is essentially about relationships and community. The essence of the kingdom for Jesus was in the Beatitudes (Matthew 5: 1–12). Here is what it means to participate in God's kingdom and here is kingdom lifestyle. The core values of kingdom living are in the Sermon on the Mount and in the Beatitudes in particular.

None of the Beatitudes is about individualistic or private faith. They can only be lived in relationship and in community. They embody essential community values and are the core requirements for good community relationships. God is profoundly concerned for the quality of people's lives together and that means profound concern for the nature and quality of community life. It is in human and community relations that signs of the kingdom appear.

The blessedness of those who hunger and thirst actively for justice and peacemaking is a community experience. The peace and charity or love, which Columba wished for his Iona community, are the basis of good relationships. Peace is total well-being, which in its Hebrew meaning is social, economic, political and therefore personal and relational. Love is only possible in relationship and in community. In public terms love is justice. Justice is about law and order, but it is much deeper and broader in its Hebrew and Christian meaning. It is about an equality of opportunity and access to power and resources. It is about fair play in social, economic and political relationships. Embodied by the Hebrew and Christian ideas of covenant and kingdom, peace and love, charity or justice are at the heart of a radical alternative vision for community.

Celtic Christianity and spirituality are community centred. In his longing for peace and unfeigned charity, Columba was expressing his community vision. Without such values and qualities, community disintegrates and destructs.

His last words still envision an alternative community for the twenty-first century. Anglo-Irish relationships have improved and more healing is still required. North/South relationships also have the need for healing and more mature relating. Relationships within Northern Ireland reflect positive signs, but also much that is as far – if not further – back than ever, even with a positive settlement.

Inter-church relations can claim to be better than they were in 1969, but no one reflecting deeply can be satisfied. There is gratitude for progress, but despair too for continued separatism and exclusiveness. Churches have created too many comfort zones and exclusion zones. Even the God who is proclaimed is an exclusive and excluding God. The 'God on our side' theology is not dead and neither are those other two sectarian components: 'the one true Church outside of which there is no salvation' and 'error has no rights'. Neither are these three planks of sectarian theology the monopoly of one religious tradition or the other.

Columba belongs to both the Irish and the Scots and remains a significant person for each. Even if the population of Northern Ireland insists on its Irish and Ulster-Scots identities (and they are perceived by some as oppositional identities, defined in opposition and each sometimes needing the other as opposition to reinforce its own identity), Columba is shared. Within our conflicting loyalties, our ancient hatreds and our deep divisions, Columba and the Celtic tradition still speak. There is a shared future, but only if we can practise his last words: 'Be at peace and have unfeigned charity among yourselves.'

Key Points from Chapter 5

- ❑ Columba was born 521 CE at Gartan, Donegal of royal lineage, which may account for his political astuteness.
- ❑ Columba became known as Columcille, Columba of the church (cille) because of his frequent visits as a child to the church to pray.
- ❑ He was fostered by Cruithnechan the priest and educated by Gemman, which provided the grounding for his later roles as poet and advocate on behalf of the bards at the Druim Cett Convention (575 CE).
- ❑ At the monastic school, possibly at Moville, Columba studied scripture, classics, philosophy, literature, science and Latin.
- ❑ Columba then attended Clonard in Meath to complete his training, where he encountered eleven other outstanding students who also became monastic founders. There he was ordained priest.
- ❑ Columba founded his first monastery at the Place of the Oaks, Derry in 545 CE.
- ❑ Controversy over ownership of Columba's copy of Finnian's manuscript led to Columba rousing the Northern Uí Néills to whom he belonged against the High King Diarmit and to the battle of Culdrevney, in which as many as 3,000 lost their lives.

❏ A synod at Teltown in Meath accused Columba of having caused the deaths at Culdrevney and he was ex-communicated in his absence. At Brendan of Birr's intervention on Columba's behalf the sentence was revoked. The synod commanded Columba to convert as many to Christianity as had lost their lives.

❏ On Molaise's advice Columba accepted the verdict. In 563 CE he left Derry for Iona to convert the Picts.

❏ When Columba arrived on Iona Connall was king of Scottish Dal Riada, an Irish dependency. When Connall died, nine years on, the way was open for independence or home rule.

❏ Columba chose Aidan and not his older brother Eogan, as king, overthrowing the natural right of succession. He consecrated Aidan on Iona, using the occasion to claim independence for Dal Riada.

❏ The Druim Cett Convention (575) was a national assembly of Irish kings and clergy. Columba attended with Aidan to achieve home rule, which he negotiated, agreeing to the compromise that Dal Riada would support Aedh, the king of Irish Dal Riada, in land war.

TEST QUESTIONS

❏ Outline Columba's achievements at the Druim Cett Convention. What qualities did he demonstrate in his negotiations?

❏ Comment on the claim that at the heart of Columba's community vision was a desire for peace and charity. Justify your answer.

6 Columbanus: Patron Saint of a United Europe

Robert Schuman, a French foreign minister, was the architect of the European Union. After the destruction of the Second World War Europe was devastated and divided, especially France and Germany. People like Schuman dreamt of a reconciled and united Europe in which old antagonisms and divisions could be dealt with and healed. A Coal and Steel Community was the forerunner of today's European project in which much of the healing has taken place. Europe is a large project in conflict transformation seeking to ensure that war between European nations will not happen again. For the first time in centuries Europe is at peace with itself. Centuries-old conflicts have been laid to rest, the last conflict regions being Northern Ireland and the Balkans. Much has been achieved in these regions towards peaceful futures. Conflicts rooted in history are being transformed, and new and shared futures are being constructed.

European history was in much need of healing and reconciliation, and today democracy and human rights have become the basis of a more just and peaceful Europe. Schuman's vision has been realised to quite a degree. It is no longer a Eurocentric world but a larger, more diverse world in which a united Europe plays its part. As Schuman articulated his dream he invoked an early Irish Christian saint, Columbanus. Columbanus, he claimed, was the patron saint of those who seek a united Europe. Described also by the late Cardinal Tomás Ó Fiaich as 'Ireland's first European', Columbanus has left his footprints over large areas of western Europe and remains very much a European saint. His influence on the civilisation of western Europe has been significant. 'In particular his influence through his continental monastic foundations has been a major factor in the development of the intellectual life of the early Middle Ages.'[1] Who was this patron saint of a united Europe?

6.1 Early Life and Formation

Columbanus was born in Leinster in 543 CE. Like all of the early Celtic saints, history and legend are interwoven. He appears to have been a young person of strength and attractive appearance. The latter quality drew the attention of members of the opposite sex, one of whom in particular drew a mutual response. The relationship might well have become permanent but for his sense of vocation to the monastic life. The relationship ended not without pain for both and not without a deep inner struggle on the part of Columbanus.

Another legend suggests a single-minded sense of monastic vocation. His mother was opposed to his becoming a monk and threw herself across the door of the family home in Leinster to stop him leaving. She begged him not to leave but he stepped over her body and with determination walked on without looking back. This may indeed strike us as harsh on his part and we may feel anger at Columbanus and pity for his mother. Whether or not it happened this way we do not and cannot know. The storytellers were not interested in factuality or literalism. The story is set in the context of reflection on a gospel saying attributed to Jesus about putting one's hand to the plough and not looking back. A life journey does at times produce difficult choices with hard decisions, and this has been part of the experience of many, whether religious or not. At the same time significant relationships ought not to be abused and there may be times when insensitivity is inexcusable. Columbanus may have been faced with difficult choices and hard decisions as a young man.

Around the year 560 CE, when he was seventeen years old he left home to become a student at a new monastery. The monastery was located on the island of Cleenish in Lough Erne, Co. Fermanagh. The abbot was Sinell, one of the Twelve Apostle of Ireland who had studied with Finnian at Clonard. Not a great deal is known about Sinell other than that he was 'famous for his holiness and for his learning in sacred things'.[2] He appears to have been a scripture scholar, which would have provided Columbanus with a grounding and formation in scripture study as well as grammar and rhetoric.

After some time Columbanus appears to have left Cleenish for his Leinster home, perhaps for a period of reflection on his vocation. He may well have had struggles with uncertainties and doubts. Difficult choices are never made quickly or once and for all. Struggle is involved, and this is the pattern portrayed by the Christian gospels of Jesus, especially in the wilderness temptation story, which according to Luke occurred again and again.

Later Columbanus returned to Cleenish and then seems to have committed himself to monastic life by moving on to Bangor, Co. Down. Here he became part of one of the great Irish monasteries of the sixth century. Its founder was Comgall, who has been included in various lists of the Twelve Apostles of Clonard. Bangor was a third-generation foundation, and life there was lived under a strict rule which reflected Comgall's own formation. Bangor gained a reputation for choral music, probably an antiphonal style carried on around the clock by various choirs. It also became known as the place of 'perennial praise' and produced one of the great liturgical books of the early Irish church, the Bangor Antiphonary, still extant in the Ambrosian Library in Milan. It was in this rich tradition of monastic discipline and liturgy that Columbanus was shaped and formed for his work beyond Ireland. His Rule, which he wrote on mainland Europe, is not only

6.1 The European journeys of Columbanus

representative of the Irish church but also 'probably reproduces the Rule of St Comgall's famous monastery at Bangor …'[3] A monk was being formed for a European odyssey.

6.2   A European Odyssey

Around 587 CE, in his mid-forties Columbanus left Bangor for mainland Europe. He was accompanied by twelve monks, probably a reflection of the normative gospel story of Jesus and twelve disciples. Included in the group was Gall, who was later to have a Swiss city and canton named after him. What motivated Columbanus to leave Ireland for continental Europe is not clear, except for the characteristic Irish wanderlust, better described as 'white martyrdom', the practice of 'living years far from home and hearth for the sake of the gospel'.[4] So many accepted this vocation that it is usual to speak of 'Irish *peregrini*' or travellers for the sake of Christ. It was a way of life chosen intentionally by a monk such as Columbanus and was considered a form of martyrdom because of its difficulty. 'The Celts had a specific word, *hiraeth*, for the extreme yearning for home associated with this latter form of martyrdom; because of their deep love of family, it was considered the hardest of all to endure.'[5]

Perhaps it was 'white martyrdom' that took Columbanus with his travelling companions to continental Europe, not primarily as a missionary but in voluntary exile for the sake of Christ.

He arrived close to St Malo and eventually came to Burgundy. The first monastic community was established at Annegray, where in the Roman ruins he found the temple of

Diana. The Irish/Celtic monks repaired the ruined temple and dedicated it to St Martin of Tours. Like the desert tradition, which had shaped Martin and influenced the Celtic monastic movement, the community at Annegray attracted so many that another community was required. Columbanus found another ruined Roman fort and established a second monastic community at Luxeuil. This foundation excelled in learning, holiness and penance, and it was probably at Luxeuil that Columbanus wrote his Rule. Choral music also became a characteristic of Luxeuil with an increasing Divine Office sung night and day. The Bangor model had been exported to mainland Europe.

Columbanus was frequently at the centre of controversy. In the Hebrew prophetic tradition, he became critical of the king's abuses of power and in particular of his sexual abuses and excesses. He refused to baptise the children of the king, considering his relationship to be unethical. This public action deeply upset the Queen Mother, Brundhilde, who took vengeance by banishing Columbanus from the region. They were escorted to Nantes to take a ship to Ireland, which three days out to sea was caught in a severe storm and eventually ran aground. The monks were returned to land, and Columbanus set off on his second European odyssey. On this journey he passed through Paris, Metz, travelled by river boat to Koblenz, then along the Rhine to Basle and eventually across Lake Constance to Bregenz in Austria. Significantly in modern times Bregenz has been twinned with Bangor.

The journey was not yet complete as Columbanus made his way over the Alps to Lombardy in north Italy. In 614 CE he was preaching in Milan and in the same year founded the famous monastic community at Bobbio. A year later he died in Bobbio.

That Columbanus and other Irish monks were responsible for saving European civilisation may be open to question. It may even be another Irish tall story! Yet they did bring learning and faith to a Europe struggling with cultural and spiritual breakdown. The monasteries became great places of culture and spirituality, attracting large numbers to a living and creative expression of faith and learning. There was undoubtedly an Irish contribution to Europe, and Columbanus was 'the typical representative of Irish monasticism on the Continent.'[6] His memory has never faded from the road he travelled. 'Today, thirty-four parishes in northern Italy are still named in his honour'.[7] Not surprisingly, 1,400 years later, he was invoked as the patron saint of those who seek a united Europe.

6.3   A Spirituality for Relationships

The spirituality of Columbanus is relational and is the basis for an ethic for living in community. Relational life is shaped by core values which he expresses in his writings and which have their roots in early Irish practice.

God – The Unutterable and Inconceivable

Columbanus had a strong sense of the transcendence of God, God in God's otherness and as incomprehensible mystery. It is not possible for a finite, human mind to get to the end of God, nor is it possible for human experience to experientially grasp or encapsulate the totality of God. To affirm this is not all there is to say about God but it is a God-dimension and part of human intellectual and emotional experience.

From a faith perspective God-talk is inevitable and words are necessary. They are also inevitably limited, and this is true when humans try to describe or express life's deepest experiences and awarenesses. There are experiences of life that are beyond words, often experiences of love, intimacy and deep connectedness. Faith is essentially mystical. Human experience is at times essentially mystical, and whilst the mystical often connects with otherness, with the deep-down mystery of things, it is not impractical. Mystical experience at its best re-connects us with the ordinary and the earthy. Columbanus was a mystic and he writes as such conveying warmth and creativity: 'Nobody should attempt to explore the impenetrable aspects of God … Believe simply, but strongly, that God is and will be as he has been, for God is immutable.'[8]

Columbanus is not advocating a passive acquiescence in mystery or a simplistic acceptance that God-talk is beyond us. He himself did not cease to push the boundaries of thought and experience. Being on the road for the sake of Christ was itself more than an outward journey, although in essence an inner journey. Yet important as 'believing strongly' was, there is that of God that is impenetrable and immutable. This is not vocabulary we would use today but it is saying something about the deep mystery of God forever beyond our finite minds and experiences.

> 'Who, I say, shall explore his highest summit to the measure of this unutter-able and inconceivable being? Who shall examine the secret depths of God? Who shall dare to treat of the eternal source of the universe? Who shall boast of knowing the infinite God, who fills all and surrounds all, who enters into all and passes beyond all, who transcends all? Whom no one has ever seen as he is. Therefore let no one venture to seek out the unsearchable things of God, the nature made and cause of his existence. These are unspeakable, indescribable, unsearchable …'[9]

Columbanus lived in a pre-scientific age and assumed a different cosmology from the twenty-first century. Yet his theology does not lead to a 'God of the gaps'; the more scientific knowledge we have, the less we need the God hypothesis and the more God is pushed to the margins. Such a theological model leads to the abolition of God. The new cosmology or universe story does not marginalise God, but we do need to acknowledge that 'God' is always constructed in human language and there is no full or final word about God. Even the Christian claim that God is truly present in Jesus does not exhaust or disclose all there is of God. At the beginning of the twenty-first century, Christians and scientists, and quite often both, are a little more humble and a lot less certain than they used to be. Faith-based or secular mysticism is less prone to arrogance, abuse of power and the construction of a domination system, religious, scientific or otherwise. Columbanus walked humbly with his God!

Speak Peace Not Destruction

Columbanus has been described as 'typically Celtic in his combination of contemporary qualities, being by turns harsh and tender, humble and haughty, innovative and conservative'.[10] He was not an uncritical observer of the ecclesial scene and openly expressed criticism of the Pope. He was concerned for the well-being and unity of the church, and if the Pope needed reminding that he alone did not have a monopoly on the interpretation of scripture, that consensus was needed if the truth was to be realised, then Columbanus was prepared to say so. He was also prepared to remind the Pope where authentic power and authority lay, and in doing so expressed a critical, dissenting Irish spirit. Rome was only important for the Irish because it was St Peter's chair and the Pope needed to remember that: 'Power will rest with you just so long as your principles remain sound.' Also the Pope must not allow 'the head of the church to be turned into its tail ... for among us (in Ireland) it is not who you are but how you make your case that counts'.[11] Are such words considered to be harsh or tender, humble or haughty?

Columbanus believed that one of the greatest Irish failings was the tendency to gossip and to be self-opinionated. In his Rule he called for two virtues, obedience and silence. Obedience was in imitating Christ while silence was the antidote to gossip and self-opinion. Better to be silent than to speak ill of another in their absence or demean them in their presence. Better also to be silent than to always express an opinion about everything, especially when one is uninformed or ill-informed on the issue. Speech ethics were important to Columbanus.

Speech ethics are addressed in Sermon Eleven where he has a number of significant things to say about the use of the tongue. He is concerned about preserving peace but it is a fragile gift and easily destroyed. Columbanus is being relational again in his ethics. Peace can be 'lost by light talk and the slightest injury by a brother'.[12] Words are weapons and can be destructive. Personal character and community peace can be destroyed by harsh or violent speech. The supreme virtue of love shapes a very different social practice.

> For those who train themselves in the perfection of brotherly love should not speak as they please, letting the tongue follow the mind, since we shall be called to account not just for harmful words but also for words that are idle. Therefore we should train ourselves not to speak too much, but to say only what is necessary.[13]

His double reference to 'training' ourselves suggests a lifetime discipline of speech, a self-discipline shaped by love which is concern for the well-being of the other in social and community relations. Columbanus is all too aware of the human tendency to gossip, telling stories, true or untrue, which demean the other, destroy character and relationships. 'For there is nothing more pleasant for us than to speak of others and their concerns, to speak idle words everywhere, and to criticise those who are not present'.[14] Such unethical speech is not only destructive of others and the peace but is also self-destructive. 'However wise we may be, we give less offence when we speak less than when we speak more, for when someone lies, curses, criticises, then they cut their own throat with their sword.'[15]

Idle speech and gossip are self-demeaning and destructive of one's character. They are also destructive of the peace of humanity:

> See what is done in the works of unrighteousness; setting and planting, which we can only established with long hours of work every day, are destroyed by a single word of negative criticism, and what can hardly be constructed by lengthy labour is brought down by the beginning of a single act of speech. Let everyone beware therefore in case their root be torn up from the land of the living on account of their hateful and negative words. For no one ever undermines those whom they love, and belittling others is the firstborn son of hatred.[16]

Sectarianism, racism and homophobia are practised by hateful and negative words. Political discourse is paralysed by name-calling and abusive speech which dehumanise the other. Many complain about political correctness, but language and speech are sensitive and are used by those with power and privilege to even inadvertently wound, offend and dehumanise. Colour-coding references to evil and negativity as black or dark conveys a destructive message about people whose skin is not white. It may even be the speech of white supremacism. The frequent and continued use of masculine language in worship and liturgy is more about patriarchal control than realised or admitted. It is speech maintaining patriarchal systems, structures and domination, all destructive of women's humanity and dignity.

Columbanus' emphasis on speech ethics is prefaced by the affirmation that 'God made man (sic) in his (sic) own image and likeness' and that the divine image of all persons is not to be destroyed or distorted.[17] The sermon on speech ethics ends with the ringing affirmation of neighbour love and a prayer that Christ the founder of peace and revealer of the God of love 'inspire us with love'.[18] For Columbanus, speech ethics matter and ethical speech is grounded in divine love, the image of every woman and man.

Travellers and Pilgrims on the Road

In Sermon Eight Columbanus reflects on life as a journey which is difficult and uncertain: 'Human life is like a road and by comparing it to a shadow, we have shown that it is dubious and uncertain, and that it is not what it seems to be.'[19] He adds that it is 'unpredictable and blind'.[20] There is realism here about life and all human experience which is never simple, much less simplistic and always complex, not least in the experiences of suffering and loss. Dubious and uncertain, unpredictable and blind are also realistically descriptive of a journey through a moral maze, where there is often no moral certainty or ethical clarity. That is life and to think otherwise is pretence. Columbanus was also realistic about 'our life's end', which for him is also part of the journey. How we deal with death, how we integrate it or fail to integrate it into the life journey has important implications for the way we travel. This is a bigger question than life after death or the emphasis on an other-worldly hope. It is a here-and-now question with this-worldly implications. Dying is part of living and an intricate dimension to the natural cycle of things. Life, death and resurrection are not a Christian invention 2,000 years ago but the archetypal paradigm of how things are.

It is not life made simple but again a complex journey and an uncertain moral maze. For travellers on the way Columbanus affirmed that 'it is natural too that they should experience anxiety on the roadway.'[21] Part of his response to this may be open to question:

> And so we too who are on the road should hasten on, for the whole of our life is like one day's journey. Our first duty is to love nothing here, but to love the things above, to desire the things above, to relish the things above and to seek our home there, for the fatherland is where our Father is. Thus we have no home on earth, since our Father is in heaven.[22]

A twentieth-century, country-and-western religious song waxed lyrical in terms of 'this world is not my home, I'm just a passing through.' Is such a theology and that of Columbanus world-denying and therefore ethically irresponsible? If this world is only a staging post on the way to the next, why care for it, and why care for the rest of the human community?

There does appear to be a strand of this in the Christian scriptures. The first piece of written Christian literature is Paul's first letter to the Thessalonians. The first generation of Christians seem to have lived with an expectation that Jesus would return soon and the end would come. For some of Jesus' followers in Thessaloniki, this meant ceasing to work and a passive waiting for the PAROUSIA. Whatever Paul believed about the imminent return of Jesus or otherwise, he had no sympathy for the voluntarily unemployed visionaries of the Thessalonian house church. Indeed he saw it as socially irresponsible, leading to a breakdown in community ethics.

Columbanus does appear to echo the Colossian letter: 'So if you have been raised with Christ, seek the things that are above, where Christ is seated at the right hand of God. Set your mind on the things that are above, not in the things that are on earth' (Colossians 3: 1–2). The letter is post-Pauline and belongs to a later generation whose expectation of the imminent return of Jesus and the end has been disappointed. The things of earth and of above are then described in terms of relationally distinctive or enhancing virtues and values. Compassion, kindness, humility, meekness, patience and forgiveness are all relational qualities and the ethical basis for shared community in the here and now. Things of earth and things above are not spatial references but negative and positive value systems which destroy or build up community. The positive values 'from above' are experienced as transcendent values or God's dream for human community on Earth.

It is not explicit what Columbanus means when he reminds his faith community that: 'governed from above we may spurn the things of the present, and thinking only of the things of heaven, may turn our backs on earthly things.'[23]

Literally understood, it is other-worldly and dangerous encouraging an ethically irresponsible attitude to human and environmental life. It discourages a celebration of life
and the response of joy and enjoyment to that which is good and beautiful. There has
always been such a strand of life-denying, other-worldly approach to faith. But it may
have over-literalised scripture language, interpreted texts not only literally but over-
individualistically and failed to see the life-affirming and creation-affirming emphasis
of the Judeo-Christian scriptures.

A more metaphorical and relational reading of faith provides a this-worldly response
and an ethically responsible engagement with life together in the world. We may wish Columbanus had been more explicit and clearer, but his words then can only be interpreted
– as all texts from the past are – by contemporary minds living in the present context.

He is realistic though about how dubious, uncertain, unpredictable and blind the life
journey is. It needs moral courage and inner strength. The moral image within ourselves
and in life within community and world is real. For Columbanus God is not a crutch in
a complex world, nor is faith an infantile dependency on a 'big daddy' kind of God. The
God who 'contains all things … God the Trinity is still known and present to us … Let
us pray to him (sic), I say, while we are here, so that we may enter in more intimately
and understand more clearly.'[24]

Columbanus' Rhine voyage produced his best-known poem, the 'Boating Song', which
captures the sense of life's journey as adventurous and robust, requiring courage, endur-
ance and struggle to the end. It is a theo-poetic expression of faith written as he and his
companions sail down the Rhine towards the Alps and the abandoned town of Bregenz
on the shores of Lake Constance. The rhythm of the poetry and repeated refrains seem
suited to rowers bending their backs and stretching with the oars. The life of faith through
the moral maze is one of 'heave' and 'still sounding heave'.

> See, cut in woods, through flood of twin-horned Rhine
> passes the keel, and greased slips over seas —
> Heave, men! And let resounding echo sound our 'heave'.
> The winds raise blasts, wild rain-storms wreak their spite
> but ready strength of men subdues it all —
> Heave, men! And let resounding echo sound our 'heave'.
> Clouds melt away and the harsh tempest stills,
> effort tames all, great toil is conqueror —
> Heave, men! And let resounding echo sound our 'heave'.
> Endure and keep yourselves for happy things;
> you suffered worse, and these too God shall end —
> Heave, men! And let resounding echo sound our 'heave'.
> Thus acts the foul fiend: wearing out the heart
> and with temptation shaking inmost parts —
> You men, remember Christ with mind still sounding 'heave'.

Stand firm in soul and spurn the foul fiend's tricks
and seek defence in virtue's armoury —
You men, remember Christ with mind still sounding 'heave'.
Firm faith will conquer all and blessed zeal
and the old fiend yielding breaks at last his darts —
You men, remember Christ with mind still sounding 'heave'.
Supreme, of virtues King, and fount of things,
He promises in strife, gives prize in victory —
You men, remember Christ with mind still sounding 'heave'.[25]

Living as Global Citizens

Columbanus lived on a large map. His travels in the latter part of his life were extensive and his achievements considerable. He may well have been Ireland's first European. Significantly the monasteries he founded in Europe were often on the ruins of old Roman buildings. He travelled to a Europe in which the Empire had declined and had indeed fallen. Not only had Roman temples and buildings fallen into ruins, the imperial culture, civil religion, symbols and values had also collapsed. It was in many ways a broken continent, not for the first or last time.

The Irish may not have saved European civilisation but they did make a remarkable contribution to renewing culture, faith and learning. Columbanus was helping to construct a new Europe on the ruins of an old Empire.

No civilisation or imperial power lasts forever. History is in many ways a series of endings and new beginnings. In a real historical sense, the end is always near. It is not the end of the world but the end of an era, the end of an epoch. It may be the end of an imperial era such as the decline and end of the Roman or British empires. Or it may be the end of a world view that has dominated thinking and imagination for a few centuries. Many feel that the Enlightenment or modern era is over. Whatever exactly is meant by post-modern, it is the shorthand description of an era, the landscape of which is not yet clear. Others speak of the post-Christian era which became more than evident during the latter half of the twentieth century in Europe. The power connections between church and state, throne and altar, which had existed in Europe since 313 CE, the Constantinian era, have now broken down in Europe with the deprivileging of Christian churches and their loss of power in the public square. Some generations live through endings and beginnings. Columbanus perhaps lived more during a new beginning and made his contribution to the reconstruction of Europe.

On the last major accession to the European community in 2002 the *Irish Times* produced a series of maps reflecting the political boundaries at different times during Europe's history. Boundaries have always kept changing, and so Europe has kept changing, not least as a concept. It has been a continent repeatedly torn by war and violence. The most catastrophic was during the first half of the twentieth century. Millions died in two horrific wars, the first of which was supposed to end all wars but the ending of which made the second inevitable. Then out of the ruins came the dream of European reconstruction which has been the story of the second half of the twentieth century and is still ongoing. Yet again Europe is being reconstructed, a task still in progress and already a model of conflict transformation. For the first time in centuries Europe is at peace and the process is at the same time a model of just peacemaking where systems of democracy and human rights ensure that war and conflict are not possible and not necessary.

We are now European citizens, reflected on our passports, in a way we have never been before. This does not mean that Europe is utopian. There are faults and flaws and justice issues which still need to be tackled, but the reconstruction of Europe is well under way, an awareness of which is probably greater in the Republic of Ireland than Northern Ireland. The United Kingdom still struggles with European ambivalence.

Modern Europe's problems have often been based on nationalism. Nationalism is an eighteenth- to nineteenth-century invention and has been at the heart of much war, conflict and violence. The orange and green nationalisms of Ireland have a rhetoric suggesting that the respective nationalisms and rights of nation states go back to the beginning of time. This fictional delusion of nationalism is writ large. We do not live in a post-nationalist context, though regional and cultural identities may be gaining strength. Thankfully new nationalism in Europe is confined mainly to the sports field.

Columbanus lived in a pre-national age, over a millennium before nationalism was invented along with flags and anthems and making the supreme sacrifice for one's country. Yet he did have a vision of human belonging that transcends all cultural and national boundaries. His Christian faith, which was already the faith of Christendom Europe at that time, convinced him that believing in Christ provided a uniting bond which transcended all boundaries. 'Do not believe that we think of ourselves any different than of you: for we are joint members of one body, whether Gauls, Britons, Irish or of any other people.'[26]

From the perspective of Columbanus, the primary identity factor was Christ, uniting people in one body transcending all other identity labels or markers. In all probability it was a Christendom perspective, possible then but not now.

Nevertheless, it is possible to continue speaking of a transnational identity and commitment. Those in the Christian community and Jewish and Muslim communities can still hold the perspective of all human beings made or stamped with the image of God. Recognising every human person as the image of the God of life, and, on the basis of this affirmation in the Genesis creation poetry and myth, as an image of God most fully realised in community, provides a primary identity and commitment transcending cultural and national loyalties. It also shapes an ethic of personal and communal responsibility, being one's sister's and brother's keeper as well as active commitment to the common good. Such is an Abrahamic social ethic rooted in compassion, justice, right relations and peace.

Europe in its history has also been shaped by the humanist tradition, rich also in its ethical roots. In a post-Christendom Europe, which Columbanus never experienced, the great humanist tradition – along with the Judeo-Christian and Muslim traditions – continues to make its contribution to a transnational identity beyond the boundaries based on our basic humanity. We are primarily human beings with moral worth and dignity which transcend all national labels and commitments. We are always more than Gauls, Britons or Irish and any diminution of human dignity is immoral.

Faith-based or humanist-based, we are in the twenty-first century global citizens with transnational commitments, living in one world with one shared future for the planet and ourselves. Columbanus had no sense or experience of that, but in his own time he pinpointed and was committed to a more primary and common identity that relativised all the other identities and crossed all the boundaries.

KEY POINTS FROM CHAPTER 6

- ❏ Columbanus was born in Leinster in 543 CE. In 560 CE he became a student at a monastery on the island of Cleenish in Lough Erne under abbot Sinell.
- ❏ He moved to Bangor, Co. Down, one of the great Irish monasteries of the sixth century founded by Comgall. Life at Bangor was strict, and it gained a reputation for choral music carried on round the clock. It produced one of the great liturgical books of the early Irish church, the Bangor Antiphonary.
- ❏ Columbanus' Rule, which he wrote on mainland Europe, probably reproduced part of Comgall's.
- ❏ In 587 CE Columbanus left Bangor for mainland Europe accompanied by twelve monks.
- ❏ He may have been responding to a personal desire for white martyrdom when he became one of the Irish *peregrini*, or travellers for Christ.
- ❏ The first monastic settlement was at Annegray in the ruins of a Roman temple, which he dedicated to St Martin of Tours. He established a second monastic community at Luxeuil. The latter excelled in learning, holiness and penitence and the Divine Office was sung night and day. It was probably at Luxeuil that Columbanus wrote his Rule.
- ❏ Columbanus continued his journey through Europe founding monastic communities, his most famous in Bobbio, Italy. At times he had to leave certain places as a result of his critique of rulers who were abusing their power.
- ❏ He died in Bobbio in 615 CE and is remembered for his contribution to the development of learning and faith in Europe, which at the time was struggling with cultural and spiritual breakdown.
- ❏ Columbanus' spirituality is relational as expressed in his writings.
- ❏ He affirmed the great mystery of God while seeking relationship with God in the ordinary and earthy.
- ❏ His concern for the well-being and unity of the church at times led him to criticise the Pope.

❑ In his Rule he calls for obedience in imitating Christ and silence rather than inappropriate speech which could harm individuals and relationships.

❑ His concern was for the well-being of the other in social and community relations, and was grounded in his belief in a God of love, who is imaged in every woman and man.

❑ Columbanus recognised that the unpredictable nature of life can create anxiety and needs moral courage and inner strength to persevere in faith and live relationally.

❑ His vision was of human belonging that transcends all cultural and national boundaries. For Columbanus Christ united people in one body.

❑ He reminds us that we are human beings with moral worth and dignity that transcend all national labels and commitments.

Test Questions

❑ What contribution did Columbanus make to the development of an ethical vision and practice in Europe?

❑ Explore the view expressed by Robert Schuman that Columbanus was the patron saint of those who seek a united Europe. Justify your answer.

7   Marginalised Women: The Struggle for Justice

Patriarchy is a local and global phenomenon, and gender equality – along with poverty, violence and environmental destruction – is one of the major issues facing the twenty-first century. It is difficult to deny the patriarchal context of even the earliest writings. The Bible is set in a patriarchal context and written and translated from a patriarchal perspective. The same can be said for the history of its interpretation. It is startling, therefore, when the question is raised as to the sex of biblical authors. Most assume that the biblical literature was written by males. Yet one scholar has now raised the question about one author and suggested on the basis of some evidence that part of the first five books of the Hebrew scriptures may have been written by a woman.[1]

The suggestion appears in a careful piece of work identifying not only the various sources or strands that make up the Pentateuch, Genesis–Deuteronomy, but the socio-political locations and identities of the different authors. These five books are a skilfully edited edition of different collections of stories and laws produced at very different times and places in Israel's history. The J collection, so called because it consistently uses the name *Jahweh* for God, emerged from the southern kingdom of Judah. The E collection, using another name for God, *Elohim*, has its roots in the northern kingdom. Deuteronomy is known as D and its author is also responsible for the Deuteronomic history found in Joshua, Judges, I and II Samuel and I and II Kings. The P literature is written from the perspective of the priests and inevitably has much to say about temple, rituals and genealogies. It also includes a history of Israel, another version from another perspective, told in I and II Chronicles.

It is in relation to the J and E collections that the intriguing suggestion is made. The E stories have a strong connection to the Levite priests of Shiloh in the northern kingdom. In Israel the priesthood was strictly male, making male authorship a certainty. The J collection is open to another gender possibility. In the Judean court women of the noble class did have power, privileges and education, certainly more than males from a lower class. The J stories are more concerned with women and more sensitive to women's issues. In Genesis 38 there is the story of Tamar, and E simply has nothing to compare with this story. What is most striking in the J story of Tamar is: 'that the story is sympathetic to a wrong done to this woman, it focuses on her plan to combat the injustice, and it concludes with the man in the story (Judah) acknowledging her rights and his own fault'.[2] This, of course, is not conclusive evidence that the author was a woman, but it opens the possibility that a woman did write J with sensitivities that a male author may not have possessed. Perhaps because of that the J stories were much valued in the southern kingdom of Judah.

There are other stories from sources other than J which are not kind or sensitive to women. Judges 19 relates the story of a nameless concubine who becomes the brutalised victim of gang rape, who was later dismembered by her master and the twelve parts of her body left in different parts of the country. The tribe of Benjamin was held responsible and put to the sword, which resulted in another urban genocide with 400 young virgins taken captivity so that the line of Benjamin would not be wiped out completely. A not dissimilar story is told in Genesis 19, where the men of Sodom surrounded Lot's home and demanded his guests, or male strangers, to use them as sexual sport. Lot offered his two virgin daughters instead. Again they are nameless.

Rigorists and biblical literalists insist that the stories of Genesis 19 and Judges 19 are to be read in terms of God allowing the women to be gang raped rather than have men commit homosexual acts. God allows the lesser of two evils, the gang rape of women being the lesser!

The Bible itself nowhere says this. It is the rigorists' and literalists' interpretation imposed on the text from a morally distorted perspective. The interpretation is distorted in three ways:

- It is misogynist treating women as less than human.
- It is homophobic in its logic.
- Its god-image is demonic falling far short of basic human ethics.

Whether biblical stories or Celtic hagiography, these three distortions provide critical test questions to be put to any text. All writers have agendas, often patriarchal and a reading or interpretative strategy needs to be critically and ethically discerning.

Women in the Celtic tradition may have enjoyed a little more equality than their mainland European sisters, but it would be unwise to push the equality agenda too far. There are stories also of the victimisation of women, a classic example being the legend of Macha from Ard Macha, Armagh. She was forced to race against horses at Emain even though she was at the point of giving birth. Like the Bible, the Lives of saints have stories of the rape and murder of women. In Celtic culture women were exposed to war and retribution given the tribal nature of Celtic society. It is against this background that Adamnan produced his Law of the Innocents or Law of Women that gave legal protection to women and children in situations of war and violence. Adamnan decreed that 'all women were mothers of equal, and supreme, cultural importance'.[3] This late seventh-century text gave motherhood a unique status but it limited women's social roles to that. In that sense the protection of women also created confusion. But his Law arose from family experience. His mother pitied the plight of women because they were enslaved by men. Men forced them to stand in deep pits holding the wooden cooking stakes upon which meat roasted. Women were thrashed and sent into battle to kill each other to satisfy men's warlike ambitions. According to the story an angel persuaded Adamnan to make a law protecting women from abuse.[4]

Early Celtic women may have been better off than their European sisters, especially in relation to laws of marriage and divorce, but it was a relative equality as can be seen in exploring the lives of early Irish women saints.

In the world of hagiography there are few stories of women. Male Lives dominate but the Lives of four great Irish women have survived. Brigid we have already looked at and along with her are Ita, Moninna and Samathann. Lesser known except for her spirited reply to Senen is Canair of Bantry. Their stories reveal either a struggle with patriarchy or ambivalence around gender relations.

7.1   Ita of Kileedy

Ita is probably next to Brigid in significance and importance in early Ireland. She is thought to have lived from 480 to 570 CE and has been described as 'the most irresistibly memorable'.[5] Some of the stories parallel those of Brigid, such as the tale of a fire blazing outside the room where Ita slept. Fire is one of those primal images of sacredness, divine presence or holiness. Ita was sometimes referred to as Deirdre and was born in Co. Waterford of noble family stock. A young male from her social class wanted to marry her but she refused him because she believed her vocation was to the religious life. Her father opposed her religious calling to follow Jesus but in a vision an angel rebuked him. The young man was disappointed as Ita followed her vocational instincts and founded a church in Co. Waterford. Later she too received directions from an angel and went to west Limerick. There she founded a monastery which became known as Cill Ide or Kileedy. A number of notable characteristics emerge from her life, most of which offer an ethical perspective.

Foster-mother of the Saints of Ireland

Ita had a reputation for being an educator – a role that is set in the cultural context of fostering. Many male saints were said to have been fostered and educated by women in religious life. Brigid is said to have fostered Tigernach and Lassair while Ita is said to have educated Mochoemog for twenty years. A more famous saint – Brendan the Navigator – spent his first five years with Ita. Foster-mothers like Ita were educators of those young boys and even into later life offered advice and spiritual guidance. In a sense Ita was a counsellor as well as an educator. Spiritual mentor and soul-friend would also describe her role. She was foster-mother to so many, forming and shaping them for religious life, that she acquired the reputation of being foster-mother of the saints of Ireland.

A deep bond of love characterised the relationship between foster-mother and child. Ita and Brendan had a 'life long relationship marked by affection, loyalty, and intellectual exchange …'[6] When Brendan returned from one of his voyages he went to Ita who scolded him: 'Ah, dearly beloved son, why did you go on your journey without first taking counsel from me.'[7] And yet in the first Irish Life of Brendan, Ita offers paradoxical if not contradictory advice: 'Do not learn of women or of virgins, lest you be reproached in regard to them.'[8] According to this Brendan was to ignore the counsel of women, yet he continued to visit his foster-mother and was scolded for not seeking her help before one of his voyages. Perhaps the story reflects the hagiographer's anxiety with sexuality and opposite-sex relations.

Sexual Politics

Ita's life contains more references to religious women's sexuality than any other Lives of women. In thirty-six chapters, four are about sexual lapses of nuns and a fifth focuses on a man who is strongly tempted. Ita appears to have clairvoyant abilities, telling nuns that they have 'fornicated in secret' one virgin when she was visiting in Connacht. All confess and repent except one thieving nun who left the community and became a harlot. The nun who had her baby in Connacht did repent and returned to Kileedy where she lived in holiness, bringing up her child there.

In Ita's Life a nun is warned by Ita to travel home with a bishop! The point is that the nun is described as being at risk from her own weakness of sexual lust. Samthann's Life has two sexual episodes, one of a nun becoming pregnant and the other of a monk who entering the community fell in love with a beautiful nun who responded. She got permission to go on an errand and met him outside the walls. Samthann brutally intervened and put an end to the relationship banning the monk from ever visiting again. There are also stories of male saints producing miraculous abortions for penitent nuns which can be seen as acts of compassion but by the twelfth and thirteenth centuries such stories were being edited out of the narratives.[9]

What are we to make of these stories? The Lives perhaps tell us less about the saints and more about the hagiographers and the monasteries in which they lived some centuries later. There does appear to be a development of sexual anxiety, a growing concern with sexuality. If the Lives were, like the Bible, written mainly, if not exclusively by males, then there may be an attempt in the context of sexual anxiety to present male monks and clerics with unimpeachable and scrupulous morals. The stories are not kind to women, advocating the avoidance of women and portraying them as struggling with sexual lust and as temptresses. Even the monk-induced abortions put men in good light, compassionate in response to penitent women. Whatever about the early double monasteries and the positive relationship between women and men, the later Lives portray a growing sexual anxiety, a growing unhealthy attitude towards sexuality and an increasing patriarchy which led to growing gender inequality in Irish Christianity and society.

Thirst for Holiness

Ita's name is said to be derived from IOTA, thirst. She became Ita because of her thirst for holiness. It may well be that it was this quality of life that drew many foster children to Kileedy and which also attracted so many women.

St Brendan once asked what were the three works most pleasing to God, and the three works most displeasing to him. Ita answered, 'Three things that please God most are true faith in God with a pure heart, a simple life with a grateful spirit, and generosity inspired by charity. The three things that most displease God are a mouth that hates people, a heart harbouring resentments, and confidence in wealth.'[10]

Holiness has to do with wholeness of living, and there is a rich holistic spirituality about Ita's response. The ethics of holiness portrayed here are essentially relational. It is in relationship to God, others and the world that faith is lived with integrity. 'A mouth that hates people' is speech that is bitter and destructive of other people. When characters and reputations are destroyed by words there is a hate motive behind it. Conflict is not only created by prejudiced and malicious words, but also words kill. People may claim not to have broken the law by destroying property or people's lives but incitement to hate or opposition has often been taken to its logical conclusion by others. Sectarianism, racism and homophobia work that way.

'A heart harbouring resentments' is self-destructive as well as destructive of relationships. It produces a bitterness that poisons feelings and attitudes and imprisons one in anger and self-pity. The inner spirit of resentment and negativity blocks the ability to relate, not only to the immediate other but also to all others. One engages in battle with oneself and other persons.

'Confidence in wealth' is misplaced trust. Life becomes centred on accumulation, getting more and eventually on greed. It is the insatiable desire for more which often convinces itself that scarcity is the perennial problem. There is not enough, which can be behind personal pursuit of success and plenty, as well as motivate imperial expansionism; more weapons, gold, land, oil. Wealth is usually gained at the expense of others. Life centred on wealth and more wealth often shuts out the poorer neighbour and diminishes compassion.

Ita's positive values enhance relationships and help build a caring and compassionate community.

'True faith in God with a pure heart' is the authentic centre and focus of confidence. Commitment to and confidence in God is to centre life and shape relationality by God's values of love, mercy, justice and compassion. The pure heart is not moral perfection, the Celtic saints were down to Earth and all too human. It is, as Jesus taught in the Beatitudes, the single-minded commitment to the life of God in the world, the blessedness of the merciful, justice seekers and peacemakers. The pure in heart, committed to these values and praxis, see God or know God. And to know God is to build a merciful, just and peaceful community.

'A simple life with a grateful spirit' is a way of life with integrity. A consumerist society imposing on us its liturgy of advertising, creating need and necessity when they are not really required, produces a life-spirit of insatiable desire. It creates an endless competition between people, a lifestyle of jealousy, envy and covetousness. Neighbour is set against neighbour, child against child, and humans against the Earth. Western lifestyle is unsustainable at the expense of the rest of humanity and the ecological systems. Ita knew nothing of our contemporary environmental crisis, but she practised simplicity of living. She only accepted small grants of land for her foundations and she was committed to the poor and marginalised. Simplicity of lifestyle is a faith commitment for the twenty-first century. It is holiness in action, and a grateful spirit is the opposite of a grasping spirit.

'Generosity inspired by charity' is Ita's third positive value towards others. At the heart of this practice is compassion. One story describes a hospice-like ministry which cares for a dying abbot, who perhaps like all humans facing their mortality has anxieties and fears. Because of Ita's caring and compassion 'St Comhganus then left this world accompanied by choirs of angels'.[11]

In another story Ita shows tremendous compassion for a murderer who seeks forgiveness and reconciliation. Ita held together justice and mercy, which not all can do, and saw justice as ultimately restorative and transformative. Ita was not prepared to leave another human to 'rot in hell' or to 'lock him up and throw away the key'. In yet another story she responded with compassion and patience to a man whose ways she had wanted to change. He was wounded in a battle against west Munster and she sent a messenger to him. 'He brought the brother back to Ita who received him kindly, and he was healed of his wounds. Later, he did a fitting penance, according to Ita's order, and died a happy death.'[12]

Caring, healing, forgiveness and reconciliation, restorative justice and transformation of relationships and life were all qualities practised in Ita's foundation at Kileedy. Her response to Brendan articulated her thirst for holiness and expressed the essence of holiness. It was not an other-worldly piety but a centredness on God which was a generous ethical relationality.

7.2   Monenna of Kileevy

Monenna was also known as Darerca, or Moninne, or even Modwenna. The prefix Mo apparently was a common Irish term of endearment found in saints' nicknames. Her father's name was Mochta and her mother Coman. Legend has it that Monenna received her nun's veil from Patrick. Whatever the truth she and nine other women set up a foundation on Beggery Island, Wexford harbour, and there they were guided by Bishop Ibar, reputed to be an uncle. Ibar was associated with Brigid at Kildare and perhaps not surprisingly Monenna went to Brigid's foundation at Kildare. Monenna impressed everyone with her selfless care for the poor and then returned to her native part of Ireland in Co. Louth. She formed a community there and soon had 150 women in residence. The story goes that Brigid, impressed by Monenna, gave her a silver vessel which she left behind at Kildare. When discovered, Brigid ordered the vessel to be thrown into the River Liffey, from which it flowed to the sea, drifted northwards until it reached calm waters near Newry. Monenna's brother found it and returned it to her.

The busy, bustling community in Louth became too much for Monenna and she sought a quieter life at the foot of Slieve Gullion in Co. Armagh. The site was Kileevy and she remained there until her death in 517 CE. There are legendary stories of her founding communities in Scotland and England, but these are more likely to be embellishments or a confusion of names.

Gender Politics

The presence of women, like Monenna, suggests that women played a significant role in the early Irish church. Yet even though there are many references to men in the Martyrologies or calendars of saints, few Lives have remained. Perhaps there were other Lives which have not managed to survive. The few which do still exist suggest that women struggled with clerics and warriors in a gender battle. Monenna herself seems to have dealt with numerous power struggles which frequently undermined and diminished her foundations. 'At one point, a bishop, threatened by her nearby foundation, instituted cloister on the nuns, leaving them with very little water during a severe drought.'[13]

In a twelfth-century document, Conchubranus told a story about Coemgen who was determined to destroy Monenna's foundation. He found out that Monenna was reading psalms with a reformed robber and his gang, and then asserted that a devil had persuaded him to attach and wreck the community. Monenna was quite calm about the whole episode and reminded Coemgen of the 'little black boy' (sic) whose advice had inspired his jealously. 'She settled the whole matter by drawing off the demon and drawing Coemgen a nice, hot bath – a reminder, perhaps, of the Ulsterman's habit of dunking Cúchulainn in an icy-cold tub when he went a little wild.'[14]

From the twelfth-century perspective of Conchubranus, Monenna's era was one characterised by antagonism caused by sexual difference. Yet in his perception of sexual politics he described Monenna as a heroine. Significantly there is a reconciliation in the story between Monenna and Coemgen, and a local king who is also involved in the power struggle is converted to more holy ways and his nephews become clerics through Monenna's influence.[15]

Though Monenna continually struggled with gender politics, there are stories which suggest an influential and formidable woman. When she was dying, she was visited by warrior chiefs. They pleaded with her not to die and leave them as orphans. 'For we know that whatever you ask from the Lord you will undoubtedly receive from him.'[16] Did they believe that her prayers would guarantee them victory in war? Monenna refused but gave them some of her personal possessions which if carried into battle would give victory. What she is reported as saying next is of huge significance. 'They should not go to war against other people beyond the bounds of their lands unless compelled by a greater force, lest the wrath of the Lord come upon them.'[17] In other words their battles are only to be in self-defence, not an invasion of others or a pre-emptive war. Women saints like Monenna did have a peacekeeping role.

Within gender politics, Monenna was a significant saint. One Life suggests a saint of major cultic importance sought out by many people for her prayers on their behalf. Many also visited her community which had a reputation for educational greatness. The profile is of a woman with significant autonomy, not answerable to male authority and making her own decisions about community foundations and life. She also negotiated the release of hostages, not immediately or easily achieved, but with determination, intervening in local politics and negotiating with kings. Her lack of land and property are portrayed as intentional, an asceticism or self-denial that refused donations of land and goods. Monenna is therefore profiled as a woman of strength and character, much sought by lay people for her prayers, wisdom and negotiating skills.

Nevertheless, she appears to have become disillusioned by gender politics. It is said that 'she never looked upon the male sex again'.[18] If she had to out of necessity, she would 'face or address men with her face covered by a veil, ever wishing to leave an example to the younger so as not to allow death to enter the soul in any way through the windows'. She also 'hid everything from men's notice except what clear necessity forced her to display to them'.[19] These responses may indeed reflect survival tactics in the hostile environment of male domination and gender politics. Women obviously struggled with marginalisation. The ethical challenge of gender inequality goes back a long way in Irish history.

7.3   Samthann of Clonbroney

Samthann's foundation was at Clonbroney, Co. Longford and was one of the three primary monasteries for women in Ireland. It continued to exist until the mid-twelfth century. Samthann herself was from a high-ranking Ulster family. At one point she was betrothed for marriage but chose instead a religious life. When she entered the monastic community, she was responsible for the finances of the community, which suggests skills in practical administration. Handling finances also gave her the opportunity for generosity, not least towards the marginalised who visited the monastery.

There are conflicting stories about who founded the community at Clonbroney. One source credits Samthann while another credits Patrick, and yet another states that followers of Brigid were responsible. Whatever the truth, it is with Clonbroney that Samthann is associated.

She was a person of considerable gifts, described as an 'abbess, a spiritual director, an educator, and a church dignitary who attended the church synods in Ireland'.[20] That she was all of this in an Irish world where male dominance was extensive and male spirituality the norm is enough to mark her out as one of the great women saints of Celtic Ireland. It is her skills in a spiritual direction that stand out in a world where male norms predominate. Yet even here there is gender ambivalence.

Spiritual Direction

Two stories related to prayer have been preserved which suggest her deep insights into spirituality. They also suggest that Samthann did not suffer fools gladly and was impatient of pious pretension. She could see through piety that was unreal and impractical.

A monk once asked her about posture for prayer. Should a person pray lying down, sitting or standing? Samthann replied that a person should pray in every position. Perhaps the monk was being over-concerned or over-anxious about fine detail, displaying a scrupulosity about liturgical practice. Samthann's reply may be affirming that there is no one way to pray. Lying down, sitting or standing, no one way is better than another, use one, use all, it is the communion with God that matters. Whatever enhances the divine-human relationship and enables the relationship to grow and deepen are what is important.

On another occasion a teacher approached Samthann proposing to give up study and give himself to prayer. She replied: 'What then can steady your mind and prevent it from wandering, if you neglect spiritual study.' Spiritual wisdom was able to see through the pious pretension. Was the teacher looking for an escape route? The next proposal confirmed Samthann's instincts, 'I wish to go ahead on pilgrimage.' He may have been deflated by her reply but she pushed him to face up to the real world. 'If God cannot be found on this side of the sea, by all means let us journey overseas. But since God is near to all those who call on him, we have no need to cross the sea. The kingdom of heaven can be reached from every land.'[21]

It is likely that the teacher was running away from himself, seeking to escape into prayer and pilgrimage rather than face a deeper issue within. Religion and piety are often ways of escape from a past or a present reality. The more intense and even extreme religious life becomes, the more certain it is a sign of escapism. A religion of absolute certainties and rigorism is often on the run from some painful reality. A wise spiritual director like Samthann had the ability to see what was really going on in the teacher's life and perhaps also in the life of the monk mentioned above. Scrupulosity and pious pretension are escape routes and unhealthy with root causes. Wise spiritual direction can help deal with the issues.

Samthann had a significant association with the Celi-De movement and was on very good terms with Maelruain, one of the main leaders of this renewal experience. The movement was based in Tallaght. It was an eighth-century reform movement which developed as the Celtic church was increasingly being challenged by the leadership of the church in Rome and when the Viking invasions were beginning to occur in Ireland. It was also a time when intense rivalry was developing between Irish monasteries, often resulting in armed conflict. A battle between Cork and Clonfert resulted in a great slaughter. In 824 CE the Kildare community was plundered by Tallaght. Christians became disillusioned, there was a distinct lack of leadership in the church and profound theological questions were being asked about God, who and where is God and what models of the holy life are available? This context had a major influence on the writing of hagiographies, the Lives of saints as models of holiness.

The Celi-De or Culdees, meaning 'friends' or 'servants of God', were also disillusioned and seeking reform and renewal. The renewal movement emphasised three themes, especially in the hagiographies:

- spiritual disciplines – solitude, prayer and simplicity of life;
- devotion to the saints;
- the value of anamchara – soul-friend for ongoing spiritual development.

Maelruain was the founder, abbot and bishop of Tallaght. Along with Dublitter, abbot of Finglas, Maelruain advocated a clear vision of spirituality. Tallaght and Finglas became known as 'the two eyes of Ireland'. Other monasteries were involved including Clonbroney where Samthann was also a key influence on the movement. She is portrayed as a 'woman of prayer', knocking frequently 'at the doors of divine mercy'.[22] Much of her prayer is in a socio-political context, especially that of release of hostages and captives. Her prayer is connected to the socio-ethical issues of her time and suggests an inseparable connection between prayer and action. Samthann's ethic of justice is rooted in her contemplation and prayer. Her spiritual direction is connected to real life, ecclesial and secular, again suggesting spirituality without dualism.

A highly significant story emerges from her relationship with Maelruain. She sent a messenger to him asking 'whether he accepts women for confession, and will he accept my soul friendship?' This was prefaced with the comment that Maelruain was 'my favourite among the clerics of the desert'. Maelruain then 'blushed down to his breast and made three genuflections, then fell silent for a long time.' After some time he agreed to receive spiritual advice from Samthann. When the messenger reported back, Samthann angrily asserted 'I think something will come of that youth.'[23] She then took a brooch and pricked her cheek until only milk came out, blood being a symbol of passion. Holding the drops of milk on her nail as proof of her purity, she declared, 'So long as there is this much juice in his body, let him bestow no friendship nor confidence upon womankind.'[24]

The story with its gender implications suggests ambivalence in relation to spiritual direction. Samthann does not believe that Maelruain has the ability to be a soul-friend to women. It would be a dangerous practice given his displaced lust. That is how she interprets his 'blushing down to his breast'. She is aware of the complexity of male spirituality but her only way of dealing with his displaced lust 'was to eradicate her own source of passion'.[25] To what extent did Samthann buy into the male norm of spirituality, accept separatism in spiritual practice and deny her own sexuality? Brigid certainly did not accept separatism. In her monastery they 'offered joint prayers to heaven', and she had no time for Patrick's practice of asceticism, standing at nights in icy pools of water. This 'form of male spirituality was not to be hers'.[26]

The issue remains since the equality of spiritual experience and norm has not been realised. Male norms and practice still dominate after two millennia of Christian history. Women still struggle to have their spirituality validated as of equal worth and value. Some have even bought into the male norms and others are ambivalent about equality of norms and spirituality. Though challenged and improving, women's spirituality remains on the margins.

7.4   Canair of Bantry

Little is known about Canair. The only source is found in the Life of Senan, whose monastery was on Scattery Island, in the mouth of the River Shannon. Canair had founded a hermitage at Bantry where she lived and prayed for many years. She died on Scattery Island around 530 CE and her partially submerged grave is marked by a flag and can still be seen in the waters off the Island. In the sixteenth century a poet claimed her as patron of sailors and her grave has often been saluted by sailors as they passed by. It is her encounter with Senan that is memorable and significant and which is told in Senan's Life.

Ireland's First Feminist?

She is described as 'Canair the Pious, a holy maiden of the Benntraige of the south of Ireland'.[27] One night at prayer she had a vision of all the churches of Ireland, and 'a tower of fire rose up to heaven from each of the churches'. The greatest fire was on Scattery off Inis Cathaig. Seeking the place of her resurrection, the place of death, she set off immediately, and from the shore of Limerick she 'crossed the sea with dry feet', arriving on the island. Senan 'went to the harbour to meet her, and he gave her welcome'. There follows an astounding dialogue, with Senan suggesting that she receive hospitality, not on his island, but on another island with a woman's monastic community. Canair will have none of his separatism and insists that hospitality will be on Scattery.

Senan replied: 'Women cannot enter on this island'. 'How can you say that?' asked Canair. 'Christ is no worse than you. Christ came to redeem women no less than to redeem men. He suffered for the sake of women as much as for the sake of men. Women as well as men can enter the heavenly kingdom. Why, then, should you not allow women to live on this island?'

'You are persistent', said Senan.

'Well then', Canair replied, 'will I get what I ask for? Will you give me a place to live on this island and the holy sacrament of Eucharist?'

'Yes, Canair, a place of resurrection will be given you here on the brink of the waves.'

Canair's persistence paid off, she stepped on to the island, received the Eucharist and 'immediately went to heaven'.

Canair's response to Senan is remarkable and it remains a powerful speech in its challenge and affirmation of gender equality. She may have been a recluse in Bantry but she had worked out a significant theology of equality. Was she Ireland's first feminist?

The dialogue needs to be seen in the context of a ninth- and tenth-century Life of Senan wrestling with the question of mixed-sex monasteries. There are issues of gender, sexual temptation and ritual purity. The Life of Senan has been read from the perspective of suspicion of women in Irish church life. It has been suggested that women were considered impure. In another interpretation Senan is not considered misogynist. Rather he suggested that she go to a neighbouring island for which he has responsibility for pastoral care and sacrament, but Scattery is closed to women, though even here he gives way to

Canair's persistence. 'That Senan was not a shunner of women is confirmed by the Life's later episodes, which recount that when he knew he was soon to die he was determined to visit for one last time his sister and also the group of nuns who lived under his rule.'[28]

Harrington, though, does not answer the question, why separatist monasteries, and why Senan's initial response? Also the strength of Canair's reply is played down. True, he did give way to her persistence, but is the Life not reflecting accepted practice and a separatist women's monastery which still requires the male rule and pastoral care? In fairness to Harrington she does draw attention to the upsurge in misogyny, certainly by the time the story of Canair's is retold in the thirteenth-century poetic Life of Senan. In this version Senan asks: 'What do women have in common with monks? We shall neither admit you nor any other women on to the island.' Canair is told to return to the world lest she become a source of scandal. 'Even if you are chaste in heart, you have sex in your body.' Canair dies and the story ends by satisfying both positions. Canair has got her wish and Senan has allowed no women on the island.[29] Senan's response that Canair has 'sex in her body' is misogynist and a variation on the interpretation of Genesis and Eve as temptress. It is difficult not to avoid the conclusion that the separatist monastic community was a male decision expressing spirituality as a male norm and women as the source of sexual temptation. Why does Adamnan's tenth-century Life report that the male saints were offended by the burial of a pregnant woman on Tory Island off the west coast of Donegal and why do eleventh-century Writings of Bishop Patrick of Dublin not even allow female birds to land on an island in north Munster? Senan was reflecting a widespread practice, a misogyny present from the beginning though challenged from the earliest days by female saints.

Christian and secular women lived on the margins, ultimately subordinate to men, kings and clerics.

> But their status, like that of secular women, always depended on the status of their male guardians and their roles remained formally supportive … Penitentials, canons, laws, annals, and genealogies all confirmed women's subsidiary relation to male clerics. While interpretation of religious women's roles changed over time, by region, by individual, and according to gendered perspective, the roles themselves remained the same.[30]

Key Points from Chapter 7

❏ The content of biblical stories and Celtic hagiography was patriarchal, as have been the majority of interpretations of these texts. More recently an awareness of a plethora of interpretative strategies that promote competing ethical practices has underlined the importance of critiquing the interpretative strategy.

❏ In the world of Celtic hagiography male lives dominate. However, lives of four great Irish women have survived: Brigid, Ita, Monenna and Samthann; also Canair of Bantry's challenge of Senan is also extant. Their stories reflect the struggle they experienced with patriarchy and general ambivalence around gender relations.

- ❏ Ita (480–570 CE) born in Waterford of noble family stock, founded a church in Co. Waterford. Later she founded a monastery, Cill Ide or Kileedy, in west Limerick.

- ❏ Ita was an educator, counsellor, spiritual mentor and soul-friend. As foster-mother to many future male saints, her role of forming and shaping them for religious life was deeply significant.

- ❏ One of her foster-sons was Brendan the Navigator, who maintained a lifelong relationship with Ita, marked by affection, loyalty and intellectual exchange.

- ❏ Ita developed a reputation for holiness and lived a life that was essentially relational aimed at building a caring and compassionate community. For Ita to know God was to create a just, merciful and peaceful community.

- ❏ Ita sought to live a simple life showing generosity toward those in need. She produced a ministry of caring, healing, forgiveness, reconciliation and restorative justice with a view to transforming relationships and lives.

- ❏ Monenna, along with nine other women, set up a monastery on Beggery Island, Wexford harbour. She spent some time with Brigid at Kildare, impressing everyone with her selfless care for the poor. She then returned to Co. Louth, her home county, to form a community. She eventually sought a quiet life at the foot of Slieve Gullion, Co. Armagh at Kileevy where she remained until her death in 517 CE.

- ❏ In her lifetime Monenna dealt with numerous power struggles which undermined and diminished her foundations.

- ❏ She played a peacekeeping role and advised war as a last resort of defence, and was much sought-after for her prayers, wisdom and negotiating skills.

- ❏ Samthann's foundation was at Clonbroney, Co. Longford and was one of three primary monasteries for women in Ireland. She was from a high-ranking Ulster family.

- ❏ She is described as an abbess, a spiritual director, educator and church dignitary.

- ❏ Samthann had a significant association with the Celi-De renewal movement, which emphasised the importance of spiritual disciplines, devotion to the saints and the soul-friend.

- ❏ Her ethic of justice and concern for hostages and captives is rooted in contemplation and prayer.

- ❏ Canair founded a hermitage at Bantry and died on Scattery Island c.530 CE. The only source of information on her is in the Life of Senan.

- ❏ Canair refused to leave Scattery, where she felt God was calling her to live, insisting that Christ came to redeem women and men and therefore she was entitled to live on the island and receive the Eucharist as a direct challenge of Senan's authority.

- ❏ Canair's persistence is rewarded and she achieves her intention, while at the same time affirming gender equality.

- ❏ The inclusion of Canair's challenge in the Life of Senan highlights the controversy over mixed-sex monasteries, which was a real issue and may reflect a developing misogyny in the Irish church. It also indicates that from the earliest days this practice and perspective were challenged by women saints.

Test Questions

❑ What evidence is there that Irish women saints struggled to fulfil their ministry within a patriarchal context?

❑ Is gender equality still an ethical imperative in twenty-first century Irish churches? Can lessons be learned from the Irish women saints in the Celtic period?

8   Holiness: Living Faithfully in the Socio-Political World

There are dangers in looking back to a 'golden age'. Many do it, almost as a way of reading history. The cultural or religious 'golden age' is always in the past, the present falling far short, but with the hope that the 'golden age' will one day be restored. It is dangerous because the 'golden age' probably never existed. It is a wistful invention often ignoring the struggles, failures, suffering and violence that were closer to the real world of the fictitious past. The danger is present when exploring the Celtic past. The sixth century of early Irish monastic life is sometimes described as the 'golden age' of Irish Christianity. It is during this and the following century that the claim is made for Ireland as the 'land of saints and scholars'. This is not altogether a fiction; there is some truth in the claim given the character of many leading Irish Christians and the levels of scholarship that were emerging from Ireland, or from Irish monks, scattered throughout Europe. But it would be misleading and wrong to claim an island dripping in sanctity and to portray a race of saints transcending real humanity, without fallibility and vulnerability. Saints are always all too human and in theological terms saints are always sinners.

The sixth century is nevertheless remarkable. It saw the development of some of the great Irish monasteries headed by very significant abbesses and abbots. There was Finnian who established the great monastery and centre of learning at Clonard around 520 CE. There is a roll call of saints such as Ciarán of Clonmacnoise, Enda of the Aran Isles, Brigid of Kildare, Columba of Derry and Durrow, Ita of Kileedy, Brendan of Clonfert, Comgall of Bangor and Kevin of Glendalough. Some heroic saints pushed out from the western coast of Ireland into the Atlantic and founded a community on Skellig Michael, characterised by beehive cells. The monastic movement – rooted in the tradition and spirituality of the desert with its austerity and solitude – had even discovered the desert in the ocean. 'By 600, more than eight hundred monasteries had been founded in Ireland alone.'[1] The monastic community had become the characteristic mark of the early Irish church. Without overclaiming their significance, they were communities of learning, culture and holiness. Within the community sanctity was nurtured in very human people.

By the seventh century hagiography as a distinctive literary genre was emerging. Lives of the Saints were being written. They were not historical biographies. Much of the material was without historical basis. The earliest surviving hagiography is that of Cogitosus on Brigid. The Kildare abbess had two other hagiographies by Ultan and Aileran. The greatest of the Irish hagiographers was Adamnan who wrote a Life of Columba. This life 'far surpasses all the other seventh-century Irish Lives both as an authentic portrait of its subject and in its value as evidence for the life of the church in Adamnan's own time'.[2] There is perhaps more of the latter along with information on contemporary political affairs in the Life. Like many of the hagiographers, Adamnan is reclaiming Columba and those who followed him to remind readers of the significant role played by Iona and its monks in spreading Christianity in northern Britain. Large claims were also being made for Armagh as the Primal See in Ireland by two Lives of Patrick from the seventh century. Muirchú's Life of Patrick is political spin described by Ó Cróinín as 'a travesty of the man and of the genre'.[3] Cogitosus was also making a political claim for Kildare. He goes over the top in extolling the beauty of the church and the many wonders of Kildare itself.

There is an element of truth in the claim that: 'With few exceptions, the saints' Lives are a dismal swamp of superstition and perverted Christianity, dreary litanies of misplaced reverence and devotion.'[4] The miracles worked by saints do border on the fantastic and a fantasy world. Read literally the Lives are often unbelievable, sometimes even off the planet! But this is a modern scientific reading which has lost the appreciation of myth and legend as vehicles of deeper truth than facticity. Beyond the political spin and even tourist attraction of the saints, the Lives are primarily seeking to draw attention to the holiness of the saint. HAGIOS is the Greek for holy, and hagiography is holiness writing. It is also the word for saint and is highlighting the sanctity of the person.

The hagiographical genre was not the invention of the Irish writers. Such literature had existed before Cogitosus and Adamnan had put quill to parchment. Very early Christians such as Peter, Paul and Mary (Magdalene) were historical figures of the first century. During the first three centuries of Christianity legends and stories developed around each of them, often heard and told as 'gospel truth'. Separating history from legend is interesting and notoriously difficult, but history and fact are far from the only thing that matters. Historical fact and legendary imagination were often combined, even in the canonical Acts of the Apostles. 'Historical memories, later embellishments, legendary expansions, and pure fabrications were all told and retold because they related truths, beliefs, views, and ideas that Christians wanted to convey and to which they responded.'[5] Such stories caught the imaginations of foundational Christians before their faith became the legal and official religion of the empire. Within such a genre the three most significant figures of the early Christian movement were portrayed and by presenting them in this way their importance for the Christians of the first three centuries was being strongly highlighted. They were models of holiness and leadership for the early church.

So too with the Irish Lives. The crossover between history and legend is not of primary significance, but Brigid, Columba, Ita and Senan are models of holiness, above all an 'imago Christi', a living image of Christ. They are portrayed as people who lived faithfully in the socio-political world of their time. Holiness is lived in the world of struggle, conflict, suffering and relationships. It is the kinship with Christ that is the heart and form of the hagiographies and the essence of sanctity. The hagiographies offer patterns of holiness.

8.1   Biblical Roots of Holiness

Before looking at hagiographical patterns of holiness it is helpful to explore biblical roots. This means looking at the core understanding of holiness in the Hebrew scriptures and then at the distinctive vision of holiness offered by the teaching and practice of Jesus in the gospels.

Holiness in Israel's Faith

In Israel's tradition holiness holds two tensions together. Separateness and righteousness are bound in creative tension. One does not exclude the other. Exodus, Leviticus, Numbers and Ezekiel express much of the faith perspective of the priests of Israel. In this priestly tradition holiness describes the person or object separated from ordinary or common use. He or it is therefore pure and set apart for careful religious purposes. The priestly tradition, with its concerns for cult and temple, emphasises purity for priests, festivals, food and sexual relationships. The priestly writings in the Hebrew scriptures took shape when Israel's identity was threatened and when it was important, certainly from the perspective of the priests, for the community to remain pure, whole and clearly separate from others around them. Community identity was separatist and purist, and this was holiness, living faithfully in the real world.

Within the priestly literature there was a particular set of writings with a very special emphasis on holiness. It has been called the 'Holiness Code' and is found in Leviticus 17–26. 'The commandments cover aspects of community life concerning food, farming, prostitution, care for the aging, holy priests, holy festivals and holy sacrifices.'[6] Again holiness, meaning set apart or purity, is important for the well-being of the community. Such social purity was essential to the community identity and purpose.

The righteousness dimension of holiness belongs to the prophetic tradition of Israel. The emphasis here is not on purity and separateness but on the quality of social relationships. Righteousness has to do with right relations based on justice, socio-political and economic justice. In this way social relationships are to be rightly ordered. Such righteousness is neighbourly. The challenge of the prophets to the community is not to overcome the threat of ritual and cultic impurity, but to face the challenge of socio-political and economic injustice. Holiness is right neighbourly relations, and Israel is a holy people through the practice of social justice and in the quality and character of social and community relations.

This understanding of holiness as separateness and social justice, being different and distinctive, is rooted in Israel's experience and understanding of God. The people are to be holy as God is holy. 'You shall be holy, for I the Lord your God am holy' (Leviticus 19: 2). Holiness is the imitation of God.

Perhaps the most awesome vision of the holiness of God in the Hebrew scriptures is in Isaiah 6: 1–8, a vision that comes to the prophet Isaiah in the everyday worship of the temple. Beyond the liturgy, action and symbols he experiences the radical otherness of God. The prophet encounters a God who is beyond all the categories, rituals and formulations of tradition and religion. God is unutterably beyond all human constructs and categories. Such an experience makes the prophet aware of personal and community uncleanness and injustice. Life and community fall far short of the otherness of God. In the prophetic tradition though that does not lead to despair or paralysis of will, but for Isaiah it becomes a sense of being impelled or sent to proclaim social transformation. He has a sense of being set apart for the purpose of enabling right ordering of community relations at the heart of which is social justice.

The awesome holiness of God in Isaiah's experience has a flip side in Hosea's experience of the intimacy of God and God's essential compassion. This prophet can articulate God as 'The Holy One in your midst' (Hosea 11: 9). The God who is radically other is also the God of compassion, intimately present and close. It was this vision of God that was to shape Israel's life as holy, an imitation of God in the life of the world.

Holiness in the Praxis of Jesus

Holiness for Israel was the imitation of God in the everyday life of the world. Jesus, as a Jew, was firmly in that tradition and the heart of his ethic was the imitation of God. It is important to recognise the Jewishness of Jesus since this core identity has been airbrushed from most of Christian history. The Jesus movement was one of a number of Jewish reform movements in the first century and may have been one of up to twenty-two movements within Judaism at that time. It is this diversity of emphases within Judaism that is being reflected in the gospels, especially in the conflict scenarios between Jesus and some of the Pharisees.

The Pharisees have frequently been given a bad press due in no small measure to centuries of Christian anti-Judaism and bias. They were fundamentally good people with a vision for the life of their people at the heart of which was holiness. The Pharisees, then, were not hypocrites and not bad people but good, virtuous and ethical. Phariseeism was one of the renewal movements committed to the priestly vision of the Hebrew scriptures. The Pharisees were a lay movement committed to priestly purity among the people in general and a key characteristic of their practice was table fellowship. Their concern in the life of Israel was legal cleanness or purity and correct tithing of agricultural produce. This represents a significant social vision, holiness as a social ethic at the heart of community life.

Here is the heart of the conflict between Jesus and the Pharisees. They both took the traditions of Israel seriously but interpreted holiness differently. Jesus and the Pharisees had competing social visions and conflictual social ethical values. For the Pharisees, the core value of their social vision was holiness as purity. The core value of Jesus' social vision, as Marcus Borg has argued, was compassion.[7] Twice in Matthew's gospel, Jesus or the Jesus community towards the end of the first century, counters holiness as purity with compassion. The Pharisees are critical of Jesus' table fellowship with 'sinners' or the unclean and later of Jesus followers for breaking the Sabbath laws by plucking grains of wheat for food on the holy day. On each occasion Hosea 6: 6 is invoked from Israel's prophetic tradition: 'I desire mercy/compassion and not sacrifice' (Matthew 9: 13 and 12: 7). Even if both these texts are Matthean reflections on the conflictual relationship between the Jesus community and the Pharisaic leadership of local synagogues, they indicate the nature of the conflict which was intra-Jewish. The use of Hosea draws attention to the repeated emphasis of the Hebrew scriptures that God is essentially compassionate and that faithful human living is also compassionate.

> Jesus' ethic, in short, was based on an Imitatio Dei, just as the quest for holiness was based on an Imitatio Dei. Moreover, just as the Pharisaic Imitatio Dei was intended as a programme for Israel's life, so it is reasonable to assume that the alternative Imitatio Dei of Jesus was intended as the guiding paradigm for Israel as a social reality.[8]

The essence of Jesus' vision is expressed in Luke 6: 27–36 and Matthew 5: 38–48. In both texts the Holiness Code of Leviticus 19 is echoed and modified, and described by Borg as the 'Compassion Code'.[9] 'You shall be holy because I am holy' (Leviticus 19: 2) becomes 'Be merciful (or compassionate) as your Father is merciful' (Luke 6: 36). Matthew has 'Be perfect' behind which is an Aramaic word meaning 'all-inclusive' or 'all-embracing' as God is all-inclusive or all-embracing. The gospel writers are being intentional and deliberate in their modification of Leviticus 19: 2.

The 'Compassion Code' deals with love of the enemy, a modification towards inclusion missing in the context of Leviticus, and in the gospel context with clear reference to the Roman imperial and political enemy. Human compassion is to imitate God's compassion. God makes the sun rise on the evil and on the good, and sends rain on the righteous and on the unrighteous (Matthew 5: 45). The inclusiveness of compassion is to be a quality of human relationships and behaviour.

This did represent a clash of social visions and conflicting models of social ethics. For the Pharisees, their holiness vision 'had narrow and sharp boundaries', and though sincere and well intentioned it was a vision of an exclusive society based on rigorous morality or purity. The social vision and ethic of the Jesus movement – as 'animated by the vision of compassion' – had broad, inclusive and very indistinct boundaries.[10] No one was beyond the compassion of God or to be an outsider in human community. All were embraced and affirmed by divine compassion and all, even the hated, violent and demanding Romans, were to be included in human compassion, the imitation of God.

Jesus radically reinterpreted holiness and centred his social vision in compassion. For him as a Jew, within Israel's tradition, compassion was the *Imitatio Dei*, and it was the core value of his social ethic and vision. Whether understood in religious or secular terms the conflict between social visions remains. There are still tensions between purist, exclusive identity and inclusive, compassionate identity. In the social praxis of Jesus holiness remains as radical compassion and compassionate community.

8.2   Holiness as the Pattern of Christ

When the hagiographers wrote their holy lives they generally followed a pattern. The Lives are shaped as an *Imago Christi*. The hagiographers borrow wholesale from other earlier Lives of saints such as Anthony and Martin. These were heroes of faith and models of holiness, but the ultimate source for hagiographers was the Jesus story. His actions and praxis became the model around which the life of God was to be lived. Character was to be shaped by the teachings and actions of Jesus and the quality of living was to reflect his. It is for this reason that the Lives of the saints were written around the pattern of Jesus' life and work. 'The basic source for the genre of the Vita is the gospels, especially Matthew and Luke …'[11] A good example of this is the later Life of Patrick by Muirchú: 'My lord, Aed, many have made an attempt to put order on this historical account according to what their fathers and those who were storytellers have handed down since the beginning.'[12]

However defective Muirchú's writing may be, he is deliberately modelling the opening of his Life of Patrick on the opening of Luke's gospel, perhaps underlining what he considers to be the sacredness of his work (Luke 1: 1–4). We may be somewhat sceptical of his motives and see ecclesial politics at work, which were really power politics, yet his starting point is familiar.

> This modelling on the gospels was more than a convenient writing convention; it was based on the assumption that the life of a saint had been patterned upon, and associated to, the life of Christ, therefore, the pattern of the two lives (Jesus in the gospels, the saint in his/her Vita) is the same.[13]

The following parallel columns may help us to recognise the pattern or the Life modelled on the *Imago Christi*.

The Saint's Life	Jesus in the Gospels
Distinguished ancestry	Matthew and Luke's birth stories
Birth preceded by events and dreams	Annunciation to Mary
Confirmation of future greatness	Simeon and Anna in Luke
Saint's human or angelic mentors	Jesus and John the Baptist in Mark
Brendan and Ita (foster-mother)	Affirmed by the Spirit at baptism
Help from angels and animals	Cared for by angels at temptations
Becoming a leader or mentor for others	After temptations Jesus calls disciples
Saint attracts following – builds monastery	Jesus teaches women and men
Stories of miracles	Jesus heals the sick, casts out demons

Saint's compassion and prayer	Jesus had 'compassion on them'
Saint travels elsewhere	Jesus travels around towns and villages
Saint on the move – outside Ireland	Jesus travels to non-Jewish communities
Saint's awareness of his/her death	Jesus prepares for last week in Jerusalem
Saint prepares followers for departure	Jesus at Supper and in John leaves a legacy to his friends
Miracles and marvels after death	Jesus' death has torn veil of temple
Columba's death calms violent storm	Earthquake and dead raised in Matthew

History and fact are not the important issues here. Whether the stories in the Lives and the gospels are always historical and factual is not the point. Over-concern may even miss the point. In Lives and gospels we are reading theologians, who in Celtic or Jewish culture are more concerned with meaning than fact, especially meaning in the life situation of a seventh- or late first-century writer. Hagiographers wrote to pattern in order to reflect the saints' relationship with Jesus. The pattern conveys the core message that these saints were people closely connected with Jesus and their lives were shaped and transformed in a profound way by his story. More to the point they were changed profoundly by his life. Holiness is *Imago Christi* and that was not just true for Patrick, Brigid, Columba or Ita; it was to be true for the hagiographer and whoever would read the Life. Lifestyle, praxis and spirituality were to be shaped by Jesus, not in some other or esoteric world, but in the socio-political world of the here and now. Holiness is commitment to God's dream and passion for social justice and right relations and to a social vision of inclusive compassion. Writing to pattern and modelling the Lives of the saints on the life of Jesus is the theo-ethical point of the hagiographers.

8.3   Holiness Motifs in the Lives

Hagiographers not only wrote with a primary pattern in mind, but also developed their Lives around shared motifs. Rich themes or threads run through their Lives which also highlight the holiness of their heroes. These too are theological themes or motifs providing theo-ethical meaning in the Life of the saint and suggesting a model of theo-ethical spirituality for all who read.

Though the word saint is widely used with reference to the early Celtic Christian leaders, only Patrick has been officially canonised by the Roman Catholic church. All the rest are popular saints and are not regarded as in any way aloof from the ordinary people. In the Celtic tradition saints are close friends, holy people who are all too human and one of ourselves. Canonisation, perhaps inevitably, creates a hierarchy, an élite, however unintended. This was not how the Irish saints including Patrick were perceived. The Irish word for saint is NAOMH which has a root meaning of 'bright' or 'good'. Saints are people of light or good people, not by any means morally perfect, but good people who are fallible, vulnerable and human. From the Christian perspective they are people trying to live faithfully in the world, seeking to follow Jesus and to pattern their lives on his, which is the imitation of God, the God he pointed to and disclosed. Mark's gospel understands this as discipleship, a key theme or motif of Mark. From beginning to end it is also a story of failed discipleship. The friends of Jesus repeatedly do not get it! At the end they have gone into hiding, hardly the image of a stereotypical saint.

The Lives of the saints are often idealised, but beneath all the stories are real human beings, and that too is evident from reading between the lines and sometimes by just reading the lines. Hagiographers write around motifs which are motifs of holiness as a model for ordinary people. They are the 'sacred version of the life pattern of all heroic or celebrated people' and they encourage all to be saints.[14]

Healings

Many hagiographers portray the saints as performing miraculous healings. Adamnan in particular has Columba performing many miracles, so many and so fantastic that we have reason to be sceptical. Adamnan's Life leads to the conclusion that an atmosphere of miracles pervaded Iona at that time, but there is much exaggeration and some stories are sheer invention. Columba 'brought to life the dead son of a Christian layman and restored him alive and well to his father and mother – a very great miracle'.[15] Many hagiographers have their saints doing similar miracles.

Columba may have been a person 'endowed with immense authority and personal magnetism',[16] but stories like the above do not ask us to be uncritical and unquestioning and pass over the story in silence. Nor can all the stories be dismissed as folklore. Adamnan, like all historians or theologians, writes out of a mental map and he may be using a literary device quite acceptable in his time to prove sanctity: 'Literary influences helped Adamnan to organise and present this material in such a way as to make it clear that St Columba was a man of God in a mould that was both biblical and universal.'[17] Putting Columba in such a context and tradition is a worthy literary device but we are in touch with folklore when we read of a sorcerer drawing milk from a bull at Columba's command. The bull wastes away as a result but makes a remarkable recovery when Columba blesses it with water![18] It is possible that Adamnan was writing allegorically, a popular interpretative method of reading the Bible at this time.

Getting inside Adamnan's mental map is difficult but whatever his literary devices and variations, healings make a holy man and he uses the motif for this purpose.

Fire and Light

Both symbols are common to the Christian tradition. On the day of Pentecost according to the Acts of the Apostles: 'tongues of fire appeared among them, and a tongue rested on each of them' (Acts 2: 3). It was a sign of the Spirit, the presence and activity of God in the world.

Light is a key symbol in John's gospel, where Jesus is described as 'the light of the world'. It is one of the 'I am' sayings in which the gospel points to the disclosure of God

8.1 Brigid's fire pit at Kildare Cathedral.

in the life of Jesus. In the prologue to the gospel the light is present in every person, and no matter how much violence, injustice and domination the light shines and has never been put out or overcome (John 1: 4). Light is also the presence of God and symbol of goodness and justice.

Hagiographers made use of both symbols in their Lives. 'Fiery manifestations and lights seen in the sky at the time of saint's births' are common. 'Sometimes the saint is described as surrounded by the mystical light of holiness.'[19]

A range of symbols are associated with Brigid, some going back to the early Irish goddess. Of the many: 'a fiery pillar rises over her head'.[20] In one of her Lives her mother leaves her home alone and the neighbours saw flames rising from the house. They rushed to the house thinking it was on fire but found Brigid peacefully asleep. They concluded that 'the girl was full of the grace of the Holy Spirit'.[21] Also in this Life the poem of Brecain is quoted: 'Brigit, excellent woman, a flame golden, delightful, May she, the sun dazzling, splendid, guide us to the eternal kingdom.'[22] In the poem both symbols are used to describe her holiness.

In the Lismore Life of Columba, Patrick foretells the saint's birth and breaks into song.

> A manchild shall be born of his family
> He will be a sage, a prophet, a poet,
> A loveable lamp, pure clear,
> Who will not utter falsehood.

Here light symbolises purity, truthfulness, goodness. The presence and power of God is the source of holiness and goodness. Brigid and Columba live God-centred lives. The sacred fire burns for centuries at Kildare, the fire of goodness and justice. The saints share the passion of God.

Crozier and Bell

Both are associated with miraculous power. The crozier is used to raise the dead, drive back a flooding river with echoes of Moses and the Exodus. Again echoing the Moses story, the crozier splits rocks. It also banishes demons and protects travellers and could even return when misplaced by flying through the air to the saint owner!

To read these instances as literal is to reduce the Lives to nonsense and stretch incredulity off the planet. The hagiographers are not so naïve or gullible. They are again using literary devices to make theological and theo-ethical points. At times we are in the presence of theo-myths, a profound way of highlighting truth.

The crozier is a pastoral symbol and draws attention to care and well-being. The saints were leaders of communities and as such were not to dominate community members. Stories of croziers and healings symbolise the caring, compassionate nature of the saint. They were committed to the well-being of their community and were responsible for creating and sustaining communities of inclusive compassion.

The travelling saint had a bell which again was used in healings and if stolen could miraculously return to its owner. The bell had a central function in religious life and was used to call people to prayer and devotion. The monasteries were communities of prayer, and if the abbot travelled to outlying places people were still called to prayer, perhaps by a river or in an oak grove.

A popular story was of the bell remaining silent until the saint's destination was reached and then it would ring out joyfully by itself! Perhaps there is something here about the presence of holiness, catching and contagious. At least compassionate care for the weak, suffering, marginalised and oppressed, arising from prayer, contemplation of and communion with God, is the hagiographer's mark of holiness.

Birds and Animals

Again and again the hagiographers portray saintly women and men as sympathetic to all creatures. There is a kinship with the animal world and the saints have a very special relationship with that world.

Colman had three pets: a cock, a mouse and a fly. They were all in partnership with Colman and each other. At midnight the cock would crow for him to call him to prayer. As Colman sang the Psalms, the fly would walk along each line of the text, stopping as Colman paused. Being human Colman would sometimes drop off to sleep during the Psalms, at which point the mouse would nibble his ear, so that he would waken up and continue the night office. A delightful story which would be spoiled by explanation.

In the Lives creation is attracted to the saints. In Cogitosus' Life of Brigid a hunted bear joins her herd, and without fear 'served her tamely and humbly'. Wolves act as a swineherd for her: 'because of their enormous reverence for the blessed Brigid'. Wild ducks come to her: 'a great flock of them flew on feathered wings to her, without any fear'.[24] Columba is movingly comforted when dying by a loyal white horse, which 'put its head against his bosom, inspired I believe by God for whom every living thing shows such understanding as the creator bids … it began to mourn like a person, pouring out its tears …'[25]

The motif conveys that goodness pervades everything and communicates itself to all life. Holiness of life, living justly and compassionately, reaches out to the animal world and all of God's creation.

Also the key point in such stories is that a holy person is in a properly balanced relationship to the world. The Lives portray a saint at peace with the environment. This image of what today we might call ecological holiness, continued for a long time in Ireland. Being in a properly balanced relationship with nature remains an imperative, not least because of an environmental crisis.

The Great Monster

Monsters are the stuff of legends. St George and the dragon come to mind. If the monster is not slain, it is banished into the lake. Both types of stories occur in Lives of Patrick and Columba. A third Life of Patrick written c. 896–901 CE has a Croagh Patrick story with Patrick at the top of the mountain for Lent. At the end of Lent the peak is filled with black demonic birds. Patrick banished them by ringing his bell and they were replaced by white angelic birds. Patrick then refuses to leave Croagh Patrick unless God gives him the right to judge all the Irish on the Last Day.[26]

Anglo-Norman Lives of Patrick invented the story of Patrick banishing snakes from Ireland. From at least a century before Patrick, the Greeks knew that there were no snakes in Ireland. Various stories have Patrick banishing monsters into lakes in various Irish locations. One major reason for the beginning of the Lough Derg pilgrimage was that Patrick banished a monster into the lough.[27]

Columba too has a monster story from the land of the Picts, which seems like the original Loch Ness monster story. The monster had snatched a human being. The bystanders froze in terror:

> but the blessed man looking on raised his holy hand and made the sign of the cross in the air, and invoking the name of God he commanded the fierce beast … At the sound of the saint's voice, the beast fled in terror ….[28]

Such stories again are the stuff of legend and in the hands of a hagiographer they become profound theo-myths. The stories have their source in the Apocalyptic writing of the Christian scriptures where the dragon is released on the Last Day and then confined to the lake of fire.

The book of Revelation draws its imagery from elsewhere, and it is a literary genre familiar to first-century Jews and is the language of myth. But the myth underlines a profound truth. Revelation is anti-imperial resistance literature. The beastly imagery, already used in earlier Hebrew literature such as Daniel with its beastly images of successive empires and domination systems, is being replicated in the bizarre language of Revelation. The dragon in question is the Roman imperial power with its militarised and economic domination system exploiting the majority of its imperial citizens for the benefit of the élite who rule and prosper at the top. Such is a patriarchal, domination system. Such oppression and injustice will not last but has within it the seeds of its own destruction. Apocalyptic literature in the Bible is literature of non-violent resistance and hope. The dragon will be cast into the fire or the deep. Holiness is opposing by non-violent means all that dominates, oppresses and dehumanises people. Holiness is political holiness, lamenting injustice and working for justice and transformation, not only of persons but systems. The great monster stories of Celtic hagiography are profound theo-myths providing theo-ethical politics.

Such are the motifs that punctuate the hagiographies. They too portray holiness, patterns and models of living faithfully in the socio-political world. Centred on God is about living justly and with compassion at the heart of socio-political and environmental life.

Key Points from Chapter 8

❏ By 600 CE more than 800 monasteries had been founded in Ireland alone and monasticism had become the characteristic mark of the early Irish church.

❏ Monasteries were communities of learning, culture and holiness.

❏ By the seventh century, hagiography (holiness writing) as a distinctive literary genre was emerging, primarily aimed at highlighting the sanctity of the saints and establishing these women and men as models for the Christian world, and living images of Christ.

❏ The Lives of the saints reveal that holiness is lived in the world of struggle, conflict, suffering and relationships.

❏ Holiness in the Israelite tradition holds separateness (priestly writings) and righteousness (prophetic tradition) in tension. Separateness is concerned with social purity and is essential for community identity and purpose; righteousness has to do with right relations based on justice that is socio-political and economic.

❏ This diversity of emphases is reflected in the gospels, especially in the conflict scenarios between Jesus and some of the Pharisees. The latter interpreted holiness as purity, the former holiness as compassion. This resulted in a clash of social visions and conflicting models of social ethics.

❏ Jesus' actions became the model around which the life of God was to be lived for Celtic hagiographers. Consequently the lives of the saints were written to reflect the life and work of Jesus.

❏ The hagiographers, like the gospel writers, are more concerned with meaning than fact.

❏ Holiness is commitment to God's dream and passion for social justice and right relations and a social vision of inclusive compassion.

- ❏ The Lives of the saints (people of light, good people) are about real human people, who even though idealised often reveal their fallibility and vulnerability; they are models for ordinary people.
- ❏ Hagiographers use literary devices – healings, symbols of fire and light, croziers and bells – to make theological and theo-ethical points and encourage imitation of Christ and a concern for God's kingdom.
- ❏ They portray the saints as sympathetic to all creatures illustrating that goodness pervades all of creation, and holiness is reaching out to all of God's creation.
- ❏ Holiness is portrayed as opposing by non-violent means all that dominates, oppresses and dehumanises people and creation, whether the evil is disguised as demonic birds, snakes or dragons.
- ❏ Holiness works for justice and is concerned with the transformation of unjust people and systems towards the recovery of a God centred, compassionate and just socio-political ethic.

Test Questions

- ❏ Outline the features of hagiographical writing, illustrating your answer with reference to the lives of the saints.
- ❏ How did the hagiographers understand holiness? What are the implications of their vision of holiness for social ethics in the present context?

CELTIC SOCIAL ETHICS

9   An Ethic of Hospitality

Contemporary Ireland, and the wider world of which we are an integral part, present us with many ethical challenges. Life, which is always life in community, is filled with endless choices. Life cannot be lived without making moral and ethical decisions. Ethics, therefore, are integral to living.

The ancient Greek ethicist, Aristotle, suggested that the Greek ETHICA, is derived directly from ETHOS. This has to do with custom, habit, practice, the way of life. Ethics are about developing standards of conduct, the struggle to determine what to do. We can speak of an ethic of doing or the practice of the moral life.

All of this takes place in community. Ethics are ultimately a community enterprise and achievement. Each of us is unique as individuals, but we are only truly ourselves in relation to others. We cannot be human apart from others. The word conscience itself highlights this 'being with' dimension of our deepest humanity. To speak of individual conscience is something of a fiction which we realise when we look at the etymological meaning of the original. *Com + Scire* mean knowing in relation or knowing together. Conscience, therefore, is the expression of character formed only in relationships or community. Community is central to the moral or ethical life.

When we speak of Christian ethics we are talking about community ethics. It is within the faith community, and within the community of life, that we make our moral choices and reach our ethical decisions. From the beginning of Christian history morality and ethics have been dimensions of community life in which a primary concern was how the faith community was to live together and with those in the wider civic and political community. Faith itself is the struggle to live faithfully or with integrity in the complex world. The earliest reference to Christians was a 'people of the way'. 'The Way' became a descriptive term for a pattern of living, a way followed together. It is possible to speak of a Christian ethos or lifestyle. Christian ethics are community ethics and are Christian praxis.

The Celtic Christian tradition is no less ethical and expresses a way of life. Here too moral formation takes place in community and ethical praxis is lived out in relationships. Celtic ethics are social ethics. In 'Celtic Social Ethics' we will explore a range of ethical challenges and concerns that were significant for early Irish Christians. These challenges, albeit in a very different context and in different ways, are still present. In each of the chapters we shall look at the contemporary challenge, bring it into dialogue with biblical insights and with Christian Irish Celtic practice. This conversation will connect contemporary, biblical and Celtic communities in which together we can make ethical judgements, decisions and develop patterns of ethical action and practice.

9.1   Ireland Today

Hospitality is central to the Christian gospel and tradition. In Ireland today there is no shortage of opportunity to practise hospitality. This is not a response to tourism, important as it is to greet people with *Céad mile fáilte* (a hundred thousand welcomes). Forty cruise ships visiting Belfast in the summer of 2007 is very welcome, not least by the economy. It is the other Ireland, the changing Ireland, which challenges our reputation for hospitality.

A current tourist attraction in Belfast is the SS *Nomadic*, the little boat that carried passengers to the Belfast-built *Titanic*. It is a remarkable piece of history from 1912 and a reminder of a terrible maritime tragedy, when the greatest ship built to date was sunk by an iceberg on its first voyage with the loss of hundreds of lives. Belfast at last is recovering some pride in its shipbuilding history and its greatest achievement in the building of a super liner. Much will be made of the centenary in 2012. At the opposite end of the island of Ireland the *Titanic* is also remembered. Cobh was the ship's last port of call on its ill-fated voyage. In the Immigration Museum in Cobh there is a telling plaque: 'More than three million people left Ireland through this port.' It is a staggering figure and a painful human story. Ireland was an emigration country, exporting people to Britain, Australasia and North America. Life was often hard for the emigrants. Hospitality was key to their early life in new lands but not all were welcomed or treated kindly.

By the end of the twentieth century Ireland had changed, and within the first decade of the twenty-first century Ireland has become an immigration country. A wave of economic and political immigrants has reached Ireland's shores. We welcome the tourists but these new 'arrivals' that are here to stay are making many uncomfortable. We display awkwardness, not just in immigration policy and legislation but also in local communities and everyday relationships. We are not sure what to call the 'new arrivals'. Asylum seekers, migrant workers or immigrants are the polite names. Racism and xenophobia have other more dehumanising ways of referring to such people. In hotels and bars the accents have changed. So too with the bus drivers. On the upper deck of a Dublin bus today, it may be difficult to hear a conversation in English and the conversational language one does hear is not Irish! Food and dress in many towns are now different. In the Co. Tyrone town of Dungannon, 10% of the population is Portuguese with over thirty languages spoken in the Dungannon Council area. There are now more than 167 languages used in Ireland from Acholi to Zulu. Instead of a culture of departure, Ireland now has a culture of arrival. The multi-cultural nature of our society, north and south, has been highlighted in 2007 with the election to the Northern Ireland Assembly of a woman from the Chinese community. It is the first for any legislative parliament or assembly in Europe.

The Christian churches in areas have shown significant increase in numbers largely due to the presence of ethnic groups. Welcome and hospitality have been expressed and rightly so. Some churches have become a little over-excited by it all, perhaps understandably in those areas where congregations were small or almost defunct. But it needs to be acknowledged that not all the 'arrivals' are Christian. In the Republic of Ireland the 1991 census declared 3,875 as Muslim. By the 2002 census the number of Muslims in the Republic had become 19,147. The numbers of Muslims and Presbyterians are now almost equal, with almost twice as many Muslims as Methodists.

The multi-faith reality of Ireland has been visible in three inaugural ceremonies for Irish presidents. These have been inter-faith ceremonies, forms of inter-faith worship. Not all Christians are comfortable with that. Inter-faith dialogue is well down the traditional Christian agenda in Ireland. Shared worship between Protestants and Catholics in Northern Ireland is still a no-go area for many, which puts inter-faith prayer beyond the pale for the foreseeable future.

And yet events take place. On Palm Sunday 2007, a Belfast Methodist church welcomed up to thirty Muslims to its morning worship followed by hospitality which shared Irish and Turkish food. The Royal College of Surgeons in Ireland has held an inter-faith service of Thanksgiving and Remembrance for those who have donated their bodies to the cause of medical education and research in the College. The service was led by Christians, Jews, Muslims, Buddhists, Hindus and Sikhs. These are significant signs of welcome and hospitality on the part of what some would describe as the 'native' or 'settled' members of the community.

Other realities need to be faced. Immigrants have left home and because of circumstances have had to make not only a geographical journey but also a psychological one. Poverty, debt, trade and tariff regulations and political corruption have caused them to arrive in Ireland. Immigrants often experience loneliness, meaninglessness and marginalisation. Old Irish songs and ballads often expressed the pathos and pain of Irish exiles. The danger is that our economic prosperity and mobility have numbed us to our ancestors' experience and to the experience of those now arriving on our shores. Immigrants often find themselves in sub-standard or overcrowded housing, doing jobs the rest of us do not want to do because they are too menial or dangerous. They also work longer hours for less pay than the locals. Racist language and attacks are increasing and most of us are silent bystanders to both.

In truth many of us feel awkward and uncomfortable about the new 'culture of arrival' in Ireland. 'Foreigners' frighten us, perhaps because we are afraid of difference, or maybe we are afraid of ourselves, insecure in our relative comfort and prosperity. Ireland today challenges us to develop and practise an ethic of hospitality.

9.2   Biblical Perspectives

The ethic of hospitality appears quickly in the biblical literature. Abraham is called to a journey into the unknown (Genesis 12: 1). Abraham and Sarah departed from all that was familiar, comfortable and safe. Apart from the call of God, which is how the storyteller puts it, Abraham and Sarah and their tribe were probably forced by socio-economic circumstances to leave home for another land. Hundreds of years later an early Christian reflected on the story and wrote of Abraham that 'he set out, not knowing where he was going' (Hebrews 11: 8). Sadly this early Christian forgot that Sarah was also without a map and that she too was a wandering nomad.

In the Semitic world the nomadic life was a normal part of socio-economic reality. People kept moving to survive and to survive they had to rely on each other. The nomadic code of hospitality was the way of life. Rest, refuge, food and water, life's basic needs, were often required and expressed the human obligation owed to other travellers. Nomadic hospitality was an ethic of life.

The storyteller(s) vividly illustrated nomadic hospitality by the story of Abraham and Sarah welcoming three strangers. Three men appeared near their tent in the midday sun. Abraham 'ran from the tent entrance to meet them, and bowed to the ground' (Genesis 18: 1–2). No matter that it was the hottest part of the day, Abraham and Sarah rushed into hospitable action. Feet were washed, rest and shelter were provided, Sarah was ordered to 'make ready quickly' cakes while Abraham continued to 'run', took a 'tender and good' calf and ordered the servant to prepare a meal (18: 6–8). Abraham then became the waiter as the strangers were fed. Abraham and Sarah went out of their way and did all in their power to provide nomadic hospitality. The ethic of hospitality was their way of life.

Hospitality was core to Israel's identity and self-understanding. The Book of Deuteronomy provides an early Israelite credo:

> A wandering Aramean was my ancestor; he went down into Egypt and lived there as an alien, few in number, and then became a great nation, mighty and populous. When the Egyptians treated us harshly and afflicted us, by imposing hard labour on us, we cried to the Lord, the God of our ancestors; the Lord heard our voice and saw our affliction, our toil and our oppression. The Lord brought us out of Egypt ... (Deuteronomy 26: 5–11). \>

This statement of faith expresses the core experience of the socio-economic slaves, and repeatedly in their writings it is this experience that becomes the central basis of Israel's social ethic of hospitality and justice, shaping how they are to respond to the weak, vulnerable and stranger. The books of Deuteronomy and Exodus have much to say about the orphan, widow, stranger and resident alien, those who lacked status, protection and were often displaced and marginalised. Israel was never to forget that once they too were strangers and aliens in Egypt. Sometimes ethical development and formation require memory and recall, if not one's own immediate personal history, then the historical experience of one's people and community. Forgetting the past can be a convenient way of blocking out the strangers in the present.

Hospitality also featured large in the Christian scriptures. When Luke and Matthew wrote their birth narratives they situated Jesus in the context of the Jewish concern for the displaced and aliens. Luke has Jesus born into a family without lodging in Bethlehem (Luke 2: 7). Matthew has Jesus with his mother and father exiled in Egypt (Matthew 2: 14). Homeless and refugees are how two gospel writers portray the early Jesus. Luke has poor, outcast shepherds as the first to welcome the birth and hear the announcement of the alternative peace to the imperial, oppressive, Pax Romana (Luke 2: 14). The whole purpose of Jesus' life and work was 'to bring good news to the poor …' (Luke 4: 18).

Luke's ethic of hospitality is further illustrated with stories of Jesus welcoming children, poor, outcasts, prostitutes, tax collectors and sinners. The last were not necessarily immoral people, but those considered outcasts by the religious leadership and élite because they did not fulfil or were unable, like the shepherds, to fulfil purity laws. These are the people Jesus had at dinner parties, so much so that he attracted criticism from the religious establishment: 'This fellow welcomes sinners and eats with them' (Luke 15: 2). Jesus practised the ethic of hospitality and even told stories about feasts where there was an open invitation. There were places at the table for those who normally never got an invitation: 'When you give a banquet, invite the poor, the cripples, the lame, and the blind … they cannot repay you …' (Luke 14: 13–14). People only threw dinner parties in those days for those like themselves and who could and would reciprocate. Jesus suggested inviting the nobodies, those who socially and economically were in no position to repay or reciprocate. His ethic of hospitality upset the cultural norms of his day.

The unknown author of the Letter to the Hebrews may well have had the Abraham and Sarah story in mind when encouraging a faith community to live ethically in a complex and difficult world: 'Do not neglect to show hospitality to strangers for by doing that some have entertained angels without knowing it' (Hebrews 13: 2). The community was also asked to be in solidarity with those in prison and those being tortured (Hebrews 13: 3). Another early community facing difficulty and suffering, including homelessness, was called as part of faithful living to: 'Be hospitable to one another without complaining' (I Peter 4: 9).

The Greek word for stranger is *xenos*. The word has been incorporated into an English word xenophobia, which means fear of the stranger. With the increase in ethnic minorities in Ireland there has been an increase in xenophobia. But the Christian scriptures written in Greek have also incorporated *xenos* into a key word, philoxenia, which means love of the stranger. When translated in English Bibles it is hospitality. Hospitality then is love of the stranger and turns xenophobia on its head.

It may be that our social and political institutions are never going to be completely open, welcoming and hospitable. Nationalism may not be the force it was but it is still strong enough to make life difficult for the 'resident alien', and even to ensure that such people remain as resident aliens. The Judeo-Christian tradition challenges those committed to it to be a counter-cultural community, to live a contrast ethic of hospitality and in biblical language to 'welcome the stranger'.

9.3   The Celtic Practice of Hospitality

Hospitality was central to the Celtic community ethic. It was not only voluntary practice, part of the cultural ethos of the early Irish world, but hospitality was also institutionalised in the legal system and in the architecture of a monastic community. There were obligations of hospitality. Travellers had rights of hospitality, and a wealthy farmer was obliged to feed and shelter a traveller no matter how often the guest demanded hospitality.[1] Hospitality was legally mandated whether informal or formal and applied to both secular and religious life.

Underpinning the legal obligations was a code of conduct rooted in an honour-shame culture. To be inhospitable was to be seriously dishonourable. Everyone knew of the 'six sons of Dishonour'. They were:

- niggardliness;
- refusal;
- denial;
- hardness;
- rigour;
- rapacity.

This also implied a reciprocal culture. To give hospitality was also to receive it: 'Hospitality assured travellers food, shelter from wind and rain, and protection, but also obliged them to entertain wayfarers who knocked their doors.'[2] Within this context the practice of hospitality was a way of nurturing social ties, developing networks and alliances, and building community.

An essential structure in any monastic enclosure was the guesthouse. It was a building within the enclosure and set apart for the particular purpose. It also stood in a promi-nent place, all of which underlines the importance of hospitality as faith in action: 'It symbolised monastic charity and the social co-operation that lay behind all hospitality.'[3] An early abbot, Molna, brought his senior monks to their new land and asked where he would build the abbot's house. They chose the best site and Molna announced that the guesthouse would be built there.

A monk was in charge of the guesthouse. He has been described as 'the man who had the care of guests and paupers', indicating not only that there was chronic poverty but also that in monastic practice the distinction disappeared between the traveller and the chronic migrant poor.[4]

On arrival the guest was formally welcomed, offered shelter and a bath, a share in Christian prayer and liturgy and food. These steps in the practice of hospitality had a theological or theo-ethical basis. Every guest represented Christ who was recognised in the face of the stranger and the poor. It would appear, though, that such a high theology of hospitality was not always practised. Monastic communities remained all too human communities. It is significant that the Penitential laid down severe penalties for the failure to practise hospitality. In the Irish Canons there are eleven paragraphs dealing with 'The Refusal of Hospitality to Persons of Ecclesiastical Rank'. The story is invoked of two bishops in the Egyptian desert, one of whom refuses the other hospitality. The penance was seven days' fasting on bread and water 'if it was his custom and he lacked human experience'. If he refused because of 'unkindness, a year would then have been assigned for each day'. Jesus is quoted from the gospel: 'If they will not receive you, shake off the dust from your feet' – that is, in excommunication. If an Irish bishop is refused hospitality and dies, then the dishonourable one 'shall pay the value of fifty female slaves … or he shall do penance for fifty years'.[5]

Apart from the Canons reflecting a very hierarchical ordering of social life, they are also patriarchal and reflect an uncritical acceptance of the economic institution of slavery. They also reflect serious problems with the practice of hospitality. They are probably eighth century and provide a window on socio-economic life and the state of Irish church life in terms of structure and practice. The ethic of hospitality was too frequently lost.

Yet the hagiographers repeatedly emphasised the ethic and practice of hospitality. The theme is implicit in Patrick's story. He was an immigrant, an involuntary one, captured with many others and brought to Ireland as slaves. Ireland's patron saint was not Irish but a Romano-Celt forcibly brought to Ireland against his will. Some years after his escape he returned to Ireland as a voluntary immigrant. This time he chose to return and spend the rest of his life in Ireland. The outsider or foreigner was embraced and accepted and made his own remarkable contribution to life and faith. Patrick the stranger received hospitality, much of it very generous. As a wandering missionary he required hospitality often and a number of wealthy patrons supported his work. He never disclosed the sources, but the generosity was such that his critics accused him of profiteering and being the equivalent of a modern tele-evangelist.

Over a century later the model of church in Ireland became distinctively monastic or community-centred. Hospitality became a core ethic and value, not just because the culture of hospitality was already there, but also because of the theo-ethical insight that the face of Christ was most recognisable in the face of the poor.

In the Lives of Brigid hospitality is a core theme. Her community at Kildare became known as the 'city of the poor', and she is frequently portrayed as providing food for them. Miracles were essential to the Life of a saint, and in Brigid's Lives there is frequent multiplication of food and drink for the sake of the poor and clerics. She turned water into beer and also multiplied the quantity of ale to supply the clergy of eighteen churches during Easter week![6] It may be that stories like these reflect earlier Celtic traditions of warm hospitality and ale parties. This was the tradition of the 'Official Hostel', and one may have existed in Kildare with a female hospitaller in charge. A much later poem, Brigid's Feast, reflects the tradition and the spirit of hospitality and ale parties.

I should take a great lake of purest ale
For the King of Kings.

I should like a table of the choicest food
For the family of heaven.
Let the ale be made from the fruits of faith,
And the food be forgiving love.
I should welcome the poor to my feast,
For they are God's children.
I should welcome the sick to my feast,
For they are God's joy.
Let the poor sit with Jesus at the highest place,
And the sick dance with the angels.[7]

The key themes are there, especially Christ present in the poor and suffering. Even before leaving home Brigid had such a reputation for hospitality and generosity that her father decided to sell her to the king of Leinster, presumably before he was left destitute: 'Of her father's wealth and food and property, whatsoever her hands would find or would get, she used to give to the poor and needy of the Lord.' While her father was negotiating with the king, Brigid, still in the chariot, was approached by a poor leper. She gave him her father's sword. Father was not amused, indeed he was 'mighty enraged'. The king asked Brigid why she did what she did. She gave a spirited reply: 'The Virgin's Son knows, if I

9.1 Entrance to Glendalough monastery

had your power, with all your wealth, and with all your Leinster, I would give them all to the Lord of the Elements.'[8] Brigid was saved from slavery.

It is said in the Lismore Life that, when Brigid was consecrated 'according to the number of the eight beatitudes of the Gospel', she chose as her motto the beatitude of mercy: 'Blessed are the merciful, for they will receive mercy' (Matthew 5: 7).[9] If there is one characteristic to describe the spiritual praxis of Brigid in her Lives, it is hospitality. In Broccan's Hymn to Saint Brigid, this old Irish cleric not only challenged the misogynistic stereotypes of Brigid found in earlier writings but also placed great emphasis on her ability to provide enormous qualities of food and her courageous action in rescuing the poor and powerless from oppressive and dominating masters.[10] Brigid embodied hospitality in the early Irish tradition.

The Lives of other saints express the ethical praxis of hospitality. Kevin of Glendalough abandoned an ascetic retreat to build his new community. He located the Glendalough community on the accessible floor of the valley with the express purpose of feeding 'companies and strangers and guest and pilgrims'. At Glendalough 'no one was refused entertainment, for the grace of the Lord is there'. It was claimed that Maedoc was seven times more hospitable than Columba because he had the best of virtues: 'hospitality unstinted for everyone'.

The hagiographer tells a story of Ciarán of Clonmacnoise to teach the importance of hospitality in the face of failure to provide it. Ciarán met a man on the road who had been refused hospitality at the house of the saint's mother: 'Enraged, the saint charged into his mother's kitchen and hurled all the food on to the ground, reviling her for her lack of charity'.[11] The hagiographer is apparently not interested in how mother felt after that outburst of rage and temper. His only point is that hospitality is a core ethical virtue and that the practice of hospitality makes a saint.

The Alphabet of Devotion is by an unknown author and probably came from Lismore, which was a famous community of learning with high-quality scriptoria. Its key emphasis is the practice of virtues, and it describes the fifteen 'virtues of the soul'. Among the fifteen are charity, mercy, generosity, hospitality and almsgiving.[12] In a sense these five are all about the practice of hospitality, a virtue believed to be essential to the life of any Irish monk.

Early Irish Christianity practised the ethic of hospitality, no doubt fully aware of its roots in the Judeo-Christian tradition, though expressed within the culture of those early Christian centuries in Ireland. Hospitality was an essential part of Celtic social ethics. It remains as a key ethical challenge in a different, twenty-first-century Ireland. There are strangers still to be welcomed, in spite of or maybe because of the limitations to immigration policy. We may well need new ideas of citizenship, hospitality, of the state, of nationalism, of belonging, of democracy. The experiment continues (has it ever ceased?) to live together in friendship and welcome, and by the ethic of hospitality.

KEY POINTS FROM CHAPTER 9

- ❏ Life cannot be lived without making moral and ethical decisions.
- ❏ Ethics is about developing standards of conduct, the struggle to determine what to do.
- ❏ Community is central to the moral or ethical life.
- ❏ Faith is the struggle to live with integrity in community.
- ❏ Celtic ethics are social ethics.
- ❏ Instead of a culture of departure Ireland now has a culture of arrival.
- ❏ Ireland more than ever is a multi-faith country.
- ❏ Ireland today challenges us to develop and practise an ethic of hospitality.
- ❏ Hospitality was core to Israel's identity and self-understanding, i.e. story of Abraham and Sarah.
- ❏ Deuteronomy and Exodus remind Israel never to forget that they too were strangers and slaves in Egypt and to practise a social ethic of hospitality and justice.
- ❏ As the gospels illustrate, Jesus practised an ethic of hospitality often upsetting the cultural norms of his day.
- ❏ Hospitality is 'love of the stranger' (philoxenia) turning xenophobia (fear of the stranger) on its head.
- ❏ Hospitality was central to the Celtic community ethic and was legally mandated and applied to both secular and religious life.
- ❏ In an honour-shame culture to be inhospitable was dishonourable.
- ❏ The practice of hospitality was a way of nurturing social ties, developing networks and alliances, and building community.
- ❏ The Penitentials laid down severe penalties for the failure to practise hospitality.
- ❏ In monastic Ireland hospitality became a core ethic and value because of the theo-ethical insight that the face of Christ was recognisable in the face of the poor. Brigid's community at Kildare was known as 'the city of the poor'.
- ❏ Hospitality remains a key ethical challenge in twenty-first-century Ireland and our response to it will be evident in the welcome we give to the immigrants seeking a new home often to escape social, economic and political injustices in their former homes.

TEST QUESTIONS

- ❏ Outline your knowledge and understanding of the evidence for saying that an ethic of hospitality was central to Celtic monastic life.
- ❏ Critically evaluate the view that in twenty-first-century Ireland the reality of immigration challenges us to develop and practise an ethic of hospitality.

10   An Ethic of Forgiveness

In 2006 the Healing Through Remembering Project completed almost two years of research, reflection and debate about truth recovery. A substantial and far-reaching report was produced entitled *Making Peace with the Past*. It offered options for truth recovery regarding the conflict in and about Northern Ireland. Dealing with the past is a major issue in any peace process. The challenge has been expressed in other ways. What happens when the fighting stops? Is there life after violence? How do we process and heal so much hurt and pain? Are forgiveness and reconciliation possible? There are no easy answers and significantly the Healing Through Remembering report offered options and not an exclusive or definitive way.[1]

Among the cluster of words on dealing with past pain and conflict is forgiveness. It is an emotive word and by no means the definitive word and concept in making peace with the past. But forgiveness may have something profound to offer within the larger context of healing and reconciliation. Minds and emotions, though, will need to wrestle with its meaning and dynamic.

10.1   An Ethic for Northern Ireland?

In the decades of conflict and violence forgiveness occasionally pierced the darkness. Victims or relatives insisted that there be no retaliation. There was resistance to anything said or done in response that would increase bitterness. Some found the amazing courage to forgive, and every now and then forgiveness found space in the midst of the killing and hate. There were those who never used the word but spoke of 'holding no grudge' or years later preferred the word healing to describe their personal journey. Some met face to face with those responsible for atrocities. Those who somehow were able to forgive created difficulties for those who struggled with their loss. People who forgave were opposed and criticised. Were they made to feel guilty for forgiving? Those who could not forgive, some added not yet, were sometimes made to feel guilty for not forgiving. Either way the F-word created guilt, was and remains emotive and difficult.

The media was too often unhelpful, sometimes inventing the word in reporting, at other times naïvely and even cruelly asking victims in the immediate aftermath of their loss if they could forgive. There were too many examples of premature forgiveness, people speaking the word and then struggling for a long time after with complex emotions, including guilt and anger. For those who spoke forgiveness it was and continued to be a struggle. Forgiveness is never offered easily. The Christian narrative has a cross at the heart of it, a reminder that forgiveness is costly. There is a cross at the heart of all forgiveness. Forgiving people travel a *via dolorosa*, a journey which may well last a lifetime.

For those who cannot forgive, at least not yet, there is also a struggle, not least with deeply wounded emotions in relation to the perpetrators of violence against them. But it is also an intense struggle within themselves. How does one not become dominated by self-destructive hate, bitterness and vengeance? Those who struggle in this way do not need moralising platitudes about forgiveness from those who often have not experienced loss at first hand.

Ironically in a context where the practice of Christian religion is relatively high, the faith community has often struggled with forgiveness. The F-word can generate a lot of emotion in religious communities. Some of those who offered forgiveness or used approximate vocabulary were bitterly opposed by members of their parish or congregation. Religious people were and are not adverse to writing anonymous letters, making abusive phone calls and even making threats. Some experienced psychological exclusion within their local faith community.

In a community such as Northern Ireland, dominated by fear and where much traditional religion, including the God-images, are punitive, the difficulty with the F-word is not surprising. Forgiveness remains a core word in Christian worship language. 'We believe in the forgiveness of sins' is a creedal affirmation, but what does it mean? Is it a piece of cheap religious rhetoric or a community ethic for healing? It may be that forgiveness has become lost in either pietism or sacramentality. Or reduced to a vertical concept, something that happens between God and the individual, often as a spiritualised experience without any horizontal reference. The 'sins forgiven' rarely touch on sectarianism, homophobia, sexism, misogyny, violent attitudes and actions or silence in the face of injustices and abuses of power. The last are often patriarchal, political, social and ecclesial. Perhaps forgiveness is pietised or sacramentalised because it gets too close to reality and touches raw nerves.

The traumas and hurts of over three decades of violent conflict happened in a political context. Any healing through remembering will take place in a socio-political context, and any practice of forgiveness will take political realities, dynamics and relationships seriously. Liturgical religious vocabulary needs to be translated into the public square and become a community ethic for healing. A theological ethic of forgiveness needs to facilitate reconciliation and the healing of broken, interpersonal relationships. Such a forgiveness praxis contributes to the restoration of social harmony and communal solidarity. Putting the F-word at the heart of the generational peace process is the best alternative to dealing with and overcoming the past. Interpersonal vengeance or institutional retribution will only offer short-term satisfaction to victims if it does not in fact re-victimise them or lock them into victimhood. Vengeance and retribution or holding on to a punitive outlook or theology will not and cannot retrieve human losses, heal injuries, repair destroyed property or recover a material or psychological world that was. Ultimately there is no alternative to forgiveness: 'In sum, forgiveness is an essential norm in building and sustaining harmonious, co-operative relationships'.[2] It is a means to promote peace and social well-being: 'a world from which forgiveness was eliminated would be nothing but a world of cold and unfeeling justice, in the name of which each person would claim his or her own rights *vis-à-vis* others'.[3]

10.2 The Jesus Model – Radical Love of Enemies

If forgiveness is to become a reality in the political context of Northern Ireland, then a socio-political reading of the Judeo-Christian scriptures is necessary. This will mean paying attention to the social, cultural, economic and political context. Every biblical book, gospel and letter is socio-politically situated. The faith community needs to take seriously the social, cultural, economic and political contexts of both scripture and contemporary society. This will take us far beyond the pietism and sacramentality in which forgiveness is held captive. To contribute to peace and social well-being the faith community needs to engage a socio-political reading of forgiveness.

This would require a more extensive study beyond the scope of this chapter. Israel's Jubilee approach to forgiveness is a socio-political model of release from the past. The core biblical theme of covenant is a model of forgiveness as restorative justice.[4] This is not to suggest that these two models and what follows translate easily to the contemporary world, which is very different from the biblical worlds. There is no direct correspondence between these worlds or the Celtic world. Yet the worlds of the Bible did struggle with the ethic of forgiveness in a social context. Modern individualism was foreign to the biblical worlds and that is our distortion and deficit in relation to forgiveness. We need to abandon modern individualism and recover a more relational and communal approach to being human, which means being human together and in community. That is not only clear to the biblical view but also more authentic in relation to the deepest human need for community and the shared future of the peace process.

When the churches confess their faith in the creeds they confess faith in a Constantinian Christ. Here is a Christology from above, a Hellenistic Christ who may even be far removed from the Jewish Jesus, who was not merely Jewish but was Galilean Jewish. The Christ of the creeds seems far removed from the oppressive world of Galilee and its geographical and economic tensions and conflict. Greek concepts and Greek vocabulary are a world away from the 'daily realities of disease, poverty and disenfranchisement that characterised the social existence of first-century Palestinians' other 95%'.[5] But then the creeds belong to a world where the church is identified with empire and where ecclesial power and imperial power merge. The world behind the gospels is a world of imperial domination and resistance to empire, or at least critical distance. There is a political, economic and religious landscape lying behind the words of the gospels. Not merely the background but the foreground of the gospels is the power of the Roman Empire, the splendour of Herodian Jerusalem and the debilitating poverty of rural Galilee and urban Judea. It is also a world of popular resistance movements and messianic pretenders.

The Palestine of Jesus was occupied territory. After almost a century of independence Pompey invaded and Palestine became another subject of the expanding Roman Empire. That was in 63 BCE. Between 40 and 37 BCE the Parthians ruled but Rome soon re-conquered Palestine and installed a client king called Herod the Great. From 37 BCE to 4 CE Herod ruled with brutality. When Herod died in 4 CE there were popular uprisings. The Romans introduced a policy of divide and rule, and then in 44 CE imposed direct rule. The so-called Pax Romana was maintained by military oppression as well as economic oppression. The populace suffered from triple taxation. There were the Roman tribute and toll taxes. Herod also enforced taxation to fund his lavish building projects. Then there was the temple tax, various tithes that enabled the high priests to live in extravagant luxury in Jerusalem. The small farmer taking his produce to the city markets was met with toll taxes and tariffs before he could even set up his stall. The 'other 95%' referred to by Ched Myers were the poor because the wealth and the land were owned by the 5% élite.

Galilee, where Jesus spent most of his time, was a province where tension was especially acute. The Herodians had built a number of Greek cities. There was a serious cultural clash between the Hellenistic cities and the Jewish towns and villages. Furthermore, Galilee was the bread basket for the Greek cities, which added to the economic oppression. Galilee and its people suffered a triple oppression. Occupied by the imperial might of Rome it was also increasingly controlled by the political and economic forces of the Greek cities. Then there was the socio-economic pressure from the religious centre of Jerusalem. Galileans lived with the military ideology of empire, the brutality of client kings, the cultural and economic conflict with Hellenism and the religio-economic oppression of Jerusalem. In the village of Nazareth, only four miles away from one of the Hellenistic cities, a young Jesus was raised. Shaped by this context, familiar with the sufferings of his Galilean people: 'Jesus came to Galilee, proclaiming the good news of God, and saying, The time is fulfilled, and the Kingdom of God has come near, repent and believe in the good news' (Mark 1: 14).

What was this reign of God? A radical alternative empire? A Jubilee time? A renewal of covenant society? A kingdom of non-violence? 'For Jesus did not believe that the Kingdom of God would arrive with fire and brimstone. And he was convinced that he would not need aqueducts, palaces, coins, marble columns, or soldiers to utterly remake Galilee.'[6]

We cannot understand Jesus and the significance of Jesus unless we understand something of the very real world in which he lived and in which he was executed by the imperial power.

> He consistently criticised and resisted the oppressive established political-economic-religious order of his own society. Moreover, he aggressively intervened

to mitigate or undo the effects of institutionalised violence, whether in particular acts of forgiveness or exorcism or in the general opening of the Kingdom of God to the poor. Jesus opposed violence, but not from a distance.[7]

This is a long way from the Christ of the Constantinian creeds where the cross was the sign of the emperor's military conquests. This is a long way from the sacramental and pietistic Jesus of our theological captivity. Perhaps not many homilies and sermons talk about the Galilean Jesus. And yet this is the Jesus whom the secular Jewish philosopher Hannah Arendt described as: 'The discoverer of the role of forgiveness in the realm of human affairs …' She went on to make a remarkable and profound statement:

> It is decisive in our context that Jesus maintains against the 'scribes and Pharisees' first that it is not true that only God has the power to forgive, and second that this power does not derive from God … but on the contrary must be mobilized by man (sic) toward each other before they can hope to be forgiven by God also.[8]

Christians might want to back away from the idea that human power 'does not derive from God', and might want to argue that Jesus was not the 'discoverer' of forgiveness in the public place. Arendt's own Jewish scriptures, which were the scriptures of Jesus, had already made the point. Yet forgiveness in the socio-political context was prominent in his teachings and in a very practical way. Societies can deal with the evils in their pasts and change for the better. Forgiveness is key to it, and this is what the controlling metaphor of the life and ministry of Jesus was about. The time announced by Jesus in Galilee – the crucial time of opportunity – was the time for humans to see the loving, liberating power of God at work in the midst of their concrete world. It was also true for Jesus that there is enough moral capacity in ordinary people to forgive and reshape their future. God is active, and humans can do things also. And there is an interdependence between God's forgiveness of us and our forgiveness of each other. The Our Father, which came out of this socio-political world of violence and oppression taught us to pray in that context: 'Forgive us our debts as we have also forgiven our debtors.' In the market squares and fields of dominated Galilee the ordinary people would have understood Jesus' story of the unmerciful servant who having been forgiven an enormous debt goes out and victimises an even poorer peasant who owes him a paltry amount (Matthew 18: 23–35). They would also have known the saying of Jesus that follows on from Matthew's Lord's Prayer: 'For if you forgive others their trespasses, your heavenly Father will forgive you; but if you do not forgive others, neither will your Father forgive your trespasses' (Matthew 6: 14).

All of this radical teaching came out of a world of oppression and conflict. So too did those radical calls to love the enemy; to take moral responsibility for one's enemies. The Jesus vision of a God is of One who makes the sun to rise and the rain to fall on the good and bad alike and who is an all-embracing and all inclusive God. Matthew's version of the outcome of this God vision – 'Be perfect even as your father is heaven is perfect' – really means 'be all-embracing, all-inclusive, even as your father in heaven is all-embracing, all-inclusive'. In the socio-political context of Jesus' world this is about breaking the cycle of oppression and the spiral of violence. It is about doing the unexpected and surprising thing in a conflict scenario. It is about taking moral responsibility for enemies. It is about liberating their humanity and our own. It is about empowering each other to build new political space; to rebuild the market square where we can all stand in equity, diversity and interdependence.

Of course Jesus did not remake Galilee, but he did shape within it an alternative community where the past was dealt with, where antagonists did take moral responsibility for each other, where justice, compassion and love were practised; where the world of conflict and repression was challenged. 'His organisation', says Shriver, 'frightened religious and secular politicians alike … it was indeed an alternative society, an alternative sphere for working out relations of leadership, power and human connection … Jesus was not just a moralist or spiritual teacher but the bearer of a new possibility of human, social and therefore political relationships.'9

Perhaps in the church we will not really know the power of forgiveness in the public place until we have rediscovered Jesus in his socio-political world. That may mean being liberated from our churchy and pietistic worlds. The liberating models are there in the church's normative text. The foundational documents do provide us with models of experience in the public place. We may have made the Bible a churchy book or a pious handbook, but it is something else. It is a book about market squares and public places where all the brokenness and messiness of human and public life are all too real. But that is where forgiveness is experienced and practised. To recover the public practice of forgiveness means engaging in a socio-political reading of forgiveness. It means rediscovering or maybe even discovering the Jubilee model, the Covenant model and the Jesus model – models that are rooted in socio-political contexts.

Forgiveness then is about liberation from the past and empowerment for the future. It is a community practice where we liberate each other from the captivity of the past, release each other from the unjust oppression of the past and empower for a new beginning. Forgiveness is about envisioning a different kind of future rooted in the practice of justice as restorative and distributive justice. Forgiveness is redressing past inequities and injustices and redistributing power relations. It is about taking moral responsibility for enemies, breaking the cycle of violence and opening up new possibilities for human, social and political relationships.

There is nothing churchy or pietistic about it unless we are prepared to radically re-vision church and redefine piety. Beyond cheap rhetoric there is forgiveness. There is a community ethic of healing. There is life after conflict and repression because we believe in the forgiveness of sins.

10.3   A Celtic Ethic of Forgiveness

A number of sources in the early Irish tradition point to the dynamics of forgiveness. The word itself is not always obvious. In many contemporary books written on aspects of Celtic Christianity the word is rarely found in any index. There is much to be said and to be explored around the themes of penance and penitentials. The rigorous ascetic tradition in early Irish Christianity cannot be ignored. Rigid discipline and bodily asceticism are key characteristics including a particular preoccupation with sex and sexuality. A Celtic ethic of forgiveness, therefore, must begin with some of the most prominent literature from the early story of Irish Christianity.

The Penitentials

The oldest Penitentials in the Irish church date from the sixth century. It needs to be noted from the outset that those rigorous documents were not for lay people, the majority of the faithful. They were written by various monastic leaders for clergy, monks and nuns. The Penitentials are characterised by detailed lists of sins and appropriate penances. They reflect the moral standards of the sixth century and the issues that were of moral concern for the members of religious community. It is reckoned that up to 45% of the Penitentials deal with sexual offences which may be one indication of the moral struggle that characterised the average monastic community. On the other hand it may indicate a faith community already preoccupied with an unhealthy obsession with sexuality in which sexuality and sinfulness have been too closely identified. If there is an obsession with sexuality it is predominately male and misogynist in relation to women. Women are already in the role of sexual objects, temptations to sin for men who in turn wrestle with sexuality as unclean or impure, and therefore a major sin to be avoided by rigorous discipline and penance. The penances themselves are indications of the intensity of the struggle and the obsession with sexuality as sin. If, as religious people sometimes complain, the twenty-first century is preoccupied with sex, then sixth-century monastic communities easily match it. Perhaps both centuries are skewed. The Western theological equation of sex with sin and sin with sex made no small contribution to the distortion of faith and sexuality. An anthropology which defines human as predominantly sexual has seriously diminished what it means to be truly human. It has also created a great deal of human guilt and unhealthy repression. Not a few in Ireland, especially of an older generation, feel that the institutional churches need more than a little forgiveness for that. 'A man who practises masturbation by himself, for the first offence, one hundred days; if he repeats it, a year.' This is from the seventh-century Penitential of Cummean and belongs to a twenty-one paragraph section dealing mainly with sexual sins.[10] These include practising homosexuality by boys and men and sex with animals. The real sin in the thought world of the time was the misuse or waste of semen. Sexual activity was solely for procreation and the rules imply a less than human view of women as mere receptacles. Put crudely it was a 'flower pot' view of women in whom the all-important male seed was planted and which grew to be a child. Thanks to contemporary science and physiology we now know differently, but the old pre-scientific view is taking a long time to die and it is probably the real issue behind the often irrational and aggressive response to male homosexuality. Lesbianism is not usually as big an issue in contemporary society.

A negative attitude towards the body is expressed in the Penitential of Columbanus:

> If anyone, desiring a bath, has washed alone naked, let him do penance with a special past. But if anyone, even while sitting in the bath, has uncovered his knees or arms, without the need for washing dirt, let him not wash for six days, that is, let that immodest bather not wash his feet until the following Lord's Day.[11]

The word 'immodest' provides the clue to a negativity towards the human body. Were these early Celtic monks trained to distrust their bodies, or dislike them? It has sometimes been claimed that Celtic spirituality involved the body in penance and forgiveness, but the Penitentials seem to point to a dislike, even abhorrence of the body. Perhaps when Columbanus warned his penitents to 'beware of mortal and fleshly sins before we may communicate ...', there was already a misunderstanding of Paul. 'Flesh' was being understood much too literally, a distortion of Paul that has persisted.

Again it is significant that the Penitentials have little to say directly about forgiveness. The F-word is rarely in the Penitential vocabulary. Penance may imply it but did the Penitentials have an adequate theology of sin, or did the religious communities engage in a reductionism, misplacing the focus and missing out on some of the real sins of early Celtic society? There is certainly little structural awareness of sin and therefore an inadequate public theology of forgiveness.

And yet one of the earliest Penitentials, that of Finnian, whether of Clonard or Moville, offers some deeper insights. Recalling John Cassian's assertion that there is cure by contraries, Finnian wrote:

> Let us seek pardon from the mercy of God and victory over those things, continuing in a state of penance ... But by contraries, as we said, let us make haste to cure contraries and to cleanse away those faults from our hearts and introduce heavenly virtues in their places: Patience must arise for wrathfulness; kindliness or the love of God and of one's neighbour, for envy, for detraction, restraint of heart and tongue; for dejection, spiritual joy, for greed liberality.[12]

This is a remarkable text full of spiritual and human insight. Pardon or forgiveness is named, and it is not a matter of cheap grace as forgiveness has sometimes been portrayed. There is a depth psychology in Cassian's contraries. Greed is overcome by liberality and generosity, and patience saves us as well as transforming us from wrathfulness or vengeance.

Finnian does focus on the more classical Celtic understanding of sin, not as breaking laws but a disease requiring healing. There is much talk in the Penitentials of 'cure'. Human beings and human community are characterised by disease, with oneself and one another. Relationships are skewed, broken, out of place. There is a social sickness, often experienced as alienation, hurt, out of sorts. The sins that Finnian names are all social sins distorting human relationships and community. Finnian reminds his penitents that: 'The anger of man (sic) worketh not the justice of God.' There is a just anger but much human anger turns to violence and vengeance and neither secures justice, social or legal. 'Covetousness is the root of all evil' is quoted from Paul. Greed, grasping, wanting and taking what does not justly belong is behind most wars, imperial expansionism and superpower domination in whatever age.

The pardon of which Finnian speaks is forgiveness as healing of disease and release from past social wrong doing. Cheap grace is again avoided in his opening to the Penitential. After invoking God as Trinity, Finnian goes on: 'If anyone has sinned by thought in his heart and immediately repents, he shall beat his breast and seek pardon from God and make satisfaction, and so be whole'[13]

Dealing with the human disease requires a process which includes the generous forgiveness of God and the making of reparation. God's gift and human effort are both involved in the healing. The pardon or forgiveness of God is given but the wrongdoer is to seek it and to show his or her readiness to be forgiven by repenting. This means turning away from the wrongdoing or from the envy, greed or violent anger, showing a meaningful remorse for what has happened and beginning to live in a different and new direction. The latter is expressed through reparation or what Finnian calls 'making satisfaction'. There is a moral responsibility on the offender to put things right, to repair the damage, to restore the relationship. Finnian does not separate the vertical and the horizontal relationship. It is through this process that the offender is made 'whole', another word for healing or restoration. In this process the victim of the wrongdoing is also restored. Dignity is given back, reparation – symbolically or materially – is made and the inequality of the relationship of power between victim and offender is equalised. Something of the good of community is also restored. Finnian might well call that forgiveness, how it works, what it involves and what it does for human and community relations.

Soul Making

On the European mainland penance was very public, humiliating and harsh. The penitent would join a penitential group and would often be expelled from the faith community and the Eucharist. He or she was allowed to return only after a rigid and severe rehabilitation process, such as publicly cropping their hair and appearing in special penitential clothes. It was a publicly humiliating process and had little room for mercy or compassion.

The early Celtic church had a different process, one characterised by 'healing, ongoing conversion and spiritual guidance [rather] than of public punishment'.[14] Again there is the emphasis on healing of disease, dealing with the social and relational sins. There is no reduction of the experience of turning around and beginning again to a single moment or experience. Conversion or turning life around is an ongoing experience, a lifetime of transformation, more a process than an event. One begins again and changes often. The spiritual guidance introduces the profound idea of the soul-friend, the wise but often wounded healer who journeys alongside the vulnerable and often struggling sinner. The soul-friend is a healer rather than a judge, a friend rather than a disciplinarian.

This is the heart of the Celtic approach to spiritual health and wholeness in the world. One is involved in a lifelong process of soul-making, seeking and experiencing healing and reconciliation with God, others and oneself. Soul-friendship was essential to this life process.

The soul-friend would often prescribe healing remedies. If one's wrongdoing had caused injustices, a pilgrimage to Jerusalem or another holy site would be recommended. This may have been the reason why Columba left Derry for Iona. His involvement in violent tribal conflict may have resulted in him leaving his homeland for 'exile and perpetual pilgrimage'.[15]

The highly influential Penitential of Columbanus uses the analogy of 'doctors of the body ... so also spiritual doctors'.[16] So Columbanus describes the healing role of the soul-friend. Again this is rooted in the pastoral theology of John Cassian. Furthermore the soul-friend is concerned with 'a complete state of health'. Soul-making is about the whole person and the soul-friend journeys alongside to enable the total well-being of the person. 'So also should spiritual doctors treat with diverse kinds of cures the wounds of souls, their sickness, offences, pains, ailments, and infirmities'.[17] Spiritual well-being and emotional and physical well-being are inseparable, which is why unresolved anger, bitterness and vengeance-seeking are destructive of the whole being. To forgive is also therapeutic, enhancing the total well-being of the forgiver.

For Columbanus the soul-friend has special qualities. He thinks it is a gift belonging only to a few. But even if only a few have the gift of soul-friendship, they do not act alone but out of the context of received wisdom. They are in touch with 'the traditions of our elders'. Soul-friends have the wisdom to draw on the wisdom received from the tradition. The received wisdom informs the soul-friend's spiritual guidance and in the discerning and healing role there is openness to learn from the wisdom of wiser people in the present as well as the wisdom handed on from the past. Learning and reflection are essential to the soul-friend's spirituality.

Columbanus also reminds the soul-friend of her or his humility. They are not people with all the answers or ready packaged advice. They have a realistic appreciation of themselves and their abilities, including weaknesses. The soul-friend journeys alongside 'according to our own partial understanding for we prophecy in part and we know in part'.[18] Far from having all the answers the soul-friend is aware of personal limitations, partial understanding and our own woundedness. The best healer in this tradition is a wounded healer. Soul-makers know the struggles of the soul in process because they have been there and are still in the spiritual and moral struggle.

The importance of the soul-friend is underlined by a number of monastic leaders and rules. In the Rule of Comgall of Bangor there are strong words: 'However self-confident you are, place yourself under the direction of another'.[19] The Rule of Ailbe – also from the eighth century – highlights the importance of someone who is 'a sure and compassionate guide in the art of good living'.[20]

Soul-friends, therefore, in the Celtic tradition were a necessary part of the life journey towards wholeness, spiritual growth and the nourishing of human greatness. Soul-making was a lifelong process and the way of holiness and wisdom. Essential to all of this was the practice of healing, reconciliation and forgiveness, not possible without the experiential wisdom of the soul-friend. In a culture where life was a preparation for dying, to die well was to have lived well. The accompaniment of the soul-friend was essential to soul-making, and soul-making was a life process of forgiving and being forgiven.

The Struggle with Forgiveness

The Celtic tradition did not always find forgiveness easy. Any difficulty we have in our contemporary context was also present in these earlier centuries. In the eighth century a collection of law tracts were brought together and the collection was known as the SENCHAS MÁR or the 'Great Tradition'. These were the laws of Christian Ireland, and as the legal code they symbolise the 'knitting together of church and kingdom'.[21] They are a reminder that the early Christianity in Ireland was within a Christendom model and that faith, therefore, was closely aligned to political power. This may be why the 'Great Tradition' struggles with forgiveness. Forgiveness clashes with vengeance, the punitive is more prominent and forgiveness is confined to the executed offender's soul: 'The example of vengeance upholds two laws'.[22] In other words the Christian era does not dispense with vengeance: 'Let everyone die who kills a man in the image of the king … Death pursues Bloodshed … When killing by foul play is pronounced, let deaths be died. Whoever releases the guilty is guilty. I sentence the guilty to death.'[23]

The ethos here is honour, personal honour being important in a Celtic society. The death sentence is required and justified: 'Thus the two laws were fulfilled: the culprit was killed for his crime, and his soul was pardoned. This was established by the men of Ireland: everyone to die for his crime, so that sin might not increase again in this island.'[24]

Collective vengeance was therefore an accepted part of the new Christian era in Ireland. It was legal practice within the Christendom model of church and kingdom. In contemporary Ireland the death penalty is no longer used, which is also true in the European Union countries. Not only did this ultimate punitive sanction fail as a deterrent, but it also produced too many miscarriages of justice as well as being a collective expression of vengeance. It left little or no room for the transforming dynamic of forgiveness. Perhaps Christendom has always had difficulty with forgiveness. In the marriage between church and state, throne and altar, it has never been a best practice model.

One of the oldest documents in the Irish language is the *Alphabet of Devotion* attributed to Colman mac Beógnse, a nephew of Columba. If so, it is a seventh-century writing and suggests a society in which not everyone is Christian. The Alphabet appears to describe a wealthy pagan who is somewhat removed from Christianity. At a deeper level it reflects the ethics of the contemplative life, what Christian ethical living might look like, or perhaps a road map for anyone seeking the spiritual life. The document may have had considerable influence on the later Celi-De reform movement. The Alphabet of Devotion spells out the four foundations of piety:

> patience to withstand every desire,
> forbearance to withstand every wrong,
> asking pardon for every deception,
> forgiving every sin.[25]

Whatever the great legal tradition of Christendom Ireland was to say in the next century, the Alphabet was clear about foundational piety, the core of the spiritual life. Both asking for forgiveness and offering forgiveness were core. Religious practice is built on forgiveness, is shaped by the ethic of forgiveness and is essentially about restoring relationships, putting right wrongs and living a transformative alternative to vengeance and the destructive power of bitterness, unresolved anger and revenge.

St Patrick Forgives

Every 17 March we celebrate St Patrick's Day. It is the celebration of a non-Irish person, an outsider or foreigner, a Romano-Celt from Britain. Behind the floats and majorettes is a painful story. Patrick at sixteen years of age was wrenched by Irish pirates from his home, family and community. Deeply traumatised by this intentional act of violence against and violation of his adolescent humanity, he became a slave in Ireland. After some years he escaped with the deep painful memory of his terrible experience. Slaves have never been treated as human beings. Somewhere Patrick embraced the Christian faith and then incredibly returned to Ireland to encounter his slave owners, to challenge the dehumanising system of slavery and to spend the rest of his life enabling the Irish to find an alternative way of living in community and in social solidarity. His was a violent abduction. He had every reason to hold an ethnocentric hatred of the Irish, every reason to seek for vengeance. He also could have denied his violent displacement, repressed his anger and resentment, avoided the past and lived in the relative comfort of his Romano-British estate. But he helped with others to bring the Irish into the mainstream of Western history. He forgave and was forgiven; he suffered the violence of slavery and overcame it; he was the outsider who stayed, or rather returned, to transform the culture of his violators and conquerors. The story of Patrick is the story of liberating and transformative forgiveness. Forgiveness can deal with the past, heal wounded persons and restore communal solidarity. Maybe this Patrick needs to be allowed to speak and be heard by contemporary Irish victims and offenders. St Patrick's Day could become an inspiration for dealing with our troubled and painful Irish history and past. From Patrick we could renew our vision of moral courage by which forgiveness and reconciliation might become our alternative story.

Key Points from Chapter 10

❏ Forgiveness is never offered easily, it is costly.

❏ In the Christian narrative there is a cross at the heart of forgiveness, the journey to forgiveness may last a lifetime.

❏ Forgiveness takes place in a socio-political context where there is a need for reconciliation and the healing of broken interpersonal relations, towards restoration of community.

❏ Forgiveness is an essential norm in peacebuilding. Holding on to the need for vengeance and retribution can be self-destructive and lock individuals/communities into victimhood.

❏ The biblical and Celtic worldview was both relational and communal, and modern emphasis on individualism has lost sight of the importance of this authentically human approach.

❏ Jesus' teaching on forgiveness came out of a world of religious, political, social and economic oppression and conflict. Jesus was concerned to break the cycle of oppression and violence, and open up new possibilities for human relating.

❏ Jesus spoke of an all-embracing, all-inclusive God who is concerned for the healing and liberation of all people. The challenge for Christians is take moral responsibility for the enemy and enable the recovery of humanity and rebuilding of relationships and socio-political space.

❏ Where justice, compassion and love are practised an alternative, healing and forgiving community becomes possible.

❏ Forgiveness is about liberation from the past and empowerment for the future. It is about redressing past inequalities and injustices and redistributing power relations.

❏ The oldest Penitentials in the Irish church date from the sixth century and written by various monastic leaders for clergy, monks and nuns.

❏ They reflect the moral standards of the time and issues of moral concern for members of the religious community: e.g. 45% of Penitentials deal with sexual offences, equating sex with sin.

❏ They also reveal a misogynist view of women, who were associated with the body and therefore with sin.

❏ The Penitentials show little structural awareness of sin and therefore an inadequate public theology of forgiveness.

❏ An exception is Finnian, who names social sins that are distorting human relationships and community. In the Celtic tradition he views forgiveness as healing of disease and release from past social wrongdoing. There is a moral responsibility on the offender to restore the relationship.

❏ In the Celtic approach one is involved in a lifelong process of soul-making, seeking and experiencing healing and reconciliation with God, others and oneself. Soul-friendship was essential to this process.

- ❏ Soul-making is about the total well-being of the person and includes the process of forgiveness, letting go of unresolved anger and the need for vengeance, which is healing for the victim.
- ❏ The honour/shame culture in Christendom Ireland often resulted in the perpetrator of a serious crime paying for it with his life and forgiveness being granted to benefit the soul after death.
- ❏ The seventh-century *Alphabet of Devotion* an earlier document to the *Senchas Mor* underlines that both asking for forgiveness and offering it were core religious practices aimed at restoring relationships.
- ❏ The story of Patrick is a story of liberating and transformative forgiveness.

Test Questions

- ❏ What information can be gleaned from Celtic writings and lives of the saints to indicate the importance of forgiveness in Celtic Ireland?
- ❏ What are the ethical implications of affirming 'we believe in the forgiveness of sins' in twenty-first-century Ireland?

11   An Ethic of Compassion

11.1 A Compassionate Society?

Compassion is the authentic mark of our humanity. We are most truly human when we live compassionately towards others and towards all of life. Disasters and tragedies seem to bring out the best of compassionate responses. The global response to the tsumani catastrophe in 2005 showed compassion to be a universal virtue in people of all faiths and none. In both the suffering and the compassionate, labels were irrelevant. Compassion was everything.

Yet this same humanity has the capacity for terrible violence and inflicting suffering. Compassionate humanity can be brutal humanity. Loving humanity can be violent humanity, destructive of life and nature.

Societies may be characterised by compassion, especially towards the poor and weak. They may also be harsh and punitive, judgemental and begrudging. Some would say that Ireland has a put-down culture. The northern part of the island has been described as a society of begrudgery. Success is quickly brought down to earth and there is little acknowledgement for achievements.

A culture of violence creates and sustains a punitive society in which the ethics of forgiveness and compassion are often in short supply. The offended want their 'pound of flesh' and the wrongdoer must pay fully for his or her crimes. Some become imprisoned in their victimhood, not merely because of terrible things they experienced (and these should never be minimised) but also because they have been shaped by a punitive society, or values, since childhood. The double tragedy is that imprisoned victims transfer their bitterness and vengeance-driven attitudes to their children and even grandchildren. Victimhood becomes generational, and compassion even towards oneself becomes non-existent or minimal. This is not universal victim experience but it is for some and it is destructive of authentic humanity in relationship.

A punitive society sees justice as punishment and the practice of compassion or forgiveness as weakness. It is usually strong on a lock-up policy and any alternative view is derided as coming from do-gooders or wishy-washy liberals. But 'lock-them-up and throw away the key' is the easy cop-out and avoids personal and collective responsibility for the common good and ultimate well-being of society. The punitive does not know the depths of the moral struggle and the efforts of moral imagination required for a more redemptive, transformative and compassionate society. It is much more difficult to build a society of just compassion and compassionate justice.

The litmus test of the health of any society is in its capacity for compassion especially towards its suffering and weaker members. This is also true of its criminal justice system, whether the system is punitive or restorative. It is not even either/or but both. Punishment and sanction are necessary and appropriate within the larger framework of restoration, which includes the victims, offenders and interdependent community.

A punitive society also tends to be a society of moral rigidity. Judgementalism is the main characteristic, especially when shaped by narrow, self-righteous religion. Sexuality becomes particularly moralistic, including homophobia which is usually rationalised as based on high moral, religious and biblical principles. All of this in an Irish society which for centuries has tolerated and accepted a high level of violence and killing, again often with religious sanction. We show little compassion towards those who are religiously, racially, economically, politically and sexually different from us. And yet the ethic of compassion remains core to the very faith tradition which is often used to justify moralism, judgementalism, violence, killing and war.

11.2   Deep Compassion in the Biblical Tradition

Compassion dominates the biblical tradition. True there are texts of terror which justify then and now terrible violence and genocide. There are strands in the biblical text where God is portrayed as utterly punitive and violent. Yet also within the text there are devastating critiques of violence, including God's violence. The prophet Elijah seems to have known nothing else but a violent strategy, demanded, he believed by a violent God. Within the same sacred text the prophet Hosea offered a devastating critique of this 'sacred violence' and did not hesitate to say that Elijah had got it all wrong. Isaiah of Jerusalem and Micah challenged the national propensity for violence and destruction, and offered more compassionate and peaceful visions of God as alternatives.

The Bible portrays the human ambivalence and struggle with faith, ethics and God as it is. The authority of the sacred text is in its challenge to us to choose between a God of violence and a God of non-violence, between a punitive God and a compassionate God. From Genesis to Revelation, all in the context of imperial domination and military, political and economic violence, the core challenge is to choose which God we are to trust and live by. To live faithfully in God's world is to live ethically, which is to live justly and compassionately.

Hosea pushed beyond the boundaries of truth, not without a moral struggle, to the vision of a deeply compassionate God. The moral ambivalence is encountered in his language and images in relation to his unfaithful wife and the analogy of God's relationship to unfaithful Israel. The language is misogynist, violent and abusive of women. Yet in the history of Israel's experience and understanding Hosea produced the groundbreaking vision of God the deeply compassionate One. Ultimately the prophet pushed beyond the destructive culture of violence to a God who was God and not human, i.e. violent, to a God of solidarity and compassion who suffered alongside and whose deep compassion would never let go or give up. Hosea highlighted the power of transforming compassion (Hosea 11: 1–9).

Jesus was in this Jewish prophetic tradition. He too pushed beyond the boundaries of truth in his own community. The faith community has often had the same problem. It more often mirrors the popular value system, the comfortable, self-serving ethics of the domination systems. The Matthean Beatitudes turn the domination system values upside down. Jesus points to God's upside-down kingdom. The fifth Beatitude pronounces the blessedness of the merciful: 'for they will receive mercy' (Matthew 5: 7). In the Sermon on the Mount in which the Beatitudes are placed, Jesus also visions God as merciful to all, without favouritism or exception. God's love, mercy and compassion are for the good and bad alike, chosen people and hated imperialists, no distinctions. Luke repeats this God vision in his Sermon on the Plain, using a word even closer to relational compassion. For both Matthew and Luke the ethical imperative is to imitate the compassion of God.

The word compassion may be a better word than mercy: '"Mercy" and "merciful" imply a situation of wrongdoing: mercy can be shown to someone who deserves punishment … In this context "mercy" is a virtual synonym for "forgiveness".'[1]

The word compassion has a different meaning. It is to 'feel with' or 'to feel the feeling of another'.[2] It is to suffer alongside and with the other and to enter into their experience and situation and with practical feeling and action. Repeatedly it is said of Jesus in the gospels that he had compassion on people. Compassion is central to the ethic of Jesus. It is at the heart of the story of the Good Samaritan who crosses the centuries-old religious and ethnic boundaries to help, bandage, take care of and ensure continuing care for a mutual enemy. When Jesus asked who was neighbour to the mugged Jew, the answer may have choked the listeners: 'The one who showed him compassion' (Luke 10: 29–37).

Luke tells stories of dinner parties. The best known is of the Great Dinner (Luke 14: 12–24). There are multiple themes in this story such as hospitality, friendship and compassion. The story is about a banquet for the poor and a call to share. It reflects the serious poverty of the Greco-Roman society of Luke's time. The ethical challenge is to be in solidarity with the poor. Do not simply throw a party for your friends; invite the poor, the nobodies, the marginalised and suffering of society! The ethic of compassion in action builds a different kind of community.

There are other stories of compassion in action. In Matthew there is the story of judgement between sheep and goats. Those who participate in the kingdom of God are those who show practical compassion to the hungry, thirsty, strangers, naked or home-less and to prisoners. Those judged are those who were so self-occupied they failed to see those suffering and who therefore lacked compassion. As in the eighth-century BCE of Amos, they may have been so busy enjoying fervent religion and lively worship, they failed to see the poor and oppressed and failed miserably to unite justice and compassion (Matthew 25: 31–46).

Matthew does not make this mistake: 'Matthew makes great efforts to unite justice and compassion.'[3] Compassionate justice in Matthew and the Hebrew scriptures, which are the basis of this gospel, is in the long term the only effective core of healthy society: 'Matthew is concerned about presenting Jesus as a model of sensitivity toward others rather than an armchair philosopher.'[4]

The Sermon on the Mount (Matthew 5–7) is placed in the context of Jesus' ministry to the sick and oppressed: 'They brought to him all the sick, those who were afflicted by various diseases, and pains, demonics, epileptics, and paralytics, and he cured them' (Matthew 4: 24). Given that the suffering of these people was directly related to the poverty and trauma of military occupation, this was truly subversive, radically compassionate and liberating activity. Then follows the Sermon on the Mount with the blessedness of those who mourn this unjust and politically induced suffering, the merciful, those who hunger and thirst for justice and the peacemakers. Jesus himself was driven by just compassion and compassionate justice. What motivates his activity is human suffering and the utterly compassionate nature of God. The Lukan Jesus whose ministry is to 'bring good news to the poor … proclaim release to the captives and recovery of sight to the blind, to let the oppressed go free, to proclaim the year of the Lord's favour' is motivated by the Spirit of the Lord (Luke 4: 18–19). This deep compassion in action is the heart of God: 'God's character is marked by compassionate generosity … Jesus speaks of compassion not only as the primary quality of God, but also as the primary quality of a life lived in accord with God.'[5] The ethical imperative in the life of Jesus and of those who would follow him is clear. It is the imitation of God through the practice of compassion.

Joseph Grassi goes beyond the inter-human dimension of compassion: 'Luke could be called the "Gospel of Animals". He mentions them more than any other gospel and gives more attention to Jesus' own compassion for them.'[6] This is hardly surprising since Jesus the Jew is rooted in the Jewish tradition. The foundational story of his people was that of the Exodus from which they identified the core quality of God as RACHUM or womb-compassion (Exodus 34: 6). This compassion of God extends not only to people but also to animals. The Psalms extend this love and compassion to all without distinction:[7]

> The Lord is good to all, and his compassion (RACHUM) is over all his works (Psalm 145: 8–9).

> For every wild animal of the forest is mine, the cattle on a thousand hills. I know all the birds of the air, and all that moves in the field is mine (Psalm 50: 10–11).

The humorous punch line to the story of Jonah sulking because God actively concerns Godself with imperialistic Assyria reminds the small-minded missionary that God is deeply concerned with Assyrian humanity, 'and also many animals' (Jonah 4: 11). Jonah has no answer to that!

This was the tradition of Jesus, the sacred text which shaped his life and view of God. In Luke's gospel, Sabbath laws must give way to compassion for humans and animals (Luke 13: 15; 14: 5). A vivid image of the pain in the heart of God is the mother hen protecting her chicks, an image of God's motherly love, care and compassion (Luke 13: 34).

Whether through imagery or practice Jesus was in compassionate relationship to the animal world. The ethic of compassion embraces both humans and animals, which is why violence towards animals dehumanises. Indeed our violence – military, domestic or against children – rarely stops with humans. God's womb-compassion, a profound feminine image, is over all that God has made. To be truly human is to imitate God in relation to animals and humans.

11.3 Celtic Compassion in Action

We know the Celtic saints through storytelling. Whether those stories are literally or historically true is beside the point. Holiness as compassionate action is the key point. To live compassionately is to imitate and to share the divine praxis in the world.

Kevin Provides Food for the Poor

One day Kevin of Glendalough was herding his sheep. He met a great crowd of poor people who were starving from lack of food. When asked for food, Kevin was deeply shamed that he had no food with him and therefore had nothing to share. The poor turned away but Kevin asked them to wait. He killed seven sheep and the poor left without hunger and satisfied. Next day Kevin visited his flock and found that all the sheep were present. There were none missing. The shame Kevin had felt when the poor asked for food and he had nothing to give them was now gone.[8]

There are similar stories in the Celtic tradition with the allusion to the biblical story of Elijah and the widow and the jar of meal and jug of oil which never failed (I Kings 17: 8–16). The story may be part of the Elijah cycle but it is the poor woman who lives out of compassion and generosity. Kevin is shamed by having nothing to give but looks for and finds a practical solution, which is compassion in action.

Adamnan's Witness to Columba's Compassion

Adamnan is also in the storytelling tradition and has a number of stories which bear witness to the gentleness and compassion of the founder of Iona.

One day Columba hurried to the church to pray for a poor Irish girl 'tortured by the pains of a most difficult childbirth'. 'St Columba was moved by pity for the girl and ran to the church where he knelt and prayed to Christ the Son of Man.' The young woman gave birth safely and regained her health.[9]

Columba responds with pity or compassion to a situation of great difficulty and pain, and significantly he connects with Christ, the Son of Man or the human one, portrayed often in the gospels as full of compassion.

Other stories of healing are told such as the healing of his servant Diarmait, who regained his full health. According to Adamnan, Columba raised a young Pictish boy to life: 'Seeing their (parents') great distress, St Columba comforted them …'[10]

Columba called on a wizard, Broichan, to release an Irish slave girl: 'having pity on her as a fellow human being'.[11]

There are many miracle stories in the Life of Columba. Again we do not need to be literalists but recognise the exaggeration of hagiographers who want to portray the holiness of a human life. Adamnan tells other stories and concludes by saying: 'This is enough of such stories about terrible vengeance on his opponents. Now we shall say a few things about animals.'[12]

There is therefore a dark side to Adamnan's Life of Columba, characterised by violence and vengeance in the name of God. Perhaps life is a struggle between vengeance and compassion. Sanctity emerges in the moral struggle and Columba was no exception. Compassion is active leading to the healing or liberation of others into greater wholeness of life. Significantly the compassionate healings of Columba were towards the suffering and the poor. Jesus too lived compassionately and healed among the socio-economically oppressed whose suffering and illness were caused by their poverty and political domination.

The 'few things' Adamnan says about animals show that Columba's compassion was not confined to humans. He offered shelter and protection to an exhausted crane which had flown in from Ireland. There is his moving response to the emotional upset of a white horse as it intuitively sensed its master's approaching death.

Columba lived compassionately towards humans and animals and with all his moral struggle, part of his real humanity, we see in his active compassion a well-rounded and whole (holy) human being.

Brigid's Love for the Poor

The Life by Cogitosus portrays a woman profoundly connected and available to the poor. Her ministry 'is not battling with druids and the forces of darkness as it is being available to those in need. Brigit responds compassionately to all sorts of people, even when she probably doesn't always feel that way.'[13]

Cogitosus affirms this as the everyday discipline and practice of her life: 'The number of her miracles grew daily, so that it is almost impossible to count them, so much did she devote herself to the duty of pity and to ministering to the poor people's need of alms, in and out of season.'[14]

Whether it was suitable or unsuitable, Brigid lived out of practical compassion towards the poor. The practice of compassion made her available to them everyday. She is portrayed as a woman of exceptional patience and generosity. She even gave away Bishop Conleath's vestments to the poor, an act which expresses a profound insight – that worship of God and social justice are inseparable: 'authentic spirituality includes outreach to the poor, the forgotten, the abused, the marginalised.'[15] This is the theme of twenty-three of the thirty-two chapters in the Life by Cogitosus.

The stories of Brigid and the taming of the wild boar and the ducks that came to her are profoundly theo-mythical, underlining the importance of compassion as an ethical response to humans and animals. Compassion immersed Brigid actively in the poverty of people and in caring friendship with animals.

Compassion as the Strength of Life

In one of the oldest documents in Irish, the *Alphabet of Devotion*, we encounter a kind of Irish wisdom literature, reflecting the practical wisdom in writings of the Hebrew scriptures. The *Alphabet* is a reflection on 'the ethics and psychology of the contemplative life'.[16] Wisdom for life is offered in succinct, summary form. It lists the fifteen virtues of the soul and includes the virtue of charity, the virtue of mercy, the virtue of generosity and the virtue of almsgiving.[17]

The word virtue is translated by an Irish word *neart*, which means strength or power. It might also be understood as energy. The inner strength of a human life, the dynamic energy and power of being fully human lies in the practice of compassion. It is in the active, practical response to others, especially the poor and suffering, that we find the power of being truly ourselves. The strength to be and to live is in compassion and in living the ethic of compassion. This is deeply connected with the Christian experience of the Holy Spirit, the power, energy and strength or *neart* of God, which creates a caring community and produces the relational fruit of the Spirit (Galatians 5: 22–23). This is not to say that the Spirit is confined to Christians. The Spirit blows where she wills (John 3: 7–8). It is the Christian interpretation of the strength, energy or *neart* at work everywhere in the world.

In the monastic Rule of Ailbe, probably written two hundred years after Ailbe died (534 CE) there is a similar emphasis on compassion. Out of eighth-century Ireland came this ethical imperative: 'He should never refuse assistance to a person who calls with insistence for it. Let him share generously and without measure with one who asks. His manner should be full of affection …'[18]

The word affection means 'kin-love'. We are all related by our humanity, a shared humanity especially when the other is marginalised, abused, oppressed. Compassion and generosity are authentically human responses to those in poverty or suffering.

Early Irish Celtic Christians were not primarily concerned with theological or mystical speculation. In contemporary terms they were less concerned (not unconcerned) with orthodoxy and more concerned with orthopraxis. The practical ethics of Jesus were important, especially in their vision of Jesus. He was the champion of the poor and downtrodden, the one who lived out of compassion for the many poor, displaced and oppressed of the gospels. This same Jesus had critical things to say to the wealthy and the powerful, and Celtic Christians had a particular literary way of making a profound ethical point. A short drama depicted rich people meeting death. It is a dialogue between a rich or powerful person and death. A powerful queen wants death to take the poor person 'who has no hope in this world, and leave me who rejoices in the world'.[19] She has not shared her joy with the poor: 'You regard the poor with contempt.'[20] Compassion as the strength of life is missing. Then follows a call to the wealthy and powerful to remember the poor:

> Remember the poor when you look out on fields you own, on your cows grazing.
>
> Remember the poor when you look into your barn, at the abundance of your harvest.
>
> Remember the poor when the wind howls and the rain falls, as you sit warm and dry in your house.
>
> Remember the poor when you eat fine meat and drink pure ale, at your fine carved table.
>
> The cows have grass to eat, the rabbits have burrows for shelter, the birds have warm nests.
>
> But the poor have no food except what you feed them, no shelter except your house when you welcome them, no warmth except your glowing fire.[21]

Compassionate Heretic!

Give a dog a bad name and it sticks! That is how one of our popular sayings sees it and there is truth in it. There may not be truth in the 'bad name', the person may not deserve it, but it sticks. This could be said of Pelagius, a lay Celtic theologian whose life spanned the fourth and fifth centuries. He may have been Irish but was probably born in Roman Britain. Wherever his place of origin he had a profound influence on early Irish theological thinking and biblical scholarship.

Pelagius is best known for his controversy with Augustine of Hippo, whose theology still dominates the Western church, Catholic and Protestant. Unfortunately Pelagius is known through the writings of Augustine and the latter's polemical portrayal of him. Pelagius is much less known through his own writings. Much of the controversy surrounds Pelagius' disagreement with Augustine's theology of original sin, including total depravity, and the double predestination theology which Augustine developed to emphasise the supremacy of God's grace and deny free will. Pelagius believed that a child was born neither good nor bad, affirmed free will and held to God's grace with which humans co-operate. Having been initially admired for his holiness and clarity of teaching, Pelagius soon incurred the wrath of the powerful Augustine, who pronounced Pelagius a dangerous heretic. In 418 CE Pelagius was condemned as such by a Council of Bishops at Carthage. Pope Zosimus excommunicated Pelagius and Celestius as heretics, and there Pelagius remains to the present day. All of this belongs to another time and the fifth-century context needs to be kept in mind:

it was in keeping with the spirit and temper of theological debate in the fifth century, when white was white and black was black, when theologians had yet to learn and admit, that there is more than one path leading to truth, that doctrine is not an end but a beginning.[22]

Heretic has stuck, and there has been no official theological rehabilitation of Pelagius. Perhaps less remembered is Pelagius' opposition to the moral decadence of many bishops and priests within the Christendom of Rome, where he lived. He was appalled by the acquisition of great wealth and power and the effect of that on the poor. Pelagius was deeply concerned for social justice and saw much of Christian practice as unjust. He believed that a follower of Jesus, especially a church leader, should imitate the poverty, humility and compassion of Christ.

He wrote a lengthy letter, 'On the Christian Life', in which he examined the meaning and significance of the word 'Christian' and the responsibilities that belong to it. After exploring the character of God, Pelagius set out ethical Christian behaviour, the Christian lifestyle. This is described as neighbourly love at all times, the generous giving of alms and the doing of good works:

> Do you consider him a Christian in whom there is no Christian act, in whom there is no righteous conduct, but evil, ungodliness and crime? Do you consider him a Christian who oppresses the wretched, who burdens the poor, who covets others' property, who makes several poor and so that he may make himself rich, who rejoices in unjust gains, who feeds on other's tears, who enriches himself by the death of the wretched, whose mouth is constantly being defiled by lies, whose lips speak nothing but unworthy, foul, wicked and base words, who, when ordered to distribute his own possessions, seizes others' instead.[23]

Following this devastating critique of those who then stretch out their impious hands to God in public worship, Pelagius pointed up the social vision of Isaiah of Jerusalem where worship and social justice are integrated (Isaiah 1: 12–17). Social justice is the public practice of compassion.

In a letter to Demetrias, Pelagius again critiqued particular emphases devoid of compassion: 'There are people who eat little, who live simply and who are celibate; yet they show no love and compassion towards their neighbours.'[24]

Faith is not about ritual perfection but generosity and love towards the marginalised:

> If you see someone who is hungry, share your food. If you see someone who is thirsty, share your drink. If you see someone weeping, offer comfort. If you see someone in despair, offer hope. If you see someone utterly confused and bewildered, try to understand the confusion and then seek clarity. Unless you are loving and generous in these ways, seeking perfection is like trying to build a magnificent palace without first putting in strong foundations.[25]

Compassion, love and generosity are at the heart of authentic Christian living for Pelagius. Christendom may have proscribed this Celtic theologian as heretical, but his life and letters portrayed a compassionate heretic. Perhaps he was closer to the heart of Christian practice than many of his detractors.

The ethic of compassion was central to the early Celtic Christian tradition and remains crucial to personal, social and political transformation. Without it in Ireland we will not transform our culture of violence, overcome our rich-poor divide, nor build new relationships for a shared future.

KEY POINTS FROM CHAPTER 11

❏ The litmus test for the health of any society is its capacity for compassion, especially towards its suffering and weaker members.
❏ The authority of the sacred text is in its challenge to choose between a God of violence and a God of non-violence, between a punitive God and a compassionate God.
❏ Hosea and Jesus envision God as compassionate, all-merciful.
❏ In Matthew and the Hebrew scriptures compassionate justice is the core of a healthy society, and it motivated Jesus' ministry.
❏ To be truly human is to live out of an ethic of compassion that embraces all life – human and animal.
❏ For the Celtic saints to live compassionately they sought to share and imitate God's actions in the world.
❏ For Kevin of Glendalough, Columba, Brigid, Ailbe and Pelagius social justice was the public practice of compassion.

TEST QUESTIONS

❏ How important was compassion in the Celtic tradition? Illustrate with reference to the lives of the saints.
❏ Comment on the claim that 'Ireland will not transform [its] culture of violence, overcome [its] rich-poor divide, nor build new relationships for a shared future' unless it recovers an ethic of compassion.

12 An Ethic of Gender Equality

Issues of war, violence and environmental destruction are key ethical concerns of the twenty-first century. The survival of the human and environmental community depends on our responses. Inseparable from these issues is that of gender relations. The relationships between women and men are skewed in many cultures and are characterised by inequalities, visible in economics, politics and religion. If the claim is true that there will be no peace in the world unless there is peace between the world's religions, then it is equally true that there is no peace unless there is peace between the sexes. The ethic of gender equality becomes an ethical imperative in the contemporary world.

12.1 The Way Things Are

As part of the Belfast Agreement, Northern Ireland was introduced to Section 75 of the 1998 Government of Northern Ireland Act. The Section 75 provision was introduced to ensure that equality of opportunity and good relations were placed at the core of public policy making. There was a radical intent to give consideration to the needs of all people, to embrace new ways of thinking and acting and to introduce a change in how public life in Northern Ireland was conducted. Section 75 listed nine categories of people for whom public authorities were to have 'due regard to the need to promote equality of opportunity'. These persons were of:

- different religious belief;
- political opinion;
- racial group;
- age;
- maritial status;
- sexual orientation;
- men and women generally;
- persons with a disability and persons without;
- persons with dependents and persons without.

These are far-reaching equality issues and if taken seriously by public authorities will change how public life in Northern Ireland is conducted. The equality agenda is an essential part of the desired shared future. Even if groups and organisations such as faith communities have no legal obligation to practise equality of opportunity in relation to the people in these categories, they have a moral obligation.

Gender equality is part of Section 75, which provides the challenge to remove the various ceilings experienced by women in church and society. Domination systems are often part of our society based on an ideology of domination. One such ideology is patriarchy, which is a pervasive idolatry within much religious thought and practice. Patriarchy in church and society has contributed to the widespread abuse and violence against women. It is responsible for a climate of gender discrimination and has led to the dehumanisation of women. When identified with God, all of this is given divine authorisation and sanction.

There are, in part, three key words that describe in varying degrees the root causes of gender inequality: patriarchy, misogyny and androcentrism.

Patriarchy

The word literally means 'the rule of the father' and it refers to systems of legal, social, economic, political and religious relations where sovereignty or rule lies with males. The status of women under patriarchy is subjugation without legal status in their own right. Husbands are heads of households; male children are preferred to female; women are not expected to have lead roles in politics, culture and religion. Much of this is seen within patriarchy as the 'natural order' of things. It is the way things are.

Misogyny

The word literally means 'the hatred of women'. Here women are thought of as morally and intellectually inferior to men and are a source of evil in the world. Aristotle the philosopher shaped misogyny in the West by his insistence that males are the normative human beings. The theologian Thomas Aquinas regarded a woman as a defective male. This has led to the dualistic notion that maleness is superior and that the body has to be rejected, especially the female body. The result is that hatred of sexuality and hatred of women are identified.

Androcentrism

Derived from Greek this word means 'male-centeredness'. From this perspective males are the norm for humanness and females only derive their humanness from males and are subordinate to them. The practical effect of this is the silencing of women and their marginalisation in church and society. The basis of androcentrism is thinking that is hierarchical, dualistic and which creates structures that are unequal in their power relations. There is an inequality of power distribution. The inequality of power also extends to nature where androcentric practice dominates as of right the rest of animate and inanimate creation. Despite the more recent insistence by theologians that God is beyond gender, much God-talk and liturgical language is still heavily androcentric.

To suggest using female images or metaphors for God, such as mother, often leads to aggressive resistance, sometimes even from women themselves.

Each of these words and what they stand for describe the domination system experienced by women in practically all areas of public life. Patriarchy, misogyny and androcentrism are all challenged in Northern Ireland by Section 75. Until these practices and ways of life are eliminated from church and society, gender justice will not be realised. There is therefore an urgency about putting an ethic of gender equality at the heart of our life together. Do the biblical and Celtic worlds provide any models of equality practice?

12.2 The Bible Says No, Yes, Maybe!

The socio-cultural context of the Bible from Genesis to Revelation is patriarchal. With a very few exceptions, even then speculative, the biblical writers were men writing from a male perspective, telling a male story from within a patriarchal culture. Men dominate the biblical story in more senses than one. There are stories of women, some named, most not, but the stories are usually told from a male perspective. As with much of history, women are screened out or filtered through male lens. To read women's stories in the Bible is often to read between the lines. Who wrote the story of Miriam in the Hebrew scriptures? Did she compose the song of liberation or did Moses? It is not clear. The song may have originated with her but was later attributed to Moses. The biblical editors were either intentionally or unintentionally ambivalent. When Miriam and Aaron questioned Moses' abuse of power, why was she punished by God and not Aaron? Who wrote that story and from what motives? Perhaps the final editorial committee could not have a woman questioning a male leader's use of power and exclusive claim to prophecy. The editors apparently had no moral difficulty with invoking God as the cause of Miriam's physical suffering, as divine punishment for questioning Moses' authority and leadership. At least they do portray the people as refusing to move on until Miriam was well again. Moses could do nothing about 'people power'.

There is no ambivalence about two men in different Hebrew stories who refuse the demands of male gangs to use male guests for sexual purposes. Instead they hand over a female concubine and in the other case a daughter. Women can be gang raped but not the male guests. In a piece of morally warped thinking these stories have been interpreted as God's no to homosexual activity. God allowed women to be raped rather than men engage together in the sexual act. Only misogynist men believing in a misogynist God could produce such a homophobic and sexist spin on an already morally warped biblical story. Biblical interpretation and translation can be devoid of ethics.

We still talk about the Abrahamic faiths as if Sarah did not exist. Traditional biblical scholarship speaks of the patriarchs Abraham, Isaac, Jacob and Joseph, even though the text does name Sarah, Rebekah, Rachel and Asenath. The last was the daughter of an Egyptian priest, ensuring impurity in the line of Jewish identity. Joseph's two sons were of Egyptian lineage. The patriarchal focus has been predominant even though the text itself has significant things to say about Sarah, Rebekah and Rachel, whose identities are tied to their relationships with husbands. That too is the patriarchal culture of the biblical social world.

The patriarchal cultural ethos continues in the Christian scriptures and even flows through the history of textual translation and transmission. From Matthew's gospel to the Book of Revelation the role of women is in dispute. In the Christian testament women are in contested space. That their role is challenged and in dispute occurs precisely because they did have a role: 'often a significant and publicly high profile role'.[1] Why else is there a gender dispute in the Christian scriptures?

The earliest Christian writings are the seven letters of Paul considered of indisputable authorship. Many letters were circulating around Christian communities from the earliest days, some still surviving but many lost. Seven authentic letters of Paul made it into the Christian scriptures. There are other letters of disputed authorship, usually thought to be the work of a Pauline school or next generation supporters of Paul. These are Colossians, Ephesians and II Thessalonians, and the three so-called pastoral letters of I and II Timothy and Titus. Language and social setting suggest a generation after Paul's death. The seven authentic Pauline letters are: I Thessalonians, Romans, I and II Corinthians, Galatians, Philippians and Philemon.

Undoubtedly Paul wrote many more letters. Letter writing was after all a key method of communication in the Greco-Roman world. In I Corinthians 5: 9 he mentions a letter he had written to the church at Corinth sometime before he penned I Corinthians. Analysis of I and II Corinthians would suggest that Paul wrote at least four letters to Corinth, and there may even be next generation additions or insertions into the canonical letters we now have preserved.

Paul's seven authentic letters pre-date the four canonical gospels and 'provide ample evidence that women held a prominent place in the emerging Christian communities from the earliest of times'.[2] They are also evidence that the dispute over the role of women in the early faith communities emerged in the post-Pauline generation.

Few public or private readings of scripture bother with Romans 16, in which Paul sent greetings to members of the Roman house churches. The list of names is intriguing. Paul named more men than women, yet the significant list of women named suggests that women were in no way inferior to men in the earliest faith communities.

The first person named was Phoebe: 'our sister … a deacon of the church at Cenchreae' (Romans 16: 1–2). Paul used two significant words to describe Phoebe. She was a deacon, translated from the Greek diakonia, also translated in English as minister of the church of Cenchreae, a significant suburb of the greater metropolitan Corinth. The Revised Standard Version of the Bible wrongly translated the word as 'deaconess' implying that Phoebe belonged to a specific order of female church workers, different from and perhaps subordinate to male 'deacons'. Apart from this translation down-grading Phoebe, the order of deaconess was not invented for another three hundred years! The suggestion that her ministry was limited to women or to the sick is another attempt to down-grade her role. The word Paul used is the same title, made without gender distinctions, which he applied to himself and others engaged in a ministry of preaching and teaching. Phoebe was in a leadership role in the whole church and not just some little part of it. She held a recognised office, was a key church official and minister of the church in Cenchreae.

The second word Paul used to describe Phoebe was *prostatis*, translated as 'benefactor of many and of myself as well' (Romans 12: 2). Phoebe was a business woman whose means enabled her to sponsor or be patron of a church, and to contribute generously to Paul's work. As such she was probably the founder of the church in Cenchreae. The word also indicates authority and points to a person in position of leadership, a president or presiding officer. Phoebe was not only the leader of an established church, but on equal footing with Paul as a co-worker, a generous supporter of many Christians. She was not defined, as women were in this culture in relation to a male husband or father, but as an independent woman of high profile and key leader in the early church. Paul does not say a great deal about her in his final chapter of greetings, but she was named first and enough is said to provide a 'tantalising glimpse of the leadership of women in early Christianity'.[3]

The tantalising glimpse of women in leadership was further underlined by Paul in Romans 16 when he names another nine women. Paul was greeting the leadership of the Roman Christian community: 'Of the twenty-eight prominent people who Paul considered it politic to greet, ten were women.'[4] That is remarkable in itself in the patriarchal Greco-Roman world. On closer examination it is even more remarkable. Eleven of the group were singled out for special praise and five were women: Mary, Tryphaena, Tryphosa, Persis and the unnamed mother. Two couples, who were presumably married, were singled out for extraordinary praise. Paul greeted Prisca (Priscilla) and Aquila and spoke highly of their work, well known among many Gentile churches (Romans 16: 3–4). Both are Gentiles and Prisca was named first. As a woman she had played a lead role in the missionary activity of the early faith community, taking a number of risks in the process. Greetings were also sent to Andronicus and Junia, 'prominent among the apostles' (Romans 16: 7). Both were Christian-Jewish missionaries who travelled, teaching and preaching from city to city. Junia has been robbed of her feminine identity by male theologians and translators, despite the fact that she was a 'heroine of the fourth-century church, and John Chrysostom's elegant sermons invoked the image of Junia, the apostle, for the Christian women of Constantinople to emmulate'.[5] Interpreters and translators changed the name to masculine, Junias, and even to the present there are those who hold to the masculine. This view is held despite the fact that the feminine Junia has been attested 250 times in ancient literature and the masculine Junias is completely unknown in literature as a male name. The real difficulty here is that the church cannot acknowledge a woman as a prominent apostle. For most of its history the church has held that apostolicity is a male preserve, and that fiction must be preserved even if it means putting Junia through a sex-change, at least in manuscript form. Junia was a prominent woman apostle, who by Paul's criteria, had encountered the risen Christ, was a hard-working church leader who also shared a prison experience with Paul. Her apostolic credentials were first class and Paul has vouched for that.

Paul also had a word for dedicated apostolic activity and it is *kopiao*, which means 'to work hard'. 'He uses it of himself twice, in Galatians 4: 11 and I Corinthians 15: 10, but four times in Romans, and exclusively for women (Mary, Tryphaena, Tryphosa and Persis).'[6]

There is no suggestion in Paul's list of greetings that these women worked in ways that were different in anyway from male colleagues in the Roman churches. A ministry of equality was practised, and women played a significant role as leaders in the churches of Paul's day. He recognised and acknowledged this especially in his Roman letter. To the Galatians he had affirmed the radical equality of the sacrament of baptism: 'there is no longer male and female; for all of you are one in Christ Jesus' (Galatians 3: 27–28). In the first-generation churches, certainly those with which Paul had contact, there was an equality of ministry and an equality in Christ which:

> may have manifested itself in the actual worship services of the Pauline communities. Rather than being silent 'hearers of the word', women appear to have been actively involved in the weekly fellowship meetings, participating, for example, by praying and prophesying, much as the men did. (I Corinthians 11)[7]

Paul recognised Junia as a major female apostle which the church of later generations disingenuously tried to avoid: 'But that problem was not Paul's. For him, women as well as men could be called by God to be apostles of Christ – equality was not only in the community but in the apostalate.'[8]

However, even Paul's yes to gender equality in the church's ministry and worship could slip into a maybe. In the Corinthian churches he had no problem with women praying and prophesying in weekly worship, but they had to do so with their heads covered, to show they were 'under authority' (I Corinthians 11: 10). Perhaps Paul like the rest of us struggled to be free from the socio-cultural norms. Christ may have set us free but not completely in relation to wider cultural practices. The early faith communities were caught in the tension between radical Christian freedom and gender equality, and the way life and relationships of power were in the wider Greco-Roman society:

> 'Paul did not urge a social revolution in the relationship of men and women – just as he did not urge the abolition of slavery, even though he maintained that in Christ there 'is neither slave nor free'. Instead he insisted that since 'time is short' (until the coming of the Kingdom), everyone should be content with the roles they have been given, and that no one should seek to change their status – whether slave, free, married, single, male, or female. (I Corinthians 7: 17–24)[9]

If Paul's yes became a maybe in I Corinthians, it was because he lived in the imminent expectation of the coming again of Jesus, a belief in which he and the early Christians were wrong. We are now in the twenty-first century and still counting!

The text of I Corinthians 14 presents a different problem. Here women are commanded to 'keep silent in church' and are reminded that 'it is shameful for a woman to speak in church' (I Corinthians 14: 33–36). The problem is that this particular text contradicts what Paul has said elsewhere in I Corinthians, Romans and Galatians. Either Paul has contradicted himself or he is seriously confused. However, neither may be the case. Paul may be the victim of later tampering with his text!

There is a close similarity between I Corinthians 14: 33–36 and I Timothy 2: 11–12. The overwhelming consensus is that Paul did not write the Pastoral Letters. The language and ethos of these letters belong to a much later time when the church had become more established and there was greater concern with church order, orders of ministry and orthodox systems of belief. All of this is reflected in the Pastorals. If the seven authentic letters of Paul are certain, and Colossians, Ephesians and II Thessalonians are probably not Paul, then the Pastorals, I and II Timothy and Titus are certainly not Paul. The most we can say is that the Pastorals have been written by second-generation followers, Pauline sympathisers or a Pauline school.

There is no doubt that Paul wrote I Corinthians, but there is doubt about I Corinthians 14: 33–36. The verses appear in different places in different Greek manuscripts, suggesting that textual scribes were unsure about where to place them in Paul's text. Since these verses appear to be heavily influenced by I Timothy, a surmise is that these are not Paul's words but are a note in the margins added by a later scribe more sympathetic to the perspective of I Timothy and the exclusion of women from ministry and leadership. The verses do not fit the context of I Corinthians 14; they seem intrusive and contradict what Paul has said elsewhere in the Corinthian letter. Paul may indeed be the victim of textual tampering by a later scribe who was both patriarchal and misogynist. He, and there is no doubt that he was male, disliked women in leadership and ministry roles in the church and believed that they should keep silent and stay at home.

The Timothy text is certainly not a yes, not even a maybe, but a big no to women in any role in the church:

> Let a woman learn in silence with full submission. I permit no woman to teach or to have authority over a man; she is to keep silent. For Adam was formed first, then Eve; and Adam was not deceived, but the woman was deceived and became a transgressor. Yet she will be saved through childbearing, provided they continue in faith and love and holiness, with modesty (I Timothy 2: 11–15).

If we compare these verses with the writings that are certainly Paul's there is a chasm in thought and perspective. On the one hand Paul has a commitment to gender equality, though on the odd occasion he is ambivalent, being pulled towards the socio-cultural norms of the wider patriarchal world. On the other hand the Pastorals reflect faith communities where battle lines are being drawn at the end and beginning of the first and second centuries, and where women are being excluded from ministry and leadership roles. They must be silent and subservient to the men of the community. The Pastorals reflect a problem and the problem is that women have a role in ministry and leadership; there are women leaders but second-generation writers invoke and interpret the Genesis Eden story to authoritatively silence these women and put them under male authority.

The use of the Genesis Eden story is extraordinary in its interpretation and applications:

> we are told that women must not be allowed to teach men because they were created inferior, as indicated by God himself (sic) in the Law; God created Eve second, for the sake of man; and a woman (related to Eve) must not therefore lord it over a man (related to Adam) through her teaching. Furthermore, according to this author, everyone knows what happens when a woman does assume the role of teacher; she is easily duped (by the devil) and leads the men astray. So women are to stay at home and maintain the virtues appropriate to women, bearing children for their husbands and preserving their modesty.[10]

If scripture is supposed to interpret scripture as some believe, then I Timothy goes well beyond the Genesis text, reads into the text what is not there and has taken literary or poetic licence to the extreme.

The Timothy prohibition 'tells us that women were praying and teaching within the community's catechetical practice and liturgical worship. But this text dismisses women from these functions and relegates them to home, silence and childbearing.'[11]

In the twenty-first century, some still insist on the text as divine revelation and authoritative. Most women no longer believe it and many happily ignore it not only through their ordination but through other forms of ministry in church and society. But the Timothy perspective was norm for centuries, a male, patriarchal and at times misogynist norm. More than any other biblical text I Timothy 2: 13–15 has been responsible for gender inequality and injustice within church and society. It has also shaped the dominant reading and interpretation of the Genesis Eve story, which has contributed further to inequality and injustice. Did the writer of the Pastoral letter abandon ethics in his interpretative approach to scripture and do we need to give attention to a more ethical, critical and prophetic reading of the biblical texts? Gender inequality is unethical and to legitimise it by appeal to scripture texts is an unethical use of and approach to scripture. For some centuries, though, the early Irish Celtic tradition had a very different reading of the Eve story, one that took ethics more seriously by refusing to demean Eve.

12.3 Equality: A Celtic Twilight Zone?

Lisa Bitel is right: 'The women of early Ireland are gone. So are their masters and guardians, the men with whom they lived, slept and struggled. No trick of light or lilt of the voice should lead us to think that the people of early medieval Ireland resembled their descendants.'[12]

The world has changed and the past is always a foreign country. The best we may achieve is to peer into a twilight zone, meeting shadows which tell us only a little of gender relations in early Celtic Ireland. The temptation to romanticise is great. The reality may be that different conclusions can be reached. Did an equality agenda exist in Celtic Ireland and did the arrival of Christianity enhance it or destroy it? Some have painted a rosy picture of early Celtic Christian women with the implication that the church improved their lot. Others have argued that the church accelerated the already diminishing equality ethic. Yet others feel that Irish Celtic women fared better than their mainland European sisters. It would be foolish to claim a full-blown equality agenda for early Celtic Ireland, pre-Christian or Christian. Yet in the twilight zone there are some shadows with shape that provide tantalising perspectives, at least on a gender struggle.

The Real Battle of the Boyne!

The 1690s are associated with a series of battles between King William and King James and have been remembered by one cultural-religious group as a glorious victory for Protestants over Catholics. The latter remember another trauma of defeat, repression, massive land loss, a broken Treaty of Limerick and Penal Laws. Less well known from the same decade are forty surviving copies of a book *Párliament na mBan*, believed to have originated in Co. Cork.

The story is that the women of Ireland, or at least from Cork, were fed up with the mess men were making of Irish life. Their response was to take political power themselves, set up their own parliament and enact their own laws. The woman who opened the parliament was very critical of the passive role of women in political and public life. She described it as 'remaining always at home attending to our distaffs and spindles, even though many of us are no good about the house'. Other women complained that the constant fighting and quarrelling of men had brought the country to ruin. They asserted that: 'If women had control of all affairs it is certain that things would be more settled and peaceful than they are.'

Debates and legal acts are also described, parliament deciding: 'that girls should be educated equally with men in the seven liberal arts and should be qualified in divinity, law, medicine and, indeed, that men's conduct should be kept under close scrutiny'.[13]

What was going on in Ireland of the 1690s? Did the parliament really happen and is this an indication of a gender equality tradition in ancient or even early modern Ireland. It is difficult to say. The author was a male priest from Co. Cork, but what was he reflecting? The ethics of *Párliament na mBan* have a basis somewhere in Irish Celtic society and were not just the aspirational invention of Father Ó Colmáin. At any rate the book was circulating in the 1690s and would have been a text subversive of war, violence and patriarchal politics, envisioning an alternative Ireland from that of the Ascendancy. Its ethical vision was of gender equality at the heart of Irish life and a prominent role for women in peacebuilding.

The Ulstermen's Pains

There is a deep gender ambivalence in the ancient myth of Macha. The story belongs to a culture in which 'men … saw themselves as the managers and interpreters of women's most important labour'.[14] They assumed the ideological control of procreation, whether as saints, clergy or jurists.

From the Ulster cycle comes the story of Macha who wanders into the house of an Ulsterman, Crunniuc. She becomes his housekeeper and soon becomes pregnant. The annual fair was where all of Ulster gathered for politicking, feasting and games. When the chariot races were being run Crunniuc boasted of Macha's speed. When King Conchobar heard this he insisted that Macha be brought to the races and compete with the horses even though she was close to giving birth. Macha appealed to the crowd for understanding and compassion, but the all-male gathering was not listening. Macha cursed the Ulstermen while she ran, finished first and gave birth to twins. She screamed that those who heard her would suffer in their times of greatest difficulty, experience the same pains for five days and four nights, and have only the strength of a woman after childbirth. Macha's curse was the basis of the Ulstermen's pains.

Whatever the meaning of the Ulstermen's pains, the male author of the myth told a story of abuse against a woman and 'almost succeeded in seizing control of reproduction'.[15] Ulstermen could not produce babies, but their pains produced something else, perhaps even more valuable: 'warriors reborn with extraordinary prowess'.[16] The myth gave birth to a cycle of Ulster war stories, invoked yet again in the most recent phase of Irish violence and paramilitarism. Men play the game of war, and though the Ulster warriors acquired the symbolic ability to give birth, through Macha's curse, they were soon reborn to play their war games again.

The Macha myth is one of violence against women and the male ideological and cultural-symbolic control of procreation and war. The ethic of the Macha Celtic myth is not kind to women nor to gender equality.

Adamnan's Law: Charter for Equality?

The hagiographer of Columba introduced his Cáin Adamnáin or the Law of Adamnan at the Synod of Birr in 697 CE. It was the centenary year of Columba's death. The context for the Law was the warrior culture of Ireland. On one occasion he invited his mother Rounat to climb on his back so that he could carry her through the mud. Rounat refused, which shocked Adamnan who asked what more she wanted him to do. Rounat acknowledged his virtues as a son and asked that he 'should free women for me' from the fighting, wounding, killing and torture that they often experienced in a warrior society. Eventually a reluctant Adamnan with his mother now on his back set off for a battlefield. What they saw was horrendous. Many women lay dead, slaughtered in the fight but most moving of all was finding the head of a woman in one place and the body elsewhere with a baby sucking the breasts of the dead woman: 'a stream of milk upon one of its cheeks, and a stream of blood upon the other'.

Adamnan was still reluctant to fulfil his mother's wish and after much suffering, described as torture, he set off to negotiate the liberation of women from slavery and war.

Apart from the issue of war, honour-price was involved where the level of fine in relation to a woman was only half that for a male. The low level of fines imposed for crimes against women reflected their low status in early Irish Celtic society. The unit of value was a Cumac, the original meaning of which was a female slave. War, slavery and inferior honour-price were the key concerns when Adamnan began to negotiate his Law. The negotiation was not easy. A society of warrior heroes had to be convinced and so too did those who held political power. He needed the support of the powerful Uí Néill and strategically arranged to be present at the annual gathering of the Uí Néill Kingdoms at Telltown. This was also where Columba in 561 CE had tried to defend himself against his involvement in a battle, and from where he had gone into voluntary exile to Iona. After Telltown Adamnan spent at least eighteen months travelling the country gathering support for his Law, often against powerful vested interests. In 697 CE a special synod was arranged on the plains of Birr.

For Adamnan the Synod of Birr was an outstanding success. In the name of the Trinity, saints and Mary, Columba and Brendan, he asked those present to signal their assent as guarantors of the Law of the Innocents.

The Law began with detailed descriptions of the horrors experienced by women in a warrior society. Women could take part in military battles and command an army. These were, however, images of women forced by a husband's flogging into battle. The prized trophies of war were the heads or breasts of women, and women were often the first to be exchanged as hostages or slaves: 'The story reflects a time when Irish women were greatly oppressed by the warrior elitist society.'[17] In relation to what was the norm elsewhere in Europe, Adamnan's Law was a remarkable piece of legislation. Women, children and clerics could not be killed in battle:

> The same securities and compensation would be required in the future from anyone injuring them. Neither women, clerics nor children would have to go to war, and their social alliance was the only real alternative there was to the all-pervasive warrior ethic.[18]

Not only did the Law protect women from the horrors of war and violence as well as sexual abuse from brutal male warriors, but it also prohibited women from becoming warriors or military commanders.

It has been claimed that 'Adamnan's Law enhances the status of women by emphasising their role as life-givers while simultaneously drawing an analogy between them and Mary the mother of God.'[19] Certainly the Law was the first of its kind in Ireland to deal with the status of women and has been hailed as an achievement which should be celebrated in Geneva, Helsinki and Birr, a kind of Geneva Convention of the Celtic peoples.

However, the freedom and equality of women came at a price. The law has also been read as Adamnan's attempt to impose Roman Christian sensitivities on a larger cultural reality. The rape of women and sexual abuse did undoubtedly take place in battles. Though as Cherici pointed out: 'any man who sexually assaulted a woman warrior would have to contend with her sword as well as the Brehon Law prohibiting rape'.[20] Women warriors and commanders might have argued that they had an inherent gender equality. But in a theology where an asexual Mary and a similar Mary of the Gael (Brigid) were becoming dominant paradigms for women, Adamnan's motives may have been mixed. Was the Law also concerned about the control of women?

More ominous was the literal price women had to pay for their freedom. The Law imposed a quarterly tax on women, which was payable to the monks of Iona. Queens were expected to give horses. Less well-off women were expected to contribute tunics, gold, cakes, pigs, lambs or linen. Failure to meet this tax led to a threat from Adamnan that their children would decay and die full of crimes. Was the Law liberating women from one form of slavery only to make them victims of a religiously imposed slavery?

The underlying assumption of the Law was that women could not determine their own destiny and required the probation of a social institution. Prohibited from engaging in one profession – the warrior class – women were to find other professions closed to them: 'It was the beginning of Christian inspired restrictions for Celtic women which would ultimately ban them from the traditional occupations of healer, scholar and judge.'[21]

Given also that the Law was ignored by numbers of Celts and had to be re-enacted many times, questions have been raised about its effectiveness as an instrument of liberation and equality for women:

> It is indeed uncertain how successful these 'laws' were even in the eighth century as they were enacted quite frequently which would appear to indicate that they did not have any great effect. The churches also gained materially from their peace initiatives since the proclamation of the 'laws' had to be paid for by means of a tribute.[22]

So the women of Ireland could be 'protected' by the church but only by being permanently indebted to Adamnan and his successors. The church would control gender relations and any equality women might have came at a price. The Law of the Innocent may not quite have promulgated an ethic of gender equality after all.

Meet Irish Eve

When Celtic Christian Ireland wrote or thought about women, it was usually as a type of femaleness. A few biblical women were highlighted: Eve, Mary, Herodias who wanted the head of John the Baptist, and the queen of King Solomon. Most revealing was the focus on Eve. It may well be possible to draw a distinction between biblical Eve and Western Eve, or Eve in traditional Western interpretation. Biblical Eve is of course Hebrew Eve and she does not have a particularly high profile in the Jewish tradition. Adam and Eve are not the basis for any developed Jewish theology of sin. Western Eve is the source of all our troubles, blamed for our fallenness, portrayed as sexual temptress and the stereotype of all women.

The constant retelling of the Genesis stories in the Irish Celtic writings included the Adam and Eve story, but for 500 years the Irish interpretation of the story, especially of Eve, offered a totally different reading to the traditional Western one. Eve has become the most celebrated sinner in Christendom! The church has described all women as 'daughters of Eve', not only sharing in Eve's sin of disobedience, but also with the propensity to lure men into sexual wrongdoing. 'Temptress' and 'seductress' are Eve's legacy to all women and it is Eve who is forever blamed for the human fall, even in the Christian Scriptures (I Timothy 2: 13–15). But it was Augustine who formalised this interpretation for the Western church with the forbidden fruit offered by Eve as sexual allurement and temptation. The consequences of this interpretation for women in terms of subjugation, subordination, sexual abuse, violence, control, especially of sexuality and bodies, and oppression in church and society remain all too obvious.

It is a different Eve on the Irish High Crosses and writings. The Fall is described in ungendered terms. Eve is not blamed or scapegoated by history. The serpent is the seducer, not Eve. Irish Eve is very different from Western Eve. How Eve is portrayed in Irish writings reflects a view of women in early Christian Irish society. Having said this: 'Eve was not a major character for the Irish in their exegetical and apocryphal writings, which date as far back as the seventh century.'[23] Much more is made of Mary, and on the few occasions where Eve is the focus she is not held up as the typical woman, nor is she cast as the seducer. Humankind is fallen but Eve has no particular responsibility for that.

The most significant portrayal of Eve is in a late tenth-century poetical reflection on Genesis. The *Saltair na Rann* is a kind of sacred history of the world and is not quite original. Its primary source is an earlier apocryphal writing, *Vita Adae et Evae*. When the *Saltair* wrote of Eve it is on terms of lover-like praise for her.

> Whose name was noble Eve, prudent, bright, fair and modest, dear, shapely, the best of the dividing, the excellent foundation of true children. After that Adam arose out of his sleep without danger, and saw the women of fair complexion, noble, famous, shapely. And he saw her dear face, he chose her above every true prize, he promised her clear wisdom, that she would be the especial love of hosts. 'It is for you, without concealment, that every man will abandon his mother and his father; from today, forever, triumph …, all of us will be completely at your disposal.'[24]

Here we meet Irish Eve, unrecognisable from Western Eve, described in such positive and fulsome terms that she appears more equal than Adam!

The poem continues, and though Eve is scolded for her eating of the forbidden fruit the transgression is shared. Eve is not the sole culprit. Adam eventually suggests that they stand in the River Tigris, Eve for thirty-three days and he for forty-seven, as penance. They went their separate ways to carry out the penitential act. Lucifer appears to Eve in the river in disguise and tells her that God has pity on her. She sets off to convey this good news to Adam who, up to his neck in water, is furious and horrified when Eve approaches with Lucifer. Adam reveals Lucifer's true identity, which leads to an angry Eve protesting against Lucifer's campaign against them. Lucifer's argument was with God, not with them as humans. Eve is not the source of human fallenness.

The *Saltair* is saying a great deal about 'the relationship between women, original sin, and the essence of femininity'.[25] Irish Eve is passed as the fair mother of future generations. She is portrayed as a beautiful woman, and though the Fall of humankind is noted there is no sexual overtone or undertone. Whatever the human sin is, it is not sexual nor is forbidden knowledge portrayed as sexual. Eve is deceived, but she is no seductress or wilful temptress. Irish Eve is no scheming woman using sexual allurement to bring down her husband and all men. Irish Eve is Adam's beautiful and cherished partner. There is no special punishment from God for Irish Eve, no special curse in the pains of childbirth, and no legacy to be paid for by future generations of women.

The *Saltair* offers a much more woman-friendly interpretation of the Genesis story, very different from the traditional Western interpretation, which still prevails. The *Saltair* avoids misogyny and patriarchy. This is all the more remarkable since the author of the *Saltair* was a male who composed this lengthy and loving description of Eve as 'noble ... prudent, bright, fair and modest, dear, shapely, the best of the dividing, the excellent foundation of true children'. This, at least, is his view of women in Irish society. Significant also is his portrayal of Eve as the voice of lament. Eve sheds tears for the way the world is, protests against the reality of evil. Eve's lament is in the same genre as Deirdre's lament expressing heartbreaking sorrow and sharp criticism. Ireland in this early Christian Celtic era did give women the role of lamenter, which was the voice of the innocent sufferers and the voice against injustice. Irish Eve 'resembles the sorrowing women, not a Jezebel'.[26]

The misogynistic reading of Augustine and much of the Western Catholic and Reformed churches is missing from the Irish interpretation. Had this Celtic reading of the Eve story become the norm, the gender conflict may not have been so characteristic of Western church and society. The dehumanisation of Eve in Western theology has also dehumanised men. The celebration of Irish Eve and her goodness offers a way to liberation for women and men in the twenty-first century.

The liberating potential of Irish Eve was not the whole story of early Irish Celtic society. Like the biblical world it too was stamped with ambivalence and often characterised by inequalities. The story of Irish Eve was counter-cultural. It was a sharp critique of the Western obsession with sin and sex, sex and sin, and its legacy of gender inequality and the demonisation of women. The spirit of Irish Eve and women like Canair of Bantry[27] provide the basis of an ethic of gender equality. It has not yet been embedded in Irish church and society. It remains an ethical imperative.

Key Points from Chapter 12

❑ Gender equality is part of Section 75 of the 1998 Government of Northern Ireland Act, which provides the challenge to remove the various inequalities experienced by women in church and society.

❑ Patriarchy (legitimates male rule) has contributed to the widespread abuse and violence against women.

❑ Misogyny (hatred of women) has equated women with the body and men with the mind; the former viewed as inferior, the latter superior.

❑ Androcentrism (male-centredness) affirms males as the norm for humanness and in the hierarchical structure females, considered subordinate, derive their humanness from males.

❑ Each of these three practices is dualistic, and abusive of women, resulting in inequality of power distribution.

❑ Identifying God with maleness is idolatrous and gives divine authorisation to unjust practices and domination systems.

❑ The socio-cultural context of the Bible is patriarchal. The stories of women are told from the male perspective, and many remain unnamed.

❑ Biblical language, story and interpretation overlook, dehumanise and often oppress women.

❑ The Christian testament illustrates women had a place in the early church; however, their role was often disputed.

❑ Women played a significant role as leaders in Pauline communities.

❑ The Pastoral Letters reflect a resurgence of patriarchal control in the late first-century and early second-century Christian churches, resulting in the dismissal of women from leadership positions.

❑ I Timothy justifies this reassertion of male rule with reference to the Genesis Eden story, which is given a misogynist twist.

❑ The patriarchal Irish context was challenged by women not always successfully; evidenced in the stories of the 1690s' *Párliament na mBan* and the myth of Macha.

❑ In Celtic society women were often the innocent victims of war, were captured as slaves and had a low honour-price, all of which provides the context for the Law of Adamnan (697 CE). The law protected women from the brutality of war and prohibited them from becoming actively involved in the fighting.

❑ Adamnan's Law is the first of its kind in Ireland to deal with women's status.

❑ The Law, however, laid a financial burden on women that left them economically vulnerable, paying dearly for their freedom.

❑ Adamnan's Law, while offering protection to women, also gave the church authority to control gender relations, which in effect limited women's roles and freedom.

❑ In contradiction to the traditional Western interpretation of Eve as 'temptress' and 'seductress', responsible for human fall, the Irish Eve is not cast as male seducer nor viewed as responsible for the human condition.

❏ The *Saltair na Rann* is a tenth-century Celtic poetical reflection on Genesis, which presents Eve in positive terms and as Adam's equal. It avoids the misogyny and patriarchy that developed in the Western church and which justifies the subjugation and oppression of women in church and society.

Test Questions

❏ What evidence is there in both the first-century Christian communities and Celtic society to support the view that patriarchy was widespread?

❏ Comment on the perspectives that counter-cultural interpretations of patriarchal texts are necessary to promote gender equality.

13 An Ethic of Environmental Care

Religion has always frightened people with doomsday warnings. The medieval world painted lurid pictures of hell, and there are still some evangelists who literally believe this next-world landscape exists and that people can be frightened out of it. God-channels on television have preachers – complete with elaborate charts – painting bloody pictures of Armageddon, soon to occur in the Middle East, when the warrior Christ will wade knee-deep in blood on his way to victory, bringing only the saved or elect with him. A divine militaristic doomsday scenario indeed, and all predicted in the Bible, or just a few verses from Daniel and the Book of Revelation. The insecure may easily be frightened into faith, other-worldly faith by either of these doomsday 'certainties'. To believe on the basis of either is to abandon ethical responsibility for all life.

A much more serious doomsday scenario with huge ethical implications is environmental destruction. The destruction of the planet and its atmosphere is something of which we humans are more than capable. We have the capacity to destroy the Earth and also the capacity to become partners in its healing. This real-life scenario, dealing with this life and not the next, is loaded with ethical imperatives. Climate change is one of the big twenty-first century challenges to all of us and its challenge is in life before death, not life after death.

13.1 Twenty Years to Turn It Around

At the beginning of 2006 a report on climate change told an audience of scientists and policymakers 'that governments have twenty years in which to act'.[1] In the same month of January, former American President Bill Clinton, in contrast to his successor at the White House, said that 'climate change was the most pressing threat we now face'.[2]

David Attenborough was, for a long time, a sceptic of climate change. Attenborough has changed his mind and has participated in a BBC documentary on climate change and its consequences. The reason given for his change of mind is significant: 'How could I look my grandchildren in the eye and say I knew this and did nothing.'[3] Attenborough, now convinced of the reality of the dangers of climate change, has a sense of ethical responsibility for future generations. There are still those who feel the threat is exaggerated or even false, but most scientists are convinced that the destruction of climate change is a reality and that humans are responsible for it: 'Scientists are adamant that, unless certain emissions are reduced by over 2.6% per annum during the next two decades, irreversible damage will be done to the life-system of the planet.'[4]

Climate change and global warming are the new buzz words and represent one of the most daunting environmental challenges with consequences for all life forms and systems. One obvious example is our consumption of fossil fuels. If this continues at the present rate of demand, there will be planetary consequences such as the melting of the Greenland ice sheet. There has been enough visible footage on television documentaries and news reporting to indicate that the world will become increasingly inhospitable.

Closer to home, in fact the relatively small island we call home, and the even smaller place we call Northern Ireland or the North, will also face the consequences. In March 2007 the *Belfast Telegraph* carried a headline: 'Flooded Ulster: devastating impact of global warming'. It reported that many parts of Northern Ireland (there are not many parts!) are likely to be permanently flooded by rising seas and storms within fifty years as a result of global warming. Fermanagh could be flooded, while Co. Down could lose its finest wetlands owing to temperature rises. The Quoile estuary and Castle Espie could shrink away. The report was published by the Republic of Ireland's Environmental Protection Agency. It was predicted that 116 square miles of Ireland's countryside are likely to be permanently flooded by rising seas within the next five decades. Low-lying cities such as Dublin, Cork, Galway and Limerick would be at particular risk. Belfast, though, may not be as hard hit by rising sea levels because of the barrage built across the River Lagan. The big question is did the designers take sea-level rise into account when the barrage was built? There would be coastal erosion and an increased frequency of forest fires, summer droughts affecting crops and depletion of fish stocks including cod. Pest infestation might be another consequence. All of this would stem from the loss of major ice sheets in Greenland and Antarctica by 2100. This could severely impact the Gulf Steam, which gives Ireland its present temperate climate. Is all of this another dooms-day or apocalyptic scenario or is something catastrophically real happening? Is the real Armageddon environmental and not some act of God but human-induced?

Humanity, especially in twentieth-century wars and violence, has already taken the power of life and death out of God's hands. It would appear that through environmental destruction we are continuing our human sovereignty over the death of all life systems, including ourselves. Those whose future destinies will be affected most are the poor of the Earth. We are still living in a one-third, two-thirds world with the majority suffering from high levels of poverty, disease and hunger. The one-third world, of which we in Ireland are a part, is consuming most of the world's fossil fuels and producing most of the carbon emissions. There is still the need for greater personal and political action from the one-third world. If the problem is human-induced, then the same humans have twenty years to turn things around. Such is the scale of the ecological crisis we now face and its challenge.

13.2 Biblical Ethics and Bio-Responsibility

For too long our worldview has been too human-centred. Underpinned by Greek philosophy we have believed that the human is the measure of all things. All things exist for our human use and all other life forms only have value in relation to our human desires and needs. Such a human-centred philosophy has been destructive of the Earth. When the Genesis creation poetry and myth affirmed that we are of the Earth, of the very soil and dust itself, the Hebrew authors had more insight than they realised. Humans are not above the Earth but part of it and in relationship to the rest of it. We are not, therefore, a superior life form but one life form in an intricate web of life forms in which there is incredible diversity and interdependence. A hierarchical worldview, which was also patriarchal, produced the illusion that we were somehow superior to lesser life forms and had the right to dominate, even abuse and misuse other forms of life in any way we pleased. The Genesis literature may not have said that but it is the interpretation we have imposed on it.

Rereading Genesis

The most obvious anthropocentric reading of Genesis has been around Genesis 1: 26–29. The words 'have dominion' occur twice and 'subdue' the Earth once. It is easy to see how the text lends itself to an anthropocentric reading, but a more subtle, contextual reading is required.

The creation poetry of Genesis 1 emerged from the sixth-century Babylonian exile. The exile experience was traumatic, shattering not only a community's infrastructure but also its ethos, deepest values and beliefs. It was not only a political and social crisis, but also a spiritual and theological crisis: 'How could we sing the Lord's song in a foreign land?' (Psalm 137: 4). Who was the Lord anyway? God the King in control of all things was no more, not in Israel's experience. If God was still to be God, then God had to be re-imagined or revisioned. In exile the people encountered the Babylonian creation myth in which the god Marduk was supreme and in which creation, including the creation of humans, emerged from violence and through violence.

Israel's poets and theologians came up with a creative and radical alternative. The creation poetry of Genesis 1 was produced and became a song the exiles could sing again. The great theo-poet we call Second Isaiah (chapters 40–55 of the book of Isaiah) produced a larger more liberating image of God. The old, pre-exile image of God as monarch or king had been destroyed, but the prophet re-worked it. The core image of God was of a shepherd-king, a more vulnerable, nurturing, caring image of God.

> Here is your God!
> See, the Lord comes with might,
> and his arm rules for him;
> his reward is with him.

He will feed his flock like a shepherd;
he will gather the lambs in his arms,
and carry them in his bosom,
and gently lead the mother sheep. (Isaiah 40: 9–11)

God is not a dominating, all-conquering warrior God, violent and destructive. The God-image is of the shepherd king who feeds, gathers, carries and gently leads, especially the weak and vulnerable.

Genesis creation poetry belongs to this same theo-poetic world. Even though Western mindsets have read 'having dominion' as domination and 'subdue' as conquer, and as a consequence exploited and abused the creation, the reading in exilic context offers a different ethic. The 'royal' language of the creation poetry is reread in the context of Second Isaiah's poetic God-talk and the shepherd-king. The human ethical response to creation is one of caring and nurturing, handling all other life forms gently.

The creation poem and the creation myth which follows (Genesis 2–3) were written by humans for humans, but they do not place humans above creation, nor do they give humans any right to dominate and treat creation as something humans conquer and rule. As an integral part of creation, part of the intricate web of life we have bio-responsibility, an ethic of care, nurture, gentleness and partnership.

Prophet of God's Covenant with Life

It is often overlooked in the biblical text that God's covenant was not merely with humanity, but all of life. In pledging Godself, God was not only concerned with human well-being but also had profound concern for the wider Earth community. The story of Noah in Genesis has significant insights, the most profound being that God makes a covenant with humans, animals and all of life (Genesis 9: 8–16). This insight itself offers an ethical framework within which to live in ethical concern for the whole Earth community. That people have wasted and continue to waste large sums of money and time looking for the site and remains of Noah's Ark in modern Turkey seems to show a lack of real ethical perspective. The story/parable is more profound than that. The real ethics of the story are that violence is destructive and the well-being of the whole Earth community is paramount. God's covenant with all life means bio-responsibility.

The eighth-century prophet Hosea offered a more detailed and concrete analysis of this covenant with all life:

I will make for you a covenant on that day with the wild animals, the birds of the air, and the creeping things of the ground; and I will abolish the bow, the sword, and war from the land; and I will make you lie down in safety. And I will take you for my wife for ever; I will take you for my wife in righteousness, and in justice, in steadfast love, and in mercy (Hosea 2: 18–19).

God's covenant with all of life or the whole Earth community suggests a theo-ethic of nature, a theo-ethic of peace and a theo-ethic of justice. Centuries after Hosea the twentieth-century ecumenical community developed the working ethic of Justice, Peace and the Integrity of Creation (JPIC). For the last two decades it has been the key theme of ecumenical councils and assemblies. Israel's prophet Hosea anticipated JPIC by a long way!

God's covenant means God's affirmation of the whole of life. There is no covenant exclusively with humanity or with humanity alone. To affirm life in such a positive way is to affirm and prioritise peace. The Hebrew word *Shalom* does not mean the absence of hostilities, violence and war, though it includes this. It is the total well-being, personal, political, economic, social, environmental, the common good which is inclusive of the whole Earth community. Such peace is peace with justice and right relations; life lived in its totality in solidarity and compassion towards all of life and the Earth. Justice is socio-economic and eco-justice. Hosea's prophetic ethic is comprehensive and astonishingly contemporary and is Israel's prophetic perspective at its best. At its heart is the image of a God pledged to the well-being of all creation. 'The God who wants to save us for life wants to save us, not only from the death that others are inflicting upon our world, but also from the death whose infrastructures we ourselves support, contribute to, and benefit from.'[5]

Jesus and Global Responsibility

Jesus the Jew was in the Hebrew tradition of creation theology where liberation and creation were held together. The tradition in the face of Babylonian destruction of human and environmental community affirmed the goodness of God's creation, saw God's covenant as being with all life, human, animate and inanimate, and developed the Jubilee tradition where there was space for the healing and restoration of the land as good ecology and economics as well as restoration of human social justice. Jubilee shaped the ministry of Jesus, and although Luke 4: 18–19 provided the basis for his Jubilee-focused ministry in mainly human justice terms 'the year of the Lord's favour' did not exclude the eco-justice dimension.

13.3 Recovering Celtic Eco-Ethics

In early Celtic society there was a high status given to the poet. In law the Irish *ollam* was of equal status with a bishop or petty king. The poet was central to Celtic society in contrast to mainland Europe, where such a person was 'generally suspect and marginal, lying on the periphery of Latin ecclesiastical culture'.[6] The centrality of Irish poets, strong also in Wales and Scotland, is an important source for understanding Celtic Christianity, not only in its Christian expression but also in the pre-Christian spirituality and world which lie behind it. This is true when seeking to recover a Celtic eco-ethics. It may be too easy to romanticise a Celtic theology of nature or a Celtic creation theology. It is not ready made and no Celtic saint or hagiographer wrote such a treatise. Yet from disparate sources, not least from nature poetry, it is possible to build a sufficient framework to more than glimpse a working theo-ethic of nature.

Eco-Poetics

The Book of Conquests or *Lebor Gabala* contains the poetry of Amairgen, the chief poet of the Milesians. The book is a mythical history of Ireland by a succession of tribes from the time of Noah to the mythical Milesians, who are the mythical ancestors of the present inhabitants. Stepping ashore at the mouth of the Boyne, Amairgen chanted his now-famous poem:

> I am wind on sea
> I am ocean wave
> I am roar of sea
> I am bull of seven fights
> I am vulture on cliff
> I am dewdrop
> I am fairest of flowers
> I am boar for boldness
> I am salmon in pool
> I am lake on plain
> I am mountain in a man
> I am a word of still
> I am the point of a weapon
> I am God who fashions fire for a head.[7]

The images used all have numerous associations in early Irish writings. 'I am God ...' goes on to ask a series of questions: 'Who smoothes the ruggedness of the mountain? Who is he who announces the ages of the moon? And who, the place where the sunset falls?'[8]

It is not based on the nature theophany of Job 38, but there are echoes. While Amairgen is not a god but a poet and mythological ancestor, there are theological echoes in the poetry:

> All of this suggests a worldview, either remembered or surviving well into Christian times, in which a human being might declare a sense of universal belonging – both to nature and to the invisible worlds of language ... and divine creativity ... It also presents a world in which the Sacred takes many forms, pervading the natural world and acting upon it.[9]

Nature poetry also emerges in the *Táin*. In pursuit of the great brown bull Queen Méabh of Connacht finds her way blocked by the three rivers of Ulster. The rivers rose up against them, the 'River Cronn rose up against them to the height of the treetops ...'[10] Later at a ford in the Cronn, Cúchulainn came to meet them single-handedly in battle. He prepares to meet them invoking the elements and saying a special prayer in the river itself:

> I summon the waters to help me. I summon air and earth; but I summon now
> above all the Cronn river:
> Let Cronn itself fall-to in the fight
> to save Murtheimne from the enemy
> until the warriors work is done
> on the mountain-top of Ochaine.[11]

Here Cúchulainn prays to the river, perceived to be a personal divine power who can help to save and protect. Nature is a source of spiritual power, a theme which also emerges in the poetry of Patrick's Breastplate, again in the context of protection against all forms of evil:

> I arise today
> Through the strength of heaven:
> Light of sun
> Radiance of moon
> Splendour of fire
> Speed of lightning
> Swiftness of wind
> Depth of sea
> Stability of earth
> Firmness of rock.

The words are not from Patrick himself but the later eighth century, yet has a Christian poet lapsed into pre-Christian thought, what some might pejoratively call 'paganism'? But Israel's poetry invokes nature and 'all the trees of the field shall clap their hands' (Isaiah 55: 12). The elements are often invoked and are part of everyday experience. People live with nature in relationship, aware of the goodness of nature and of the raw, sometimes destructive power of nature. This is not just personal experience from BCE but also of the twenty-first century CE. Tornadoes, earthquakes and tsunami are life experiences. Nature is not above humans but part of what it means to be human beings. Pre-Christian and Christian Celtic nature poetry clearly saw nature as a relational power, and therefore as a source or instrument of spiritual power: 'the sacramentality of the universe is one of the chief characteristics of primal religions throughout the world, together with the belief that the physical can be a vehicle for the spiritual and that there is no sharp distinction between the two.'[12]

It is the dualistic worldview that abolishes the sacramentality of the universe, creates the sharp distinction between physical and spiritual and diminishes ethical responsibility. Celtic nature poetry did not make that mistake.

Eriugena on Nature

John Eriugena was one of the great spiritual and intellectual giants of the ninth century. He was born in Ireland *c*.820 CE. Nothing is known of his family life, except that he probably left Ireland *c*.846 CE. He travelled to mainland Europe and settled in the Court of Charles the Bald, Emperor of the West, who lived close to where Paris now stands. Eriugena was a cosmologist, philosopher, scientist and theologian, and much more. John Scotus, as he was sometimes known, was the greatest Celtic scholar, and certainly the greatest Celtic theologian. 'Rediscovered today, John Eriugena's ideas seem refreshingly and surprisingly relevant. He presents a creation-based cosmology with a holistic view of nature and humanity's place in it.'[13]

For Eriugena, Christ walked among us in two shoes. One was scripture and the other creation, and if we want to know Christ we need to be attentive to Christ in the scriptures and in creation. Eriugena was much influenced by the mysticism of John's gospel. The writer of the gospel had listened attentively to the voice of God, the Word through whom all things are made and from whom all comes. God is the essence of life and is in all things. In his homily on the prologue to the Gospel Eriugena opposes the Manichaean heresy: 'that the world of the physical senses was created by the Devil and not by the Creator of all that is visible and invisible … he who contains all things exists in the world.'[14] God is present in physical senses and the material world, and there is not a spirit/matter dualism. When reflecting on the 'light' theme of the prologue, Eriugena experiences the eternal light in two sources:

> Now the eternal light manifests itself to the world in two ways, through the Bible and creatures. For the divine knowledge cannot be restored in us except by the letters of scripture and the sight of creatures. Learn the words of scripture and understand their meaning in your soul; there you will discover the Word. Know the forms and beauty of sensible things by your physical senses, and see there the Word of God. And in all these things Truth itself proclaims to you only he who made all things, and apart from whom there is nothing for you to contemplate since he is himself all things.[15]

The world for Eriugena was a theophany, a visible disclosure of God. We know the Creator by contemplating the creation. God within all things and all things in God is the source of the material and the physical. The spiritual is at the heart of the material, and the deeper we look into matter the closer we come to God. There is a nature-mysticism in the reflections of Eriugena.

His greatest work was known as the *Periphyseon*, a Greek word meaning 'about nature'. In this complex work he divides nature into four parts or into that which creates and which does not create. God, he affirms, is the alpha or origin of everything. God is also the ultimate objective, the omega or end of the creative process. God is perceived by Eriugena as cosmic origin and cosmic destiny of all creation. The middle two divisions of nature are rooted in philosophical discourse in which he affirms that the 'divine creativity stamps itself on the material world'.[16] These marks of the divine are real virtues such as 'goodness, life, truth, peace, health and innumerable other things in a similar vein'.[17] Here we encounter the ethical values of Eriugena's nature theology and nature-mysticism. His other 'division' of nature is the material world itself 'forward of the four elements of earth, air, fire and water'.[18] Centuries ahead of Copernicus, Eriugena located the sun at the centre of the universe. By 700 years he anticipated the decentring of Earth and at the same time produced a vision of cosmic harmony and symmetry, all of which was a divine theophany.

Eriugena was accused of pantheism, God is all and all is God. That is a misunderstanding of the subtlety and depth of Eriugena's thinking. His position is better described as panentheism, God is in all things and all things are in God. For Eriugena 'God is thus simultaneously present in all things and infinitely beyond all things …'[19]

His theo-ethics are consistent with his God vision in the material world. There is no division between natural and supernatural. The Devil has no physical reality; evil is the absence of good and sin has its source not in an external reality but in the will of the human. Creation or nature is essentially good, and God's goodness is the essence of the entire universe. Take goodness out of creation and it would cease to be. When of our own will we destroy the Earth, we destroy goodness and Godself. Sin against the environment is sin against God. To live out of goodness in relation to an essentially good creation is not only to know God, but also to generate life in a creative way.

Eriugena may have had his work on nature condemned by the Pope in 1225 CE and in 1685 had it placed on the Index, the papal list of forbidden writings, but his nature spirituality has lived on and his contribution to Christian thought has been a significant and creative contribution from the Celtic stream, which refuses to go away.

God of the Elements

Many early Irish texts speak of the elements of God or God of the elements. The elements are all nature combinations – sun, moon, sea, stars, earth, wind and fire. They all act together, and like many of the Hebrew Psalms Celtic poetry gives these powers of nature a prominent place and a vision of God at their heart. Celtic Christians had a deep respect for the elements of nature and experienced them as wild and unpredictable. They were invoked in poetry, as in Patrick's Breastplate, not a mere metaphor but as real, sometimes frightening forces of nature with which life had to be lived in respectful relationship. There was creative energy at the heart of nature. Life was dependent on these elements and it was essential to harmonise with the rhythm of the four seasons. At the heart of the rhythm was *neart*, the creative energy that filled everything, integrated everything, constantly changed everything. All of life and nature were dynamic. These after all were the elements of God and life was to be lived in relationship with the God of the elements and the elements themselves.

The Christian editor has no difficulty telling of the mythical Amairgen, chief poet of the Milesians, chanting a poem to ward off a strong wind which is preventing the people landing on Ireland. Pre-Christian and Christian prayer and ritual were important in relating to the elements and living with them rather than against them.

Adamnan's Law was passed by the Synod of Birr in 697 CE. We have already noted that a law to protect women from war, violence and rape was not as liberating as might first be thought, because it imposed a tax on women. But the Law nevertheless struggles for justice. The tax may not have been just, but guarantors are listed in the text as those responsible for upholding the law and ensuring justice. Adamnan's contemporaries are listed first followed by a spiritual guarantor list. 'These are the securities: sun and moon and all the other elements of God; Peter, Andrew and the other apostles; Gregory, the two Patricks, the two Cíaráns, the four Fintans …'[20]

Twenty-five names follow, providing an interesting spiritual guarantor list in which the elements are invoked along with apostles and saints. The early Celtic Christians may well have thought of the elements as personal spiritual powers. Again the Breastplate invokes sun, moon, fire, sea, wind and earth, but by the Christian era the elements have become the 'elements of God'. Pre-Christian and Christian approaches to nature merge and provide an ethic of environmental relationship and responsible care.

Christ-Mysticism and Nature

The early Irish awareness of nature made another connection from the heart of its Christian faith. It developed a Christ mysticism in relation to nature. This too was found in the Hebridean tradition. The Christ who surrounded them was also the Christ in

1.2 Crucified Christ on the Cross of the Scriptures at Clonmacnoise. The figures at the end of the extended arms may be earth and ocean.

nature, a suffering and risen presence at the heart of all things. Two sources develop this deep insight.

Blathmac was an eighth century monk-poet who wrote a long poem about the crucifixion of Jesus. Using the cultural practice of his time he has all the elements of nature keening their dead hero. Those who first listened to his poem would have recognised the custom and emotionally appreciated its power. The poetry is in the tradition of lament, both a cultural expression and familiar to faith from the Jewish Psalms, most of which are laments. The poem is not only about the crucifixion, but also the rehearsal of God's salvation story. In the crucifixion part, Blathmac picked up the reference to the elements already in the gospel story. Matthew and Luke referred to darkness and earthquake, not in a literalistic way. The gospel writers were more profound than that, and they articulated poetic or mythical expressions of the faith story. Blathmac picked up the cry of abandonment from the cross, the big 'Why' question expressing the deep, impenetrable sense of God-forsakenness by Jesus. At that point in the poem all of nature is thrown into turmoil and the elements keen their dead hero. The cry of lament by Jesus becomes the painful cry and lament of the elements:

> The sun had its own light; it mourned its Lord; a sudden darkness went over the blue heavens, the world and furious sea roared.
>
> The whole world was dark; the land lay under gloomy troubling; at the death of noble Jesus great rocks burst asunder.
>
> Jerusalem swiftly released the dead from ancient burial; when Christ suffered slaying the veil of the temple was rent.
>
> A stream of blood gushed forth – severe excess – so that the bark of every tree was red; there was blood on the breasts of the world, in the tree-tops of every great forest.
>
> It would have been fitting for God's elements, the beautiful sea, the blue heaven, the present earth, that they should change their aspect when keening their hero.
>
> The body of Christ pierced by points warranted severe lamentation – it would be fitting – that they should keen in a stronger manner the man by whom they were created.[21]

It is a profound poem connecting the death of Jesus with the turmoil and suffering and solidarity of nature. Blathmac may well be drawing on pre-Christian beliefs in the elements as personal powers. He was, however, in no doubt that the cross is an act of violence and brutality and nature is involved in 'severe lamentation', darkness, turmoil and in 'keening their hero'. The crucifixion and nature-mysticism have been connected. Nature shares in the suffering of its hero.

The brutality and violence of the crucifixion is experienced by nature in the twenty-first century. Suffering creation has become an issue of our time, in the form of environmental destruction, extinction of species and global warming. There are sins of destruction and violence against the elements and there are close connections between poverty, violence, war and environmental destruction. Blathmac's Christ nature-mysticism becomes a basis for ethical reflection and action. An ethic of environmental care enters into the experience of nature's abandonment and suffering, laments the violence and destruction of environmental and ecological systems and is committed to healing, restoring and renewing the harmony of creation. In Blathmac's Christ-mysticism and nature, the body of Christ is still being abandoned and destroyed in the ecological crisis. The body broken in the Eucharist or Holy Communion is of the very elements themselves. The central Christian act is an environmental lament, a sacrament of the planet and a hopeful pointer to healing and new creation.

The Christ and nature-mysticism theme is taken to another level by another early Irish writing, the *Evernew Tongue*. This creative piece was probably written in Ireland during the tenth century. It is written in the form of a dialogue between the Apostle Philip and Hebrew sages gathered on Mount Zion. A dazzling light appears in the sky and the sages hear a voice speaking a language all can understand including the birds and animals. It is the voice of Philip, the Evernew Tongue who is to explain creation to them. The dialogue takes place on Easter Eve, and Philip is able to go on explaining creation even though his tongue has been cut out seven or more times, hence the Evernew Tongue. This is a creation dialogue in the context of the Easter story of resurrection. If Blathmac connects the elements and the crucifixion, the Evernew Tongue connects the elements with the resurrection of Jesus. The vision is of a cosmic Christ whose 'resurrection body' brings all the elements to newness and wholeness.

Philip's story began with creation in a resurrection context:

> For that tale (the Genesis story) tells of the making of heaven and earth ... and of the formation of the world, which has been brought about by Christ's resurrection from the dead on this eve of Easter. For every material and every element and every nature which is seen in the world were all combined in the body in which Christ arose, that is in the body of every human person.[22]

Philip went on to speak of wind and air, heat and burning fire, the sun and the stars, stones and clay, the flowers and the beautiful colours of the earth: 'All the world rose with him, for the essence of all the elements was in the body that Jesus assumed.'[23]

The Evernew Tongue is not speaking the language of science but poetic theology. This is not about anatomy but poetry seeking to express theological and ethical insights:

> it is ecologically exact in its insights that human beings are not a separate creation but very much part of nature. In the Bible, the first human is made from the dust of the earth, brought to live by the breath or Spirit of God. This tradition was certainly known in Ireland...[24]

The Hebrew creation poem and story are not science either but are a theo-ethical insight into the inseparable relationship between the human and earth. All share the elements of nature. The human body is 100% of nature.

Low referred to the sense of delight in the *Evernew Tongue* text: 'a delight at explaining things, and a delight at the ingenuity of God and the intricacy of creation. The elements are intimately present here as part of our human frame, the raw materials of our physical and emotional make-up.'[25]

Again, God is in all things and all things are in God. The ultimate mystery is present in all nature, including humans. All are the body of God, intricately and intimately related and interdependent.

The Easter story is not a spiritualised event apart from the material elements, the essence of nature. The language is not literal or scientific but that which can only be expressed poetically and the profound poetry of resurrection is that all the elements of nature were taken up into the newness of all things, the new creation. All the raw materials of nature are healed and restored. Christ becomes the cosmic sign and hope of a 'new heaven and a new earth', or in Paul's words 'a new creation'. For the Evernew Tongue, the whole creation, human bodies, the elements, all creatures and life forms, are gathered up into glorious and cosmic newness, the fullness of life in God. The elements are not incidental, of lesser or secondary importance, there only for human use, exploitation, abuse, waste or destruction, of no ultimate value in God's vision of things: 'They are the building blocks of the creation, indispensable and bound for glory in a way which western theology has never really come to terms with.'[26]

Western theology has been too anthropocentric, and Catholic and Reformed traditions have too often disconnected creation from redemption. The death and resurrection of Jesus have been narrowed to human-centred outcomes projected on to the next world. The early Irish Celtic tradition had another, larger perspective, a poetic theology of the elements, an Irish eco-theology which was an eco-ethic. Of course they lived in another time. We live in the same world with a very different set of ecological challenges. Yet from the Celtic theo-poetics there are insights which become the basis for eco-ethics, a living, caring partnership with all creation.

Key Points from Chapter 13

❑ Climate change is one of the big twenty-first-century challenges to all of us.

❑ We are discovering the dire consequences of global warming and the responsibility on all of us, but especially the one-third world, to reduce carbon emissions and put a stop to environmental destruction.

❑ Our human-centred thinking and focus have been destructive of the Earth, leading to a false sense of superiority to all life forms that loses sight of the interdependence and diversity of all life forms.

❑ A rereading of Genesis 1 in the post-exilic context sheds new light on its poetic imagery. The Western mindset has interpreted 'having dominion' and 'subdue' the Earth as conquering it, which has resulted in the abuse of creation. The shepherd-king imagery in second Isaiah reveals a God who cares for and nurtures all life forms, and it is this perspective which informs Genesis 1. Humans therefore are called to practise an ethic of care and partnership with creation.

❑ God's concern, as underlined in the covenant with Noah, is with all of creation (Genesis 9: 8–16); the whole Earth community is paramount.

❑ Hosea reinforced that God's covenant is an affirmation of the whole of life and a call to practise an ethic of peace and justice, and integrity with creation.

❑ Jesus was in the Hebrew Jubilee tradition that recognises the need for healing and restoration of land and human social justice.

❑ Pre-Christian and Christian Celtic nature poetry saw nature as a relational power and therefore as a source or instrument of spiritual power.

❑ John Eriugena (820 CE), the greatest Celtic theologian, emphasised the presence of Christ in the scriptures and in creation. The world was a visible disclosure of God.

❑ Eriugena's greatest work *Periphyseon* (about nature) affirms God as the beginning and end of all created things. God's marks are visible in creation – goodness, life, truth, peace, health etc. – and give the natural world its ethical values.

❑ For Eriugena God is in all things and all things are in God (panentheism); God is present in creation and infinitely beyond all created things.

❑ Eriugena rejected dualism; there is no division between the natural and supernatural. Creation is essentially good, take God's goodness out of creation and it would cease to be. Evil is the absence of good, and when human beings destroy creation, they destroy goodness and Godself. To sin against the environment is to sin against God.

❑ Celtic Christians believed God's creative energy (*neart*) was at the heart of nature. All of life was to be lived in harmony and relationship with God of the elements and the elements themselves.

❑ Blathmac, an eighth-century monk-poet, in his poem about the crucifixion of Jesus connected the death of Jesus with the turmoil, suffering and solidarity of nature. Nature laments the violence and brutality of the cross, sharing in the suffering of Christ. The Eucharist is a sacrament of healing and new creation.

❑ An ethic of environmental care laments the violence and destruction of ecological systems and is committed to healing, restoring and renewing the harmony of creation.

❑ The *Evernew Tongue*, a tenth-century creation dialogue, connected the laments with the resurrection of Jesus. The vision is of a cosmic Christ whose 'resurrection body' brings all the elements to newness and wholeness.

❑ Celtic tradition connects creation and redemption; this formed the basis for an Irish eco-theology which was at the same time an eco-ethic. Western theology needs to recover this vision if it is to recover a caring partnership with all creation.

Test Questions

- ❑ What biblical resources challenge an anthropocentric view of creation? Justify your answer.
- ❑ Critically evaluate the view that to meet twenty-first-century ecological challenges we need to recover an Irish eco-theology that connects creation and redemption.

14   An Ethic of Justice

Closely connected to the ecological problem is poverty. It is one of the worst forms of violence because it literally kills. Poverty is not a new problem; it has always been present, but the gap between rich and poor in the world is becoming wider. The great worry is that we are at a point in history when the wealth of the Earth is not enough to meet the basic needs of the planet's population. The problem is not one of scarcity but of just distribution. Every three seconds, in some part of the planet, a child dies from hunger and malnutrition. This means that 30,000 children will die today, which is more than any sports stadium capacity in Ireland with the exception of Croke Park. Half of the world's population lives on two euro a day. People living in poverty cannot meet their basic needs. They are hungry, malnourished, drink contaminated water, have no access to basic health care, are therefore vulnerable to diseases, live in overcrowded spaces in inadequate housing or none at all, are poorly clothed and often illiterate.

The gap is one between north and south, and it is a matter of injustice, expressed through lifestyles, foreign policies and economic structures: 'Until the misery of degradation of billions of brothers and sisters is alleviated there will be no justice and there will be no peace.'[1] To live justly, personally and structurally in the world is one of the key challenges of our time.

Understanding Justice

Any attempt to fully understand justice has a built-in difficulty. Our life situation will shape our definition of justice. Living in the world of the 'haves', our place, privilege and entitlement do not make us neutral in applying principles of just distribution. Our vision of justice is shaped by a particular social location and social context. A Cuban-American professor of ethics highlights the difficulty in his book *Doing Christian Ethics from the Margins*. The margins provide a very different social location and context:

> The reality from the margins of society is that those with power impose their constructs of morality upon the rest of the culture …. Virtues, no matter how desirable, can be imposed to ensure the subservience of the marginalised …. Ethics from the margins insists that racism, sexism and classism are the end products of the exercise of power.[2]

The poor are the powerless, dominated by the powerful who hold the wealth. Ethics from the centre and ethics from the margins will be very different, as will the respective visions of justice:

> The system of ethics constructed from the margins is an ethics that proclaims a God who exists in the midst of the people's suffering and that seeks to be faithful to the praxis of the gospel message in spite of existing social structures that thwart the faith community's struggle for justice.[3]

The Ireland of the Celtic Tiger, at least those who gained from it, and the now more peaceful North, hoping it seems to have the Tiger cross the border, will not construct an ethics from the margins. North and South has its marginalised and a shared Celtic Tiger will increase their numbers and marginalisation, but will they be allowed to shape an ethic of justice? How much space will the marginalised of Ireland and the world have to be moral agents? Unless those of us whose social context is more privileged and powerful find a way to be in solidarity with the marginalised poor, our vision of justice will be skewed and our moral perspective clouded.

Attributive Justice

This form of justice is the justice of entitlement. It is a hierarchical model of justice. Each receives what they are or claim to be according to social status. Justice in this form belongs to the status quo.

Retributive Justice

This form of justice is the 'pound of flesh', 'an eye for an eye'. It is about retribution and punishment, repaying a wrong with another wrong. The repayment can often exceed the original act. It is penal, punitive justice and may even be motivated by retaliation and revenge.

Distributive Justice

This form of justice gives to each in equal proportion. It is the justice of share and share alike. There is a certain amount of equality in distributive justice but the 'equality' is determined by the needs and social location.

Redemptive Justice

The attempt is made here to bring the person to equal well-being and to the place where potential fulfilment can be realised. It is the justice of reparative equal rights, repairing what is broken or injured. It will seek the liberation of the oppressed, pay attention to the victim but rarely the offender or oppressor.

Restorative Justice

Justice in this perspective will address both oppressor and oppressed in the context of transformative change. Restorative justice recognises injustice at many interrelated levels, the oppressed, oppressor, the community, economic system, legal system and whatever other systems are involved. Restorative justice 'has a communal goal, a vision of harmony and health in relationships, a concern for equal opportunity and mutual privilege'.[4]

Critical reflection on all of the above is required, not least by those from a privileged social location. Those on the margins experiencing the poverty of the world may well see the above as an academic exercise avoiding praxis. Again the ethics and vision of justice that resonates with the oppressed, disenfranchised and the marginalised will be different. Those from the margins of the world, society, race, class and gender will insist on concrete ethical praxis, a justice that transforms and liberates. Those of us whose ethic of justice is formed and shaped from where we stand in the present structures of power need to learn a radical self-criticism. We need the uncomfortable reminders that poverty is violence against human dignity, is a seedbed for terrorism, is a major consequence of war and imperial expansionism and that global poverty is one of the major challenges to our twenty-first-century world. From a faith perspective there is an unavoidable challenge which has to do with the peace of the planet and the very nature of God:

> Ethics for the Christian must become the means to dismantle structures that privilege one group at the expense of another. Christian ethics also is the path by which God is known, by which justice is created, by which liberation for the oppressed is chosen ... For a system of ethics to be Christian, it must be forged contextually within the margins of society, specifically within the faith community.[5]

Let Justice Roll Down

The Jewish-Christian scriptures have much to say about justice. Four different words are used for justice – two in Hebrew and two in Greek – and they are used around 1,060 times in the biblical text. The impression is often given that the Bible has a lot to say about sex, that it even has an obsession with sex. Perhaps the church in its desperate attempts to control sexuality created this impression, but it is a distortion. The words for sexual sin are found only about ninety times, while words for justice are found more than one thousand times. The Bible has an obsession or, more correctly, a passion for justice.

The two Hebrew words are the basis for what is found in the Christian testament, but English translations have found it difficult to convey the depth of meaning in the original Hebrew.

Tsedaqah is often translated as righteousness, which struggles with a narrow morality perspective and against the negative self-righteousness. The word means liberating community, restoring justice, right relations in which things are put right. *Mishpat* often appears as judgement, but again not as a narrow judgementalism or punitive judgement. The word is related to rights and is judgement in a very active sense which vindicates the right of the poor and powerless. Their right to justice is upheld in a world of injustice. When Paul wrote in Romans and Galatians of justification he was far removed from the juridical interpretation that later Christian centuries imposed on him. Paul wrote out of his Jewish roots, and justification – or the Greek *dikaiosyne* – is closely related to the Hebrew sense of vindication of the rights of the poor and oppressed. Later interpreters have spiritualised Paul instead of recognising God's concrete act of social justice for those without justice. Paul has suffered from those who interpreted scripture from within structures of power, social privilege and status.

14.1 Clonmacnoise Cross of the Scriptures with its biblical themes.

Hebrew Roots

The event that shaped Israel's vision of justice was the Exodus from Egypt. The historical nature of the Exodus is probably beyond us, but something of significance happened to an oppressed people. They experienced liberation from an oppressive, domination system which memory identified as empire. The biblical text does not offer an eye-witness, camcorder record, but a profound theological reflection on just liberation, shaped and reshaped by some centuries of reflection always in situations and experiences of oppression, domination and empire, right up to the Book of Revelation, which is also a reflection on the exodus theme.

The story is told in socio-political terms in the context of theological reflection. What we have is a theo-political model of life in liberated community. The Exodus models an egalitarian society, or at least the vision of an egalitarian society. Israel probably never achieved in reality this high vision of justice, but at least did at times organise society in a less stratified way than neighbouring peoples. There is no doubt that Israel was patriarchal with women in a subordinate role. Slavery also existed in pre-monarchical Israel. But Exodus was a socio-political vision of God's purpose:

> The divine revelation holds the potential of liberation from any oppression that undermines human dignity and from any force that prevents human beings from reaching their full development in an environment of freedom, justice and peace.[6]

Exodus is a model of justice and freedom which enabled the critical tradition in Israel to critique any situation of injustice and which helped people to affirm their human dignity and moral responsibility in the face of domination systems and imperial power. Social, economic or political oppression is an injustice, and God is with the oppressed and marginalised as the God of justice who acts to vindicate and liberate. For biblical writers through to the Book of Revelation, Exodus is not a unique, unrepeatable event, but a permanent task, a perennial task. God's liberating acts of justice and the building of a just society and world is an Exodus that never ends.

Prophetic Tradition

Justice was central to the eighth-century Hebrew prophets. Amos was located in the Northern Kingdom, and his writings reflect a sharp contrast between the dominant, well-off urbanites and the many poor who lived in the hills and small towns. Amos did not address his words to the poor but to the people of privilege, power and wealth, kings, priests, rich landowners, prosperous traders and business people, including rich, indulgent spouses. These were also people given to faithful and colourful religious observance and ritual. But it was worship disconnected from ethics; elaborate liturgy divorced from justice:

> I hate, I despise your festivals,
> and I take no delight in your solemn assemblies.
> Even though you offer me your burnt-offerings
> and grain offerings,
> I will not accept them;
> and the offerings of well-being of your fatted animals
> I will not look upon them.
> Take away from me the noise of your songs;
> I will not listen to the melody of your harps.
> But let justice roll down like waters,
> and righteousness like an every-flowing stream. (Amos 5: 21–24)

Both Hebrew words for justice are in the text. Liberating justice is what God wants, and for Amos the lack of justice and equality in the Northern Kingdom was a serious matter since it was contrary to all that God is and wants, namely a society of justice and equality.

Hosea was no less committed to a vision of liberating and inclusive justice. During the last decades of the eighth century Hosea critiqued the violation of covenant with its social and political vision. Worship also came in for scathing criticism: 'I desire steadfast love and not sacrifice, the knowledge of God rather than burnt offerings' (Hosea 6: 6). Two important Hebrew words are used in the text. *Hesed* or steadfast love is the covenantal solidarity with neighbour, especially the suffering neighbour. *Da At* is the active commitment to God's will and purpose for community. Knowledge of God is never intellectual, scholastic or confessional, but concrete praxis in the world of socio-political realities. The absence of solidarity and committed praxis makes religious worship unacceptable to God.

Hosea called for a return to God (6: 1–2). This was no spiritualised return. Like Amos, Hosea stated that a true conversion includes the practice of equity (*sedaqa*) and steadfast love (*hesed*) in social relations (10: 12, 12: 6). Such practices make it possible to have order (*sedaq*) in the community.[7]

Isaiah of Jerusalem was another eighth-century voice for social justice. He spoke from within the royal court, the place of privilege and social power. Yet from this social location he critiqued the oppressive misuse of power endemic in the court system and destructive of social relations. Authentic worship has a moral dimension. The vision of God's holiness in the Temple is also a vision of social justice (Isaiah 5). Those addressed are to:

> Cease to do evil, learn to do good;
> seek justice, rescue the oppressed,
> defend the orphan, plead for the widow. (Isaiah 1: 16–17)

If the monarchy was true to Israel's social tradition embodied in the covenant, then:

> With righteousness he shall judge the poor,
> and decide with equity for the meek of the earth; ….
> Righteousness shall be the belt around his waist,
> and faithfulness the belt around his loins. (Isaiah 11: 4a–5)

Not surprisingly after that follows a vision of peace inclusive of all creation where nothing shall hurt or destroy.

Meanwhile in the Southern Kingdom of Judah, Micah was also concerned with social justice. Not just royalty, but priests and powerful land and property developers at the expense of the weak, hear Micah's thundering critique. The professional prophets or theologians of Judah are also responsible for the injustices of society, producing theology and God-talk unrelated to social, economic and political injustices. Their comfort-zone theology and status-quo or establishment religious utterances only served to perpetrate the injustices. In what is undoubtedly the ethical high water-mark of the Hebrew scriptures, Micah's God has a controversy with the people. What are they to bring to God in worship divorced from social realities?

> He has told you, O mortal what is good;
> and what does the Lord require of you
> but to do justice, and to love kindness,
> and to walk humbly with your God? (Micah 6: 7)

Micah ends with a God-vision. God is all-compassion and the God of faithfulness and unswerving loyalty (Micah 7: 19–20). That is how God's people are to be in their relations with the weak, oppressed and marginalised.

Jesus in the Prophetic Tradition

Jesus was a prophet in the tradition of Amos, Hosea, Isaiah of Jerusalem and Micah. What Jesus had to say in the context of his own time and place was rooted in the prophetic tradition. The people recognised him as a prophet and had the great prophets of their history in mind when they made that identification.

The prophetic tradition is involved in his repeated attacks on the Jerusalem Temple, including the prophetic action in the Temple itself, which was a strong protest against injustice and its cover-up by the very religious institution and its leaders. Like Jeremiah, who is quoted in the Temple story, Jesus was a Jew disturbed by the social injustices of his own religion.

Core to his teaching was the reign of God. The reign or kingdom of God was centred on justice. What Jesus is recorded as saying about the reign cannot be understood without a grasp of the Hebrew prophet quoted most often in the gospels. These quotes or references are from the book of Isaiah. Seventeen passages are used which mention the reign of God, God's activity in liberating people. They all speak of deliverance, salvation or liberation. Sixteen of the seventeen are about righteousness and justice.[8] In the book of Isaiah and for Jesus 'justice was a key characteristic of God's Kingdom'.[9]

It becomes important to identify what these passages mean by justice and therefore what justice meant for Jesus when proclaiming God's reign:

> If we look carefully, we discover that justice has four dimensions: (1) deliverance of the poor and powerless from the injustice that they regularly experience; (2) lifting the foot of the domineering power off the neck of the dominated and oppressed; (3) stopping the violence and establishing peace; (4) restoring the outcasts, the excluded, the Gentiles, the exiles and the refugees to community.[10]

Further examination of the gospels show that this was exactly the life-work in which Jesus was involved, pointing always to God's saving, liberating activity. When Jesus confronted the Temple authorities he was challenging public authorities which with Roman imperial help and support were exploiting and oppressing people. Jesus attacked the public, socio-economic and political system of his time: 'We count forty times in the Synoptic Gospels, not including the parallel passages when Jesus confronted the powers and authorities of his day.'[11] He opposed the injustice of violence, not just the Roman imperial violence, but also the violence of the guerrilla movements emerging then in opposition to Roman domination and economic exploitation. Agreeing with Isaiah he taught that violence and war are unjust and that God is passionate about justice and peace: 'Because of Jesus' teachings and practices, the Christian movement became a Jewish peace movement...'[12] It was for this reason that the Jesus movement, which was Jewish, did not participate in the Jewish-Roman war of 66–70 CE, something which led to an intra-Jewish split.

The dinner-party stories of Jesus in the gospels and the touching and healing of outcasts are all stories of inclusion against the exclusion of otherwise good and well-meaning religious practices. When religious purity separates people into us and them, pure and outcasts, it creates outsiders to God and community and becomes an injustice. It was a form of social ostracism, dehumanising people and destroying authentic community. The justice of the reign of God was about inclusion and the restoration of humanity and community.

The centrality of justice to God's activity in the world and the basis for ethical praxis were rooted in the Hebrew prophetic tradition. Ethical praxis was from the margins which is essentially what Israel's prophetic tradition was about. The powerful, wealthy and the domination systems were the causes of injustice and the need for an ethic of justice to be at the heart of community.

The Celtic Struggle for Justice

The early Celtic era in Ireland should not be romanticised or idealised. There were abuses of royal and monastic power and relations were not always just, especially in a stratified society. Women saints struggled against misogyny and for equality. The frequent stories of saints caring for the poor suggest that the poor were many and that some of the population were rich. Economic parity was not, therefore, a characteristic of early Irish society. The widespread reality of slavery, St Patrick's own experience and the necessity for a strong letter to Coroticus through his soldiers also suggest an exploitative and brutal practice and a high level of injustice. Justice needed to be pursued with vigour and was a permanent task for monks and saints. In Celtic society the social reality fell far short of the ideal. Yet within much monastic practice there was justice and charity, kindness and hospitality:

> Social involvement of an active and even determinative character was a constant feature of Celtic religious life. Like their spiritual forebears in Egypt and Syria the monks, even the hermits, did not as a rule locate their 'cells' so far from human habitation as to be impervious to the spiritual and often material needs of their neighbour. Stories from the lives of the saints indicate that they took the initiative in defending the rights of the poor as well as their own.[13]

Patrick's Anger for Justice

Patrick's letter to the soldiers of Coroticus can be described as an angry letter, much like Paul's letter to the Galatians. The reasons for the anger in each case were different, but when people especially the vulnerable are being abused, exploited or oppressed there is justification for anger. Such anger is a sign that people like Patrick and Paul are morally alive. Anger is an appropriate response to injustices against others.

Patrick had just baptised a great number of Irish over the Easter period, when Coroticus and his soldiers raided the area and carried off many Irish people as slaves. Others were killed in the raid. All of this was part of the economic practice of the day. Slavery worked in both directions, and chiefs, kings and armies saw it as big business and lucrative at that.

Patrick is seething with anger, and though he has no wish to utter harsh or rough words: 'the zeal of God forces me and the truth of Christ raises one up for the love of neighbours and sons …'[14] (para. 1). Patrick described the soldiers and Coroticus as 'servants of the demons' and accused them of being 'bloodthirsty for the blood of innocent Christians' (para. 2). Patrick listed various enemies which are against people and God. Greed is a 'deadly crime', obviously destructive of others, as are coveting your neighbours goods, killing and murder and hatred of another, which may result in the other's death, certainly the moral and spiritual death of the one who hates (para. 9). Anger is again evident as Patrick lamented that freeborn people are sold into slavery: 'indeed slaves of the worst and most unworthy of men, apostate Picts' (para. 15). Coroticus and his soldiers may claim to have faith but their unjust and violent practice puts them outside the reign of God: 'Outside are the dogs and sorcerers and murderers and liars and perjurers, their lot shall be in the lake of everlasting fire' (para. 18). The allusion is to Revelation 22: 15, another angry outburst from John of Patmos against the injustices and oppression, political and economic, of imperial Rome. Domination systems and structures are destructive of human community and life and the source of great injustices.

Patrick's angry protest against the injustice of slavery is not a private letter, but a public protest meant to be read publicly, to be read aloud so that everyone and Coroticus himself will hear. Patrick's letter can be read as a direct attack on the economic institution of slavery. It has been claimed that he is the first human being in the history of the world to speak out unequivocally against slavery. Nor will any voice as strong as his be heard again until the seventeenth century.[15] Allowing for hyperbole, Patrick's voice is still a cry for justice which arises from his anger at serious wrongdoing against the weak and innocent.

Lives of Patrick are not historically reliable, the Confession and the Letter being alone considered authentic. The ninth-century Tripartite Life of Patrick told of outlandish exploits and stories of highly questionable moral value. It did tell one particular story portraying Patrick as being forcefully and aggressively against slavery.

A group of slaves were cutting a yew tree and Patrick asked why their hands bled so much. The explanation was that they were not allowed to sharpen their tools. Patrick condemned the cruel slave owner who did not allow Patrick to enter his house. In keeping with Celtic culture, Patrick fasted outside the gate but was still refused entry. He then spat on a stone, spitting stones being a feature of ninth-century monasteries. He cursed the slave owner and publicly declared that the family would never produce a king: 'Later the owner drowned in a lake.'[16] The picture of cursing is morally questionable especially when the story suggests death as punishment. Whilst the story is in all probability fictional, it does suggest a Patrick morally aware of the need for social justice and in total opposition to slavery.

Adamnan and Justice for the Innocents

In a ninth-century Irish writing there is reference to four laws:

There are the four laws (cana) of Ireland:
Patrick's law, not to kill the clergy;
And Adamnan's law, not to kill women;
Daire's, not to kill cattle;
And the law of Sunday, not to transgress thereon.[17]

Adamnan had travelled to his native Ireland to give the Law of the Innocents to its people at the Synod of Birr, 697 CE. Women were no longer to be war combatants and were excluded from capital punishment, while the mutilation and rape of women in battle were serious crimes. There are positives here but as noted in chapter 12 the law did not lead to the liberation and equality of women. Perhaps it was as much as Adamnan could have achieved in the socio-political culture of the time. While not gaining full justice and containing ambivalence, the Law was an attempt to limit injustice. The abbot of a monastery was not concerned only with relations within the monastic community but also with power relations in the wider community. Celtic monastic communities were not isolated from the wider community, but were open and engaged with them.

Adamnan's concern for justice was also expressed in his trips to England on behalf of hostages. Two of his trips were to King Aldfrith of Northumbria, there being a very close relationship between Iona and Northumbria. Aldfrith had a strong reputation in the Irish tradition as a person of learning and, according to Bede, the church historian 'he was a man most learned in the Scriptures'.[18]

The first visit was after a battle in 685 CE and Adamnan's task was to bring sixty hostages back to Ireland. His second visit was for a similar purpose – to bring back captives. The release of hostages required negotiation skills and undoubtedly these were required of Adamnan. He was an intermediary between political factions and deeply concerned as a humanitarian for the well-being of hostages and for justice to be done.

It was the passion for justice that Adamnan highlighted in his Life of Columba. The latter is portrayed as a prophet to kings and rulers, declaring to them the just requirements of God in socio-political life. Book One of the Life ends with Columba's response to the offerings collected by Conall, Bishop of Coleraine. Columba was on his way home from a meeting of kings surrounded by a great crowd. He blessed the gifts and especially pointed to those of a rich man, commending him for his generosity. He was less impressed by another offering and publicly said so:

'Of this offering, the gift of a man both wise and greedy, I cannot so much as taste, unless he first truly does penance for his sin of avarice.' This word was at once circulated among the crowd, and Columb Mac Áido, hearing it, recognised his guilt and came forward, to kneel before the saint and do penance. He promised too that henceforth he would renounce avarice, mend his way of life and practise generosity. The saint told him to stand, and from that hour his sin was healed and he was no longer grasping.[19]

That Adamnan highlights stories like this in his Life of Columba, and with his own Law of the Innocents and hostage negotiation, all indicate how important he saw the work of social justice in the life and work of community leaders. Living faithfully was and is to have a passion for justice.

Just Saints

The passion for justice is central to the Celtic saints. Columbanus has justice as a key theme in one of his sermons. After affirming humanity made in the image of God he goes on to ask:

> What does the human race have in common with God? What does earth have in common with spirit? For God is spirit. It is a great honour that God bestowed on men and women the image of eternity and likeness to his own character. And it is a great adornment for men and women if they can preserve a likeness to God, while the defiling of the image of God is a great condemnation … But if they use the virtues implanted in them appropriately, then they shall be like God.[20]

For Columbanus the image of God is essentially love. Love is the heart of God's holiness, and love is therefore the heartbeat of our relationships. Love is not just spoken, it is action and truth. We do love, and love is the essence of living and practice. Columbanus is clear that this is the image of God and what it means for humanity to be made in the divine image.

We can 'paint the image of another'.[21] As with the image of God, the image of another is action and doing. Columbanus offers contrasts: 'For truth is distinguished from falsehood, justice from unrighteousness, love from malevolence, commitment from carelessness, fairness from injustice, affection from pretence, and both paint images upon us which are mutually opposed.'[22]

Justice is contrasted with unrighteousness or wrong relations, often abuses of power and division. Fairness is contrasted with injustice, highlighting the need for the fair treatment of others, equality and respect for the rights of others. To live justly is to live in the image of God. Holy lives are lives rooted in the practice of justice. The passion of God is the passion for justice, and it is this love in action, just action, that is to paint the human image. For Columbanus we are to 'train' ourselves in just words and actions. In a more daring image Columbanus, when affirming true love in action, suggests that we 'restore to God our Father his own image …'.[23] This mirrors the prayer of Jesus that we 'hallow God's name on earth', or make holy God's character by our love in action for justice.

The Penitential of Cummean has been described as a classic of the Celtic penitential tradition. It 'makes considerable use of Welsh sources and is the most comprehensive of the Celtic Penitentials. It follows the eight capital sins of Cassian in its structure.' It also draws from Cassian the important principle of 'healing through opposites'.[24] Cummean was the bishop of Clonfert and died in 662 CE.

In section three Cummean deals with avarice. Greed leads to the stealing of another's property. Penance involves restoration: 'restore four times as much to him whom he has injured'.[25] Penance may even involve being generous with one's gifts to the end of one's life: 'A cleric who has excess of goods shall give them to the poor.'[26] Again: 'One who lies on account of greed shall make satisfaction through generosity to the one he has cheated.'[27]

Living justly for Cummean has two significant elements. Justice is restorative in that it repairs and puts right relationships that have been distorted or broken by injustices. The restoration is not cheap or an easy option since justice requires reparation. Four times as much may need to be paid to the injured party. It is also worth noting that stealing the property or goods of another is not just an inter-personal action; it is the practice of imperial powers always bent on expansionism. This has been characteristic of every empire in history including the sole superpower of the present. Imperial powers do not do penance or reparation, nor are they good at restorative justice.

Cummean's second element of justice is simplicity of living; a simple lifestyle. The greedy cleric is to give his wealth away to the poor. Simplicity of living is about generosity, sharing and solidarity with the poor. It is ensuring that the economically and socially disadvantaged have access to fairness and a more equitable life and that they have a voice at the round table of life. Justice is ensuring that scarcity does not exist and that life's resources are fairly distributed. Cummean has something important to say about distributive or redistributive justice.

Pelagius and the Theology of Justice

Pelagius, possibly an Irish theologian, certainly a key influence on early Irish biblical studies and thought, may not have been branded a heretic and excommunicated from the church solely on the basis of his theology of goodness and free will. Given that much of what is popularly known of Pelagius is from the pen of his theological opponent Augustine, a polemical and therefore skewed perspective, it is still reasonable to ask, how Pelagian was Pelagius? Was Pelagius a Pelagian? He appears to have been the victim of vicious theological attack, not all of which fairly represented his theology. Augustine may well be guilty of assuming that only his interpretation of faith was correct and that anyone who expressed things differently was unorthodox, at least:

> In astonishing streams of diatribe, personal invective, and ad hominem arguments, the Latin Fathers accused Pelagius of diminishing or even dispensing with the necessity of divine grace. What Pelagius actually taught was that human perfection was a possibility, and because God intended human beings to achieve their full measure of maturity, striving for such maturity was morally obligatory.[28]

Pelagius was a person of considerable moral fibre for whom Christianity carried a strong moral imperative. However imperfect his theology of perfection was – and like every theologian he was flawed and limited by his finite mind – living ethically and living faithfully were core to his vision of being Christian. In his writing *On the Christian Life* and his letter to the widow Demetrias, he constantly appealed to Christian virtue and to Christian faith as active. Central also was his emphasis on communitarian values as essential to Christian living. One lives ethically in community and for community. The Christian responsibility is to contribute to the common good.

Pelagius was therefore disturbed by what he met and experienced in the Rome of his day, especially the lifestyle practised by ecclesiastics. Abuses of power and social injustices were rife and like a Hebrew prophet he said so in strong critical terms and called for an alternative social vision and practice. He was uncompromising in his cry of indignation at the fashionable and morally soft Christianity of Rome. His vision of Christianity as moral demand and ethical imperative may have been more theologically objectionable than his theology of free will, human collaboration with divine grace. Social prophets have never been popular, nor have calls for a radically alternative social vision.

Pelagius on the Christian life articulated his ethical vision when he wrote on how holy the people of God should be. The model is being holy as God is holy, hearing God's words and acting upon them: 'Those who worship and serve God should be gentle, serious-minded, prudent, devout, blameless, undefiled, uncorrupted...'[29] God is truly glorified by 'our works of righteousness', our building just and right relationships in community.

He then dealt with love of neighbour and quoted the golden rule: 'So, whatever you wish that others should do to you, do so to them' (Matthew 7: 12). There is a critical edge and directness about his words: 'Those who have not done works of justice and mercy cannot reign with Christ. Those who have not been humane, devout, hospitable, full of good will, and compassionate shall not escape the fires of hell ... whoever has done evil is the enemy of God.'[30]

At the heart of the Christian life and loving God is a remarkable list of ethical virtues. Significantly justice and mercy are together, each needing the other in the symbiotic relationship of just mercy and merciful justice. Being humane and compassionate are not only also communitarian and relational, but they also suggest that the Christian life is about being authentically human, not super pious or religious.

For Pelagius there are prayers to which God does not listen. Such are the prayers of the person who:

> boldly enters the church, brashly and without a thought stretching out hands which are dishonoured with elicit gains and with the blood of the innocent, pouring forth prayers to God with a mouth that is polluted and made unholy with the recent utterances of untruths and shameful things, as if wholly unaware of anything amiss.[31]

He went on to quote Isaiah 1: 15–16, one of the great Hebrew prophetic calls for social justice as authentic worship. After a critique of those blinded by avarice and who are robbing the poor and acquiring elicit gains, Pelagius showed that faith without works has no value. It is a lengthy and strongly biblical section. Then he asked, 'Who is truly a Christian?'

But do you actually consider a Christian whose bread never fills the stomachs of the hungry, whose drink never quenches anyone's thirst, whose table is unfamiliar to all, whose roof never affords protection either to the stranger or to the pilgrim, whose clothes never cover the naked, who never comes to the aid of the poor ...[32]

Having exposed the negative or pretence at being Christian, Pelagius filled out authentic Christian living.

That person is a Christian who is merciful to all, who is not motivated by injustice, who cannot endure the oppression of the poor before their very eyes, who comes to the aid of the wretched, who helps the needy, who sorrows with those who mourn, who feels the suffering of others as if it were their own, who is moved to tears by the tears of others ... whose goodness is known to all, and at whose hands no one suffers injustice ...[33]

There is no cheap grace in the theology of Pelagius. The gospel is both grace and demand, and authentic faith is ethics. Pelagius' Christian lives in community from an ethic of justice. His is an active and concrete theology of justice, a radical social justice without which community is dysfunctional and flawed. Officially he might be a condemned heretic, but he was an authentic Celtic prophet of justice. 'God', he asserted, 'has always been pleased with justice and offended by injustice.'[34]

KEY POINTS FROM CHAPTER 14

❏ To live justly, personally and structurally in the world, is one of the key targets of our time. Global poverty is one of the major challenges to our twenty-first-century world.

❏ Our vision of justice is shaped by social location and context, ethics from the centre and margins will be very different. The privileged need to find a way to be in solidarity with the poor to allow the marginalised vision and experience to shape an ethic of justice.

❏ The challenge is to critically reflect on our definition of justice and the consequences of our perspective for those on the margins of the world in which we live.

❏ The Bible has a passion for justice and has two words for it: *tsedaqah* is concerned with liberating community, restoring justice and righting relationships; while *mishpat* is about vindicating the rights of the poor and powerless.

❏ The Exodus shaped Israel's vision of justice, which it understood as liberation from an oppressive domination system. In contrast to empire the Exodus creates a vision of an equalitarian society, a socio-political vision of God's purpose. From this standpoint injustice is critiqued. Exodus is a perennial task, affirming God's liberating acts of justice and the call to create a just world.

❑ The eighth-century Hebrew prophets Amos, Hosea, Isaiah of Jerusalem and Micah were scathing of those in positions of power, privilege and wealth who ignored the suffering of the poor, the covenant commitment to liberating justice and equality. They connected knowledge of God and doing justice and rejected religious worship divorced from justice with no moral vision.

❑ Jesus was a Jew disturbed by the social injustices of his own religion, in the tradition of the Hebrew prophets.

❑ For Jesus justice was at the core of God's kingdom which was concerned with: deliverance of the poor from oppression; putting an end to dominating power; ending violence; and restoring the marginalised to community.

❑ In Celtic society abuse of power, inequality, economic disparity and violence were characteristic features called into question by monks and saints who pursued justice with rigour.

❑ Patrick's Letter to the soldiers of Coroticus was a public and angry protest against the injustices and abuses of slavery.

❑ Celtic monastic communities were open and engaged with the wider community on justice issues. Adamnan's concern for justice was expressed in his Law of the Innocents, hostage negotiations and his Life of Columba.

❑ Columbanus believed that when human words and action are just and rooted in love then we image God. The passion of God is the passion for justice; we are therefore to 'train' ourselves in just words and actions.

❑ Cummean (d. 662 CE) in his Penitential reflected on the importance of both restorative and distributive justice for the individual and community. The former heals relationships broken by injustice by making reparation; the latter is a recognition that when we each live simply there is enough to share.

❑ Living ethically and faithfully in community and contributing to the common good were core to Pelagius' vision of being Christian. Like the Hebrew prophets he condemned those who abused their power and acted unjustly, especially clergy, which made him unpopular. In this view God is worshipped by those who build just relations in community and offended by those who act unjustly.

Test Questions

❑ Outline your knowledge and understanding of the different types of justice, and with reference to biblical texts illustrate the connection between justice and holiness.

❑ Comment on the view that the early Celtic struggle to live justly, personally and structurally in the world remains one of the key challenges of our time.

15   An Ethic of Peacebuilding

In Ireland we are products of a long history of violence. The deep irony of our history is that we have a long religious tradition, 1,700 years of being shaped by the Christian story, yet at the same time an equally long tradition of violence. To narrow historical perspective to modern Irish history, from the 1600s to the present, is to encounter a period in which religion and violence are the key characteristics. It is very difficult, if not impossible, to separate religion and violence in modern Irish history. To be aware of this reality is to be concerned with peacebuilding. To be painfully aware is the beginning of a commitment to an ethic of peacebuilding. In exploring social ethics in the Celtic tradition, it will be important to identify the practice of such an ethic in the early monastic tradition. In contemporary Ireland peacebuilding skills have been developed as we try to move from the burden of our violent past to a more just and peaceful future.

15.1   A Road Map to Peace

On 9 May 2007 Northern Ireland achieved a political settlement. It is fragile and in the first term of a newly devolved government there will be difficulties. They have already surfaced around a number of issues, such as the decision to withhold funding from the loyalist paramilitary body and its associates. Nevertheless, the remaining political issues were dealt with through a fully inclusive process and a political settlement was achieved. The peace process will take a lot longer – at least another generation. The political process was itself a carefully worked strategy which learned lessons from elsewhere and has something to contribute to other conflict regions as part of the process of peacebuilding. Northern Ireland does provide a road map to peace and it is possible to identify key signposts.

No Winners Through Violence

The current phase of conflict lasted for thirty-five years. It is important to ask if this conflict could have been moderated or ended sooner than it was. However reflection on the past may answer such a question, a stage was reached in the conflict where all parties concerned realised that there would be no winners. No one was going to win the war. One of the most professional armies in the world, the British army, was never going to defeat the paramilitary movements, republican or loyalist. Neither of the paramilitary wings was going to defeat the state and its forces, nor would they defeat each other. Perhaps it was war weariness and a desire not to put another generation through the nightmare that brought about change. It was again a realisation that there are and would be no winners through violence. No one was defeated either but implicit in the realisation was the reality that violence was and is counter-productive and cannot ultimately achieve goals.

Communications between Government, Politicians and Protagonists

From an early stage in the violent conflict communications were taking place. They were informal and unpublicised and had leaks occurred government would have denied all. This is a familiar pattern recognisable in the South African process, where Prime Minister Botha repeatedly went on air saying he would never talk to terrorists, but his officials were already doing it. As far back as 1974 when the Irish Republican Army (IRA) called a temporary ceasefire, British government officials were engaged in dialogue with the leadership of Provisional Sinn Fein. At that time people generally perceived the IRA and Sinn Fein as identical. Later in the 1990s, as political talks progressed, the IRA was seen as the military wing and Sinn Fein as the political wing of the organisation. Messages were being exchanged and the British ambassador was assuring the Irish Minister of Foreign Affairs that the ongoing contact was 'to explain British policy and not to negotiate.'[1] Gerry Adams and Martin McGuinness of Sinn Fein were involved in early contacts and discussions.

In 1989 Secretary of State Peter Brooke 'conceded that the British and the IRA were in a military stalemate.'[2] This led to round-table talks with constitutional representatives, and by 1993 the *Observer* newspaper leaked that the British government 'had had a secret channel of communication with Sinn Fein and the IRA for three years.'[3] Meanwhile John Hume, leader of the Social Democrat and Labour Party (SDLP), opened up dialogue with Gerry Adams, not without opposition from within his own party.

However distasteful such contacts were to many, they were an important part of the process and opened up new possibilities for resolving the conflict. Without communications, however secret, a political settlement would not have been achieved.

Ceasefire for Formal Talks

Secret negotiations and talks could not continue indefinitely. Sooner or later the process had to move towards more formal negotiations. There was, however, little confidence for talking while the paramilitaries were still active. Any compromise was not possible against the backdrop of violence. Government made it public that the IRA would have to decommission arms before Sinn Fein could be admitted to all-party talks. By 1994 the IRA was ready to declare a ceasefire and this was followed by a loyalist ceasefire. There were tensions still as some republican leaders believed that the British had signalled a withdrawal within ten years. The weapons remained but at least for the moment were silent. In February 1996 the IRA ended its ceasefire by bombing Canary Wharf in

London, and when Prime Minister Tony Blair and the Labour Party swept to power in 1997 the ceasefire was reinstated. Sinn Fein was offered a place at talks. The ceasefires were necessary to allow for inclusive talks and for the confidence building required for any success.

Talks Process More Important Than Substance

What followed between 1996 and 1998 was in every sense a significant process. It was characterised by a number of features.

Inclusivity was always going to be important. Talks about a settlement were never going to succeed unless everyone was at the table. Exclude any party and failure was the price. Even though early talks were 'talks about talks' and often characterised by 'corridor diplomacy', lines of communication were opening up between all of the elected representatives of Northern Ireland. By 1998 the Democratic Unionist Party (DUP) had excluded itself from the process, on the basis of never talking to terrorists. Full inclusivity was not realised until post-Belfast Agreement when the Assembly collapsed and another process of truly inclusive talks leading to the St Andrew's Agreement was engaged. The Belfast Agreement was reached on Good Friday 1998. It dealt with the totality of relationships, those between Unionists and Nationalists in Northern Ireland, North–South relationships between Northern Ireland and the Republic of Ireland, and East–West or the British–Irish relationships. Structural bodies such as the Northern Ireland Assembly, North–South bodies and the Council of the Isles were put in place. Policing and criminal justice reforms as well as equality and human rights legislation were set in motion, and the difficult issue of prisoner release was also included.

The St Andrew's Agreement was not a renegotiation or replacement of the Belfast Agreement. By 13 October 2006 there was an outlined agreement rather than an actual agreement itself. The outline depended on Sinn Fein and the Democratic Unionist Party adhering to a timetable of events and implementing a 'to do' list. The St Andrew's timetable had to be endorsed by the electorate, so an election was held on 7 March 2007. On 8 May the new Northern Ireland Assembly met, power-sharing government was restored and devolution was returned to Northern Ireland. There was and is no peace without inclusivity.

Intensity of talks was another characteristic of the road map to peace and the process. Representatives were paid to attend talks and there was a full team of negotiators who worked for two years. Offices and a secretariat were also available. All of this came at an economic cost but without an intensive structure a political settlement would not have been realised.

Parity of esteem was crucial. Inequalities had been characteristic of Northern Ireland's history, including inequality within the loyalist community who were often as socially and economically deprived as the republican/nationalist community. There had to be a level playing field. Each party had the same number of places and the same rights to speak. Everyone was to be treated with the same respect, no matter what their personal or party history had been. There were those responsible for atrocities, but at some point a peace process required an equality of treatment if it was to succeed. Parity of esteem was necessary and remains an important equality issue for the continued building of a peace process and community ethos.

There was also a complexity about the process. The very structure of negotiations was complex, combining plenary and working groups. The agenda was also of necessity comprehensive. Nothing was out of bounds. Whatever the partners wanted on the table was there for discussion. These included prisoners, education, constitutional change, justice, discrimination and human rights. Not surprisingly when the Belfast Agreement was reached equality and human rights were central to it.

The process also changed organisational or party positions. Sinn Fein accepted devolution within Northern Ireland, and more to the point, still within a British context. The Unionists accepted power sharing and devolved government on such a model, though it did take the DUP another eight years to overcome its 'never never' to enter into power sharing with Sinn Fein. The process has discredited the word 'never' in Northern Ireland politics.

International mediation was crucial to the process. This is the concept of the third party enabling the parties in conflict to enter and sustain a process of intensive negotiations. President Clinton invested considerable energy and time in Northern Ireland, and it was he who provided a special envoy as the crucial third-party mediator. Senator George Mitchell had the intellectual and moral standing to chair talks and win the trust and confidence of all parties. With amazing skill, patience and good humour Mitchell kept the parties at their task and on Good Friday 1998 the Belfast Agreement was in place.

The third party was crucial. Left to themselves it is doubtful if the local politicians could have made it. Yet they did have to essentially produce their own agreement and feel that they owned the talks and the Agreement. It may be true that the solution was obvious and could have been written in a short time on a postcard, but it had to take at least two years, indeed all of the 1990s, to reach the momentous point of 1998, significantly Good Friday in the Christian calendar.

In many ways there was only going to be one settlement. This was a settlement of 'balanced constitutional change by the British and Irish, a Northern Ireland Assembly, a replaced Anglo-Irish agreement, and a British-Irish Council linking the Assembly to other United Kingdom bodies and North-South structures'.[4]

There was much ambiguity and difficulty, and the Assembly did collapse in 2002. It required the St Andrew's Conference to be truly inclusive and deal with the remaining two crunch issues. Would Sinn Fein accept policing and would the DUP accept power sharing? Both did and in 2007 the political process was settled. Without the road map to peace it would not have happened. Peacebuilding requires a strategy, and it is possible to see the strategy at work in the political process of Northern Ireland, transforming conflict, dealing politically with the totality of relationships and opening up space to more actively pursue a generational peace process and build the desired future.

15.2 *Shalom* as an Enduring Vision

Ever since the development of city-states in ancient Babylon *c*.3000 BCE, violence has been a way of life. City-states needed to be defended from each other or needed to expand power and influence by the conquest of others. This necessitated standing armies, social and political élites, patriarchy as males ruling over, and the violent subjugation of women. From ancient Babylon there emerged the original myth of redemptive violence, the earliest surviving version is 1250 BCE. The *Enuma Elish* was a propagandist piece of literature for the god Marduk. Like all myths this was an attempt to proclaim the supremacy of Marduk and to explain the way things are. Violence is at the heart of the myth. Marduk is supreme because he has defeated all the other gods including the brutal elimination of the goddess Tiamat. Out of this bloody violence comes creation itself and the human is the product of violence. This is how life is. It is violence that made Marduk supreme, violence that births the Earth and the human. Here is a theology of violence that achieves, liberates, creates, defends and pays. In the theo-politics of ancient Babylon violence is all-pervasive. The ethic of violence is supreme.

The myth of redemptive violence lives on in children's cartoons, video games, movies, governmental foreign policies and national security arrangements. It remains all-pervasive and is a way of life. The myth underpins our culture of violence and is at the heart of our Irish history of violence, whether that of state power, colonialism, risings, rebellions, physical force traditions and paramilitaries. This myth that violence achieves, defends, liberates and pays has been believed and is still upheld.

The myth of redemptive violence and the supremacy of Marduk was still alive and experienced by the exiled Hebrews during the time of a Babylonian superpower. The *Enuma Elish* was written by ancient Babylonian priests, connecting religion and violence in a deep way. Israel's exiled priests wrote their own myth of creation. It too pointed to the supremacy of Israel's God and offered an alternative ethic. Israel's God was good and birthed creation and continued to be present in a creation which was very good. Creation was not out of violence but from a good God who in contrast to Marduk was non-violent. Humans were created in the image of the good, non-violent God. Humans, therefore, had a God-given ethical responsibility to partner and care for the Earth. The priests of Israel in exile wrote Genesis 1 as their counter-myth to the Babylonian myth of redemptive violence. It pointed to an ethic of goodness, non-violence and responsibility as an alternative way of life in the world. It is part of Israel's ethic of peace, SHALOM, which the community's prophets, poets, priests, ethicists and wise ones were to spell out as their enduring vision for life. However much violence we encounter in the biblical text itself, the enduring vision is *Shalom*. Like ourselves there were those in the Hebrew and early Christian communities who projected their own violence and longing for vengeance on to God. When they and we do that we lose sight of the enduring vision of *Shalom*, the radical alternative to the myth of redemptive violence.

Out of Israel's experience of violence and suffering in Babylonian exile came an alternative vision of God and ethics. In Genesis 1 the priests affirmed that God's original creative intention was not violence and suffering: 'the creation was not originally intended by God as a place of suffering for created beings, as a place where violence is continuously perpetrated'.[5] Out of the chaos of exile in Babylon, Israel encountered the non-violent God whose creation and purpose was and is very good. Violence and chaos are not the final experiential word, but God's non-violent goodness and peace. Life can be lived not by the myth of redemptive violence but from the enduring vision of *Shalom*, the liberating vision for creation and humanity.

Shalom *as Holistic Well-Being*

It is not only difficult to translate *Shalom* with a single English word or even an idea, but the Hebrews also found it impossible. They used a cluster of words to bring out its multi-dimensional meaning. *Shalom* is the 'persistent vision of joy, well-being, harmony and prosperity …' The cluster of biblical words is 'love, loyalty, truth, grace, salvation, justice, blessing, righteousness'. *Shalom* is the controlling biblical vision, a vision of wholeness: 'the substance of the biblical vision of one community embracing all creation'.[6]

One of the prophets of exile, himself a priest and possibly one of the creative minds behind the alternative vision of Genesis 1, wrote of God's 'covenant of peace' (Ezekiel 34: 25–29). It is not a vision of well-being for individuals. Biblical writers do not think in modern Enlightenment ways! The vision or covenant of peace is for the whole Earth-human community. *Shalom* 'is well-being of a material, physical, historical kind, not idyllic "pie in the sky", but "salvation" in the midst of trees, crops and enemies …'[7] The whole Earth-human community is included. All of life is in together, all receive and we receive it all, personal, social, political, economic, environmental. God's covenant of *Shalom* is all-embracing and all-inclusive: '*Shalom* comes only to the inclusive, embracing community that excludes none.'[8]

Multi-Dimensions of Shalom

Shalom embraces all reality including the environmental and the human. Again in Genesis 1, *Shalom* includes all creation, and especially embraces and transforms chaos. All that is void, formless and dark in life, such as experiences of exile and displacement, of a physical and psychological nature, are to be brought into harmony, order and peace. There is movement from all forms of chaos to *Shalom*.

Mark's gospel includes a story of Jesus rebuking the wind and stilling a storm at sea, the latter a symbol of chaos in Jewish thought: 'Peace! Be still!' (Mark 4: 37–39). The echo is from the Creation story, and disorder is brought into harmony, *Shalom* is established. '*Shalom* also enters the historic political world. Absence of *Shalom* and lack of harmony are expressed in social disorder as evidenced in economic inequality, judicial perversion, and political oppression and exclusivism.'[9]

The Hebrew prophets had strong words for all that was socially negative and anti-community. Amos, Micah and Isaiah all speak out against socio-economic and political injustices, not just as unethical, but as practices and policies destroying God's intention of *Shalom*. Righteousness or right relations and justice are the foundations of good community where all have dignity and a fair share of resources and power. This is *Shalom*: 'In historic community, the forces of injustice and exploitation are opposed by God's will for responsible, equitable justice, which yields security.'[10]

Justice is at the heart of *Shalom*, but in many societies people disagree about the meaning of justice. For some it is about equality, fair play, social justice. For others it is about law and order and security. Both definitions are needed but the division reflects where people are on the power spectrum. Justice is about the distribution of power and access to power. In the Christian gospels there is particular dynamic in the foreground. The world of Jesus and the first Christians was a world dominated by the Roman superpower. Its slogan was *Pax Romana* and 'peace and security'. The Roman peace was through militarism and force underpinned by a state theology. Roman imperial theology had four programmatic themes: religion, war, victory, peace.

The Roman superpower's 'gospel' was peace through victory.[11] Jesus, however, proclaimed an alternative empire – the kingdom and reign of God – and God's empire had an alternative gospel with four programmatic themes: religion, non-violence, justice, peace. Jesus offered a counter-programme to that of the Roman Empire. Rather than peace through victory, he proclaimed peace through justice or first justice, then peace, all by non-violent methods.

Paul did not proclaim a different gospel nor was his a polemic against Judaism, as too frequently portrayed. Paul, working in urban centres rather than the rural areas of Jesus, proclaimed: 'the already present kingdom of God in his own language for that wider world'.[12] Paul spoke the language of Roman imperial theology, such as 'Son of God' and 'Saviour of the World', and used it subversively against Roman discourse. For Paul faith was the choice between Caesar Augustus or Jesus Christ, and that was a choice between alternative programmatic themes: 'Since the Romans did not roll over laughing, I trust their judgement about what it was. Over against "peace through victory" came again the alternative "peace through justice".'[13]

Ethical living from the shared perspective of Jesus and Paul is living faithfully in the world of superpowers and domination systems in the way of non-violence, justice and peace. *Shalom* is multi-dimensional and is the primary, enduring biblical vision.

15.3 Celtic Peacebuilding

It would be wrong to imagine the Celtic world, pre-Christian and Christian as peaceloving and constantly engaged in peacebuilding. It was a violent world of warrior heroes. Adamnan introduced his Law of the Innocents at Birr in 697 CE, changing the conventions of warfare: The Law 'is a monument to his dedication and desire to be at the service of those who most needed protection and gives us that warm feeling for the man that we have for humanitarians who work to limit injustice'.[14]

The Law may not have legislated for the full equality of women, but it was necessary because of the culture of violence in a society where the Christian story had already been heard. Adamnan did not try to eliminate war and violence but to limit the effects, especially against women. In his careful strategy to ensure Ireland had such a law, and in his activity as a hostage mediator in Northumbria,[15] we meet a Celtic peacebuilder. It was humanitarian work and more. Adamnan believed that he had a divine mandate drawing on the Jewish Jubilee texts of Isaiah 61: 1 and Luke 4: 18–19. Peacebuilding and humanitarian activity were part of Adamnan's apostolic witness. In more contemporary terms we would describe it as a 'faith imperative', or 'gospel imperative', what one is commanded and commissioned by God to do.

The Violent Context

Any exploration of Celtic peacebuilding needs to be serious about the violent context and culture against which it takes place. Violence is often at the heart of the myths and legends. One of the greatest myths is that of Cúchulainn, the mythical champion who dominates the great Ulster Cycle. The traditional interpretation of his name is 'the hound of Culann': 'Cú (i.e. hound) was a common designation for a warrior in Irish literature, and whatever the original import of the second part of his name it is clear that he had his source in a cult of martial prowess.'[15]

In the Táin Bó Cuailnge, Cúchulainn single-handedly defends the province of Ulster against the great army of Queen Méabh of Connacht. His whole body is transformed into a battle-frenzy. The myth contains many rituals of war, and it is not just about arms and battles. The warrior hero had mystical significance:

> In order to delay the enemy army, for instance, he twists an oak sapling into a hoop and writes a message on it while using but one arm, one leg and one eye. This was apparently a ritual of war employed by magical poets, and parallels the pose adopted by LUGH during battle.[16]

Mysticism, piety and religion in myth or history are frequently connected to war, violence and blood sacrifice.

Fedelm, the young woman poet of Connacht, recites a poem to her queen celebrating the exploits of Cúchulainn:

> A giant on the plain I see,
> doing battle with the host,
> holding in each of his two hands
> four short quick swords.
> I see him hurling against that host
> two gae bolga and a spear
> and an ivory-hilted sword,
> each weapon to its separate task.

He towers on the battlefield
in breastplate and red cloak.
Across the sinister chariot-wheel
the Warped Man deals death
— that fair form I first beheld
milled to a mis-shape
I see him moving to the fray:
take warning, watch him will,
Cúchulainn, Sualdam's son!
Now I see him in pursuit
Whole hosts he will destroy,
making dense massacre.
In thousands you will yield your heads.
I am Fedelm. I hide nothing.
The blood starts from warrior's wounds
— total ruin – at his touch:
Your warriors dead, the warriors
of Deda mac Sin prowling loose;
torn compass, women wailing,
because of him – the Forge-Hound.[17]

Not surprisingly Cúchulainn has appealed to both republicans and loyalists during the most recent phase of violent conflict, at times appearing to be historicised on wall murals. Both he and the hound have a place of honour in the Post Office in O'Connell Street, Dublin, a warrior hero, central to Ireland's culture of violence.

Fionn mac Cumhaill has been described as 'the most celebrated hero in Irish literature and folklore. Stories about him are continuous in the literature for well over 1,000 years'.[18] More comical tales are associated with the Giants Causeway and Fionn building a causeway to Scotland in a battle with another giant. Or Ireland's Eye, an island off the Dublin coast, being a sod torn from the ground by him in Co. Wicklow, thereby creating the large lake at Glendalough. A similar story is told of the Isle of Man as a sod thrown by Fionn in a fight and creating not only the Isle of Man but Lough Neagh.

In all of the collection of stories Fionn is a great warrior-seer. Battles and violence are key characteristics. He was associated with the Boyne valley, and his stories were adopted by Leinster leaders in the third to fourth centuries. In the battle between Uí Fhailghe of Leinster and the Uí Néill for possession of the Boyne valley, Fionn was portrayed as a great war leader.

Leinster and Munster combined to create an eighth-century corpus of stories in which Fionn carried off a woman called Badhamair, who was then beheaded by a Leinster warrior. Fionn beheaded her assassin in revenge, which led to a spiral of violent conflict with the assassin's half-brother Fothadh. Peace broke out between them but did not last long. Fothadh refused to drink ale at a shared feast unless 'it be in the company of white faces'. Fionn went off to Killarney and murdered the husband of Fothadh's sister, bringing the head of the man back to the feast. Unsurprisingly that created more hostility, which was ferocious: 'This type of lore is quite crude and savage, no doubt reflecting the life of young warriors of the time …'[19]

Irish mythology is inherently violent, whatever other qualities it portrays. Whilst there is no historical basis to the myths and legends, they do reflect the cultural values of the myth-makers, and the myths have a tendency in subsequent Irish history to be historicised and used as inspirational motifs in historical struggles. The violence of the 1916 Easter Rising drew heavily on the Cúchulainn myth and the myths of the Fianna, a large group of stories relating to a band of young warriors led by Fionn mac Cumhaill. It also drew on Christian theology related to the sacrifice of Jesus and a sacrificial understanding of Eucharist.

In historical life violence was widely practised. The culture was dominated by warrior heroes. Irish monasteries and monks were involved in the violence of society. Monasteries and monks became involved in power plays and political games. Family power politics were often at work or monks were driven by ambition. These dynamics rather than ethical ideals shaped activity. If myths depict the way things are and are an attempt to explain how it is, then violence was all-pervasive and monasteries and monks became caught up in the culture: 'For, predictably, the pervasive violence of early Irish society infected the role of the monks themselves. Many holy men were as guilty of violence as their secular brothers and sisters, either directly or by supporting vicious warrior-kings.'[20]

There was no law to govern the power of kings. They needed power if they were to get things and they created their own authority. This often led to violence – if not physical violence, then psychological and verbal – as the pursuit of power and authority often do. Peace in this situation would often be imposed, a microcosm of the Pax Romana.

The monks of Clonmacnoise provide a classic example of patronage relations with a king, which led to military protection and a secondary role for ethical ideals. In 900 CE an agreement or treaty was signed between the abbot and King Flann. Flann's house was within the monastery and was placed 'under the protection of the peace of the congregation of Ciarán'.[21] Flann had been at war with the king of Connacht, and violations and outrages followed, including the profanation and destruction of churches. Yet the monks of Clonmacnoise continued to bless Flann, who paid for the great High Cross there. Flann's destructive exploits brought too many gifts to the monastery as well as his protection. The monks were not prepared to disturb the *status quo* in the name of a higher ethical critique.

There was nothing extraordinary about this, since others beside Flann were involved in similar violence and destruction of monastic enclosures. Monastic communities were at war with each other. Monasteries were destroyed by other monasteries, largely because of the wealth they held. There was another story though, and to that we must turn.

Peacemakers and Pilgrims of God

Not all the monks were engaged in violence, nor were they all compromising a peace ethic. There were those who saw a higher ethic in creating political calm with the security and well-being that would accompany it. Building peace was for their own good and that of others. There was a common good to be served by peacebuilding: 'The religious élite of Ireland became professional political mediators.'[22] This, of course, was possible because in many cases the monks were related to kings and friendly with them. These relationships they put to good use:

> The abbots of Ard Macha, as sons, brothers, and in-laws to kings, besides being alleged keepers of the relics of Patraic, Peter and Paul, were highly regarded negotiators. Similarly, abbots of Cluain Moccu Nois carried more political weight than other communities in Mide and Connacht ...'[23]

The latter claim highlights the difficulty in following a pure or absolutist ethic in all circumstances. The real world of politics and power is often a grey area, and there are sometimes lesser ethical choices to be made.

Early Irish laws describe a monk as 'pilgrim of God' and an essential part of that is defined as having 'the special ability to ensure treaties, negotiations and contracts.'[24] There was an expectation in wider society that monks would be engaged in peacemaking and peacebuilding.

In all of this the monastery played a crucial role, because it was the only safe place. Negotiations, treaties and contracts needed safe space, and this could be guaranteed by the monastery. It is said that the 'abbot of Ard Macha and the successor of Finnian at Cluain Iraird made peace and amity between the men of Ireland'. The monks of Lis Mór used their moral authority to persuade Diarmait to quit his fight for the Munster kingship. Diarmait and his brother made 'peace and a covenant in Caisel', witnessed by the bishop of Caisel.[25] Much of this was accompanied by rituals, no doubt of a religious nature. Peacemaking and peacebuilding need to be ritualised, and this involves symbolic gestures and actions that go beyond the mere signing of pieces of paper.

Ard Macha especially seems to have had a reputation for peacebuilding. According to the annals, most of the peace negotiations in Ulster were facilitated by senior monks, and their skilful work appears to have included 'some treaties involving the major political leaders of all Ireland'.[26] In 1126 CE, a time of violent conflict in Ireland, leaders were away from Ard Macha for over a year 'pacifying the men of Ireland and imposing good conduct upon everyone, both laic and cleric'.[27]

Some individuals acquired peacebuilding reputations. One such was Ciarán of Saigher, founder of the monastery of that name near Birr. He has been called 'the firstborn of the saints of Ireland'.[28] From the fifth and early sixth centuries he is mainly associated with Cape Clear, Co. Cork, having been posted there, and he is still remembered in Cape Clear's folklore. He has been described as 'sower of peace and calmer of quarrels' and stories are told of unconventional means of preventing battles. He would invoke the elements, tearing up trees and replanting them on the battle area. Also he is reputed to have caused the river to overflow its banks, making terrified armies retreat. In the latter the Ulstermen returned home and the Munstermen went to Saigher where Ciarán threw a huge party.

Other stories have Ciarán involved in hostage release. Reputedly Patrick went to Munster, where Ciarán joined him. Patrick's horse was stolen and the king of Munster imprisoned the thief. Ciarán ransomed the man for his weight in gold. Apparently Ciarán paid cattle to ransom his namesake Ciarán of Clonmacnoise from a local king.[29]

There is a common Irish theme of water monsters being banished by saints. One such story is told in the Life of Columba or Colum Cille. When he arrived at Loch Ness he met a group of people preparing to bury a man who had been bitten by a water monster. Columba told one of the men to swim to the other side to collect a boat, but midway the monster reappeared roaring and rushing at the man with wide open jaws. The saint made the sign of the cross: 'and invoking the name of God, he commanded the fierce beast saying: "Go no further. Do not touch the man. Go back at once." At the sound of the saint's voice, the beast fled in terror so fast one might have thought it was pulled back with ropes.'[30]

This may be the oldest story of the Loch Ness monster, but no historical claims can be deduced from it. There are many water-beast stories in the Lives of Irish saints and they are based on folk tales with a biblical influence. The Apocalypse of John or Book of Revelation has such a myth, probably with even earlier roots. There is a dramatic description of a great dragon being thrown into a lake of fire. The last book of the Bible is the often mythical portrayal of a struggle between faithful people and domination by the oppressive system of the Roman Empire. The superpower, like all superpowers in history, imposed its peace, Pax Romana, by militarism, political and economic means. The dragon thrown into the fire is the mythical end of the oppressive system and imposed lie of peace, conveying a message of hope to a beleaguered people.

The theme and biblical allusion are found in the *Altus Prosator*, 'one of the literary and theological gems of Hiberno-Latin writing'.[31] It is late sixth or seventh century, and in all likelihood was written on Iona, traditionally by Columba, providing a panorama of Christian faith. Reference is made to the great dragon of the Apocalypse in all its destructive power:

> The great Dragon, most foul, terrible, and ancient, was wiser than all the beasts and more ferocious than the animals of the earth. He was the slippery serpent who pulled down with himself into the abyss of the lower places and its many dangerous one third of the stars of heaven. Those who flee the true light are there thrown down headlong by the Parasite.[32]

The allusion here is to Revelation 12, and later in a judgement scene the *ALTUS* alludes to Revelation 6: 15 with its faith claim: 'Then armies will flee away in the caverns and recesses of the mountains'.[33]

The imagery is of God's peace, *Shalom*, in contrast to the militarised and politico-economic oppressive peace of empire. If Columba was the author, then we can envisage him declaring God's peace as the enduring vision in a world of destructive powers. By holiness of life expressed through peacebuilding, the destructive, oppressive dragon can be consigned to the depths. Columba, pilgrim of God and peacebuilder at Drumcaet and in the *Altus*, believed that in a world of violence *Shalom* is the enduring vision and ethic. That also may be the point of the motif of saints banishing monsters. The Celtic myths contain violence, but there were counter-myths holding up the vision of peace and the practice of an ethic of peacebuilding. The monster myth is such a contrast myth.

A hagiographer might describe a saint's efforts to control political rulers in this way: 'Indeed, kings were always enemies to him, but by divine power they were forced to obey him.'[34] 'Forced' may be an unfortunate word, because the power of God paradoxically is not that of the king or his royal authority. The saint was concerned with moral authority or moral force in contrast to physical force. In much of Irish history we have put our ultimate trust in physical force. Alternative voices have always been present, pointing to and embodying an ethic of peacebuilding, echoing the early Celtic monks.

KEY POINTS FROM CHAPTER 15

A Road Map to Peace

❑ 1974 – British government officials in dialogue with leadership of Sinn Fein.
❑ 1989 – Secretary of State Peter Brooke conceded British and IRA in a military stalemate.
❑ British government continued secret talks with Sinn Fein and IRA.
❑ John Hume (SDLP) opened up dialogue with Gerry Adams (Sinn Fein).
❑ British government made public statement that IRA would have to decommission arms before Sinn Fein admitted to all-party talks.
❑ 1994 – IRA ceasefire, followed by Loyalist ceasefire, declared.
❑ February 1996 – end of IRA ceasefire – bombing of Canary Wharf in London.
❑ 1997 – Tony Blair and Labour Party in power, ceasefire reinstated.
❑ Sinn Fein offered place at talks.
❑ 1998 – DUP excluded itself from peace process, on the basis of never talking to terrorists.
❑ Good Friday 1998 – Belfast Agreement.
❑ 2002 – Assembly collapsed.
❑ 2006 – All-inclusive, multi-party talks at St Andrew's Conference.
❑ May 2007 – Northern Ireland achieved political settlement.

Shalom as an Ending Vision

❑ Myth of redemptive violence had its origins in ancient Babylon *c*.3000 BCE reflected in the Babylonian creation myth in the *Enuma Elish*.

❏ Hebrew creation myth in Genesis 1 was a counter-myth to the Babylonian myth of redemptive violence, affirming the goodness of God and creation.

❏ Genesis 1 is part of Israel's peace ethic, *Shalom*; offered as an alternative way of life based on the principles of goodness, non-violence and responsibility.

❏ *Shalom* has a multi-dimensional meaning of joy, well-being, harmony, prosperity, wholeness that results from love, loyalty, truth, grace, salvation, justice, blessing and righteousness.

❏ The covenant of peace – *Shalom* – is for the whole Earth-human community.

❏ Absence of *Shalom* is apparent in socio-economic and political injustices that are anti-community and oppressive of life.

❏ Where the empire proclaimed peace and security by military might and violence, Jesus proclaimed an alternative empire – the reign of God which established peace through justice.

Celtic Peacebuilding

❏ The Celtic world was a violent world, which required peacebuilders such as Adamnan, whose Law of the Innocents at Birr in 697 CE and activities as a hostage mediator in Northumbria were efforts to limit the effects of war and violence.

❏ Violence is at the heart of Celtic myths and legends: e.g. the story of Cúchulainn in the Ulster Cycle renowned for his military prowess; and the warrior-seer Fionn mac Cumhaill.

❏ Mysticism, piety and religion in myth or history are frequently connected to war, violence and blood sacrifice. The violence of the 1916 Easter Rising drew on Celtic myth and a particular view of the sacrifice of Jesus.

❏ Celtic monasteries and monks became involved in power plays and political games which bought them in contact with the violence in society: e.g. the monks of Clonmacnoise.

❏ Some within the monasteries sought to create political calm and the security it would accomplish; consequently a number of monks became professional political mediators.

❏ Monasteries could provide safe space for negotiations and treaties between warring parties.

❏ The Celtic myth *Altus Prosator* – of the late sixth or early seventh century, attributed to Columba – is an example of a counter-myth to Celtic tales of violence. It holds up a vision of peace and an ethic of peacebuilding in contrast to the way of violence.

Test Questions

❏ Outline your knowledge and understanding of the essential ingredients necessary to reach a peaceful political settlement. Illustrate your answer with reference to the peace map for Northern Ireland.

❏ Discuss the role of myth in promoting both violence and an ethic of peacebuilding.

16 Celtic Spirituality for Ethical Practice

My interest in Celtic spirituality was awakened when I was appointed by the Methodist church in Ireland to work in west Cork. I made a double discovery in west Cork. From the elderly man who served me petrol I discovered that I knew no Irish history, that it had not been part of my formal education. He had been a member of the old IRA, and west Cork had been a violent place from 1916 to 1923. He awakened my interest in Irish history which also convinced me that I could not do theology with credibility and integrity unless I knew the historical narrative as the context of meaningful reflection on God and life.

In west Cork I also discovered the early Celtic Irish traditions. St Finbarre was alive and well. Gogane Barre was a beautiful setting, mountains, forest and lake with a little oratory by the lakeside. It was the place associated with Finbarre's origins, and it was and is a wonderful place of reflection, quiet and prayer. The Celtic spirit was awakened in me, and in a strange, mystical way I felt that I had arrived home, and that this spirit I had always known.

So Irish history and Irish Christianity became life passions, and both have shaped and continue to shape the way I do theology, God-talk, reflection, and the doing of theology in such a way as to earth it in the practical and public issues of Irish life, especially in the north. In other words theology is life; it is praxis, doing and reflecting, reflecting and doing. Theology is ethics, and ethics is theology and living; ethics and theology are social. They are worked out and practised in community, in the social and public context.

16.1 Celtic Spirituality: A Deep Well for Our Time?

Celtic spirituality seems to be like an underground stream. Every now and then it bubbles up to the surface. Or it may be that every so often it is reinvented. Reinvention can often mean that we project our contemporary needs on to a perceived past. Over the last two decades at least, there has been a resurgence of interest in things Celtic, inclusive of both prayers and jewellery! Much has been written around Celtic spirituality with the development of communities, liturgies and symbols. An underground stream bubbling to the surface again or current mythmaking? Either way the renewed interest in Celtic spirituality may be an indication of spiritual poverty, disillusionment with many traditional expressions of faith and a longing for depths and roots which can provide meaning within our often fragmented lives, communities and world.

It is possible to romanticise a Celtic past, even invent one. Some writings do that very well. Others dismiss the resurgence as nonsense or as belonging to something suspicious called 'new age'. But Celtomania and Celtoscepticism are inadequate responses, both failing in historical rigour and critical analysis of the present. Original source materials have been recovered and translated. We now have quite a wealth of early Irish and Welsh religious writings along with rich Scottish and Hebridean material, much of it poetic. The recovery and availability of such writings include penitentials, religious prose, the lives of saints or hagiography, liturgies, creation hymns, hymns or poems of faith, lament and community rules or ways of life. As with secular history and biblical and theological studies, so with these early writings we are paying careful attention to context, social, political, economic, cultural and gendered. Now we do have a sense of what these crucial writings meant for the people who cherished and handed them on. Contemporary Celtic spirituality has historical roots, even though some may question the word 'Celtic' itself. From the roots we can draw insights and inspiration for the present, reinterpreted for our time.

The renewed interest is not confined to the Celtic regions in these islands. Mainland Europeans and north Americans find a deep-down resonance. The indigenous spiritual traditions of Australia, New Zealand, parts of Africa and Asia recognise primal echoes. Recently an email from Switzerland requested papers I had written on the Celtic tradition, the person having been introduced to it through some lectures and seminars I offered at a Dublin conference seven years ago. His prayer has been nurtured by Celtic prayers ever since. The bilingual New Zealand Anglican Prayer Book – rich in Maori spirituality – sounds more Celtic than the Irish Prayer Book! So what are the themes and insights that connect with people in different parts of the planet? Are there eternal echoes in Celtic spirituality that harmonise with other deep primal spiritual traditions and offer a lively Christian spirituality in a contemporary world?

Spirituality, though, tends to be an elusive word. It even appears to mean anything and is by no means confined to the Christian tradition. It is possible to talk of the spirituality of an organisation or institution. There is the outward form, the structure and systems, committees and boards, management and rituals. There is, however, more to an organisation or institution than these outward and visible forms. There is the inner ethos, the core values, the heartbeat of the organisation, what makes it tick. This is the spirituality, the inner dynamic that energises and drives the organisation. It may be negative or positive, destructive or creative. It is the organisational heartbeat, ethos or spirituality, and any meaningful transformation or renewal of an organisation or institution is not merely about changing the structures and systems. The inner ethos, the core values or spirituality, is where real transformation takes place.

All of this is true for the person, group or institution. Transformation is inner, or transformation of the heart. The person or the institution becomes driven by a new energy, dynamic and deep-rooted resources.

There is a spirituality in all religious tradition. At the heart of the institutional forms and structures is the spiritual dynamic, again the inner ethos. This is also true of theological systems. There is always more to a statement of belief than meets the eye. Creedal formulations are not the last or ultimate word about a faith tradition. The sacred text or holy scripture is far from being all there is to spiritual reality. What is it that really energises, drives, shapes the religious tradition and its texts and creeds? We might ask the question another way: what is the spirit of Christianity, Judaism or Islam? Creeds and texts often set boundaries and may even develop into imperialistic dogma. But there is always something that overflows the boundaries, is prior to the creedal and textual formulations and will not be confined by them. Perhaps the elusiveness of spirituality is appropriate.

Spirituality is 'felt experience' and 'lived practice'. In Christian terms it is our experience of God and our way of life, each of which is inseparable from the other. Experience of God and ethical living in God's world are two sides of the spiritual reality coin. Mysticism and action belong together. It is in the social context that we experience God as gift and demand, and it is in the social context that we live faithfully or ethically. The Hebrew prophet Jeremiah was as clear as anyone when he put it to his community that knowing God is doing justice. The passion for God is the passion for justice, and the passion for justice is the passion for God. At this point Jeremiah and Celtic spirituality are at one. What, therefore, is the heartbeat of Celtic spirituality, the inner dynamic of social ethics in the Celtic tradition?

16.2 The Heartbeat of Celtic Spirituality

The Vision of God

On our pop chart of hymns and songs 'Be Thou My Vision' ranks high. This eighth-century Irish hymn goes to the heart of Celtic spirituality, the vision of God, the great 'heart of our own heart'. In every generation we need to recover anew the God vision. The hymn visions God as 'High King of Heaven'. In early Irish society the Ard Rí, or high king, was not remote or above the people. He was elected or chosen from among the people, was one of the people and remained close to them. God visions have too often over-emphasised the transcendence, otherness, aloofness, other-worldliness of God. This has often been a God without passion, pathos, above our suffering. Celtic spirituality acknowledged the mystery of God and also experienced the immanence of God, God with us, close and in solidarity with our struggles and sufferings. The metaphor for God drawn from cultural and political experience did not perceive a distant monarch, dominant or oppressive. The metaphor of the Ard Rí shaped a vision of God in all things and all things in God. This is a relational and suffering God.

The suffering God is important in the twenty-first century. Over sixty years ago Dietrich Bonhoeffer was a key leader in the German Confessing church. He actively protested against the brutal elimination of Jews in Nazi Germany and was hanged by the Nazis because of his opposition to Hitler and the Third Reich. It was an era of war and suffering and called for ethical responses. The era led Bonhoeffer to assert that only a suffering God would do.

The bloody and violent twentieth century was responsible for the cultural death of God in Europe, certainly it was the end of belief in an omnipotent, all-powerful God who died in the trenches of warfare, the death camps and the genocidal campaigns of totalitarian leaders. Suffering of all kinds carries on into the twenty-first century with still no intervention from an omnipotent God. Only a suffering God will do, which means a vulnerable God in solidarity with all who suffer from poverty, oppression, violence and war.

Yet powerful nations, superpowers or those in power have great difficulty with a suffering, vulnerable God. They prefer a God made in the image of empire, a superpower God. Ireland has never been an imperial power but has for centuries experienced colonisation, and Protestants of the north-east have identified through much of the nineteenth and twentieth centuries, politically and theologically, with British imperialism. Within all of this individuals and groups have built and enjoyed power bases within church and society. A suffering, vulnerable God has been and may remain for some an uncomfortable and challenging idea.

16.1 The pilgrim at Clonmacnoise.

Yet the primary early Celtic God-image, the high king of Heaven, was of the people, among the people and one of them. It was a God-image also shaped by the cross. In the suffering of Jesus Celtic Christians encountered a suffering God, and it is this vision of God that shapes and energises the passion for justice.

This vision was also expressed by another eighth-century Irish hymn, 'St Patrick's Breastplate', a prayer for dressing in the morning. Here the key metaphor is Trinity, the primary way in which Celtic Christians experienced God. The Trinity, metaphor for a relational God, was also their model for community. Within God and authentic community there is mutuality, reciprocity, unity in diversity and the harmony of difference. The God vision is our social vision. A world of fragmentation, division, suffering and where we fear differences needs to recover a dynamic vision of God reflected in Celtic spirituality. This too will provide a spirituality of community essential for conflict transformation and peacebuilding.

Not only does the 'Breastplate' provide an image of God as divine community and therefore a model of community to be developed in social context, but it also offers a vision of God present in all things and the presence of all things in God. The God of the elements is invoked in sun, moon, fire, lightning, wind, sea, earth and rock. The mystical experience of God is possible in and through the elements of creation.

The great Christ stanza affirms Christ with, before, behind, in, beneath, above me. Christ is also on my right, left, when I lie down, when I sit down, when I arise, in the heart of every person who thinks of me, sees me and hears me, both friend and stranger. In Christian experience Christ discloses the presence of God. It is God we meet in everything and everyone, who in Celtic terms 'encircles' us. We encounter God in the human other, which opens up a different way of seeing others and relating to others. It is the vision of God which shapes an ethic for enemies as well as a peace-based community ethic.

Faith as a Journey

Migration for Celtic peoples was not just a necessity. For early Irish Christians it was integral to their experience of faith. They expressed their faith by travel – sea voyages that often set out without knowing where they would arrive. The best known, and one of the classic pieces of European literature, is the *Voyage of Brendan*. Early Celtic Christians were travellers for the sake of Christ. The journey was the great metaphor of faith, and the greatest journey was the journey inwards and into the liberating mystery of God. Here is a model of spirituality which never stands still, is always moving on, always questing, always going beyond the horizons. We do not arrive, there is no last word or rigidly fixed boundaries, together we journey on.

Stories suggest that Irish Christians travelled to Rome and Iceland to name but two places. If true, they are remarkable journeys. The long journey to Rome may have been made by some to claim Rome's ecclesial authority, or a purer pilgrimage may have been to a location made sacred by its past. An Irish poet did write to warn that there was little profit in a journey to Rome in return for all the trouble it was. Unless the God you seek travels with you and within you, God will not be found in Rome. It is the clue to the real motive which is not a journey into a Christian past, or to a site hallowed by many who have journeyed before. It is the journey deep within and above all into the unknown. It is the Christian scriptures' assessment of Abraham as a person of faith who travelled into the unknown. Most prefer to know and many to know with certitude, but neither the biblical nor the Celtic tradition experienced faith as that kind of knowing or certitude. For Paul, we walk by faith not by sight. Faith as a terminus puts an end to creativity, doing things, moving beyond horizons. We become static, stuck in traditionalism, more concerned with conservation than conversion, are content with a culture of death rather than ongoing rebirth. If the latter is the work of the Spirit, then we do all we can to close down the Spirit. The biblical God who is always making all things new becomes the God of the past, in the box and a God under our control.

With its core image of faith as pilgrimage or journey, always into the unknown, Celtic spirituality both lives and drives us on to larger visions of humanity, the world and Godself.

The Brendan voyage offers the classic metaphor for faith. The voyage itself is not a piece of authentic biography. It draws on earlier myths and is itself more mythological than biographical. Brendan himself was born in Tralee, Kerry and at an early age was fostered by Ita and then continued his education under Bishop Erc of Slane. Ita remained his spiritual guide and mentor. Brendan's dates are 486–575 CE. His feast day is still celebrated in west Kerry on 16 May, when pilgrims climb Mount Brandon, a more anglicised version of his name. Brendan is associated with monastic foundations at Annadown, Inishadroum, Ardfert and with Mount Brandon itself on the Dingle peninsula. His best-known foundation is Clonfert dated c.559 CE. Despite the lack of historicity Brendan is best known as the navigator from the epic tale of his voyage with thirty-three monks. The Book of Leinster claims thirty-six as a crew – the numbers varied depending on the telling!

The *Voyage of Brendan* was one of the most popular stories of the Middle Ages with 116 Latin manuscripts surviving and the myth being translated into various languages. The journey described in the voyage was proved possible when Tim Severin in the 1970s constructed a craft on traditional medieval lines and sailed to the Hebrides, Faroes, Iceland and Newfoundland. His story, published as *The Brendan Voyage*, suggested that Brendan's voyage was possible and that an Irish monk could have reached the Americas centuries before Columbus in the fifteenth century. The latter was more invasion than discovery with all the negative legacy of colonisation. If there is any kind of historical truth in Brendan's voyage, it was discovery and peaceful. But Severin's reconstructed journey only proves the possibility; the medieval story with all its popularity is still myth. Like all good myths it is true in the deeper sense.

The first appearance of the myth is around two hundred years after Brendan's death, and the earliest surviving manuscript dates from the ninth century: 'It is an abridged copy, so it is witness to at least one earlier manuscript, of uncertain date.'[1] The speculative guess is that it is the work of an exiled Irish monk of the late eighth century: 'The six earliest surviving manuscripts all come from the Rhineland or the Low Countries.'[2] Irish monks were known to have settled in this area so in all probability we have a story from an Irish author originating on the European mainland.

The author is aware of the Life of Brendan, and is familiar with Irish hagiography. He has also borrowed from earlier myths such as the Voyage of Bran and the Voyage of Maeldúin. Celtic literature has a propensity for odysseys and voyages into the unknown in search of fantastic islands in the western ocean. These were often islands 'ruled by fairy women, whose trees were hung with silver blossom and golden fruit. There was hunting and fighting and horse racing by day, feasting and music at night. All hurts were healed and no one ever grew old.'[3] Not surprisingly these pre-Christian myths were transposed by Celtic Christians into Paradise, though with a significant symbolic shift: 'So rich is early Irish mythology in tales of westward voyaging that it sometimes seems there might have been no one left behind to mind hearth and home.'[4] This richness made the symbolic shift all the more significant. On mainland Europe Christians looked for heaven in the sky above, the Irish looked beyond the sea horizon. The difference lies between a vertical and horizontal dimension to faith. The vertical emphasised the transcendence of God with the gaze upwards also emphasising the fallen earth. The horizontal has more to do with the immanence of God, the God within all things and therefore a God present in the world and an ethic that offers the vision of divinity in matter and the material as well as humanity. These theological visions have significant implications for creation and anthropology: 'What a surprise, then, to discover among the Irish Christians of Brendan's era a horizontal vision, a gazing into sea fog and rolling waves, a celebration of the here and now, a longing to pass across, not upward but westward.'[5]

The voyage westward is in itself the metaphor for the discovery of and encounter with God in this world rather than beyond it, an experience of divinity in the here and now rather than in the next world. The key metaphor lies in the myth of an adventurous sea voyage. The quest is for the Land of Promise of the Saints. Brendan chooses fourteen from his large community to prepare for the journey westwards. They were faced with a choice and made a response that catches the essence of faith. With one voice they said:

> Father, your will is ours too. Have we not left our parents and set aside our earthly inheritance in order to put ourselves completely in your hands? We are prepared to come with you, no matter what the consequences may be. We seek to do one thing alone – the will of God.[6]

It is in the journeying that the will of God is done, and so they set off on their sea adventure with forty days' supplies. Numbers in the Brendan myth, as in the Judeo-Christian scriptures, should not be taken literally. They too are symbolic.

Exhausted they rested on an island which then moved. They had landed on a whale! There are many experiences of nature with sea creatures and birds joining in the Eucharist and the various Offices. Monks and birds sing the Psalms, and the journeys are built into the Christian year and its festivals, Christmas, Easter and Pentecost.

They encountered people on the journey, sometimes shadow types. They found Judas Iscariot, sitting on a lonely rock, lashed by gales and tormented by demons trying to snatch him and eat him, his enduring punishment for betraying Christ. A hermit called Paul is also met, very old and clothed only in his long white beard. Paul told them he had been educated by Patrick who had directed him to this isolated place. For thirty years another had caught fish and fed Paul.

Whales, icebergs, volcanoes, sea creatures, sheep and birds as well as Judas and Paul plus other shadow figures, all male, offer an imaginative and exciting myth. The myth reaches its conclusion with Paul blessing the monks and their sailing southwards.

During the whole of Lent their little barque was carried hither and thither over the ocean and their only source of nourishment was the water they had brought with them from Paul the Hermit's isle. Yet they were quite content: one drink every three days perfectly satisfied their appetite for food and drink.[7]

On Holy Saturday they arrived on the Island of Birds and stayed there until Pentecost. The birds sent them on their way and eventually they reached an island surrounded by mist yet lit by a great light. Enveloped in darkness, it was an hour later before 'a brilliant light shone round them'.[8] A young man came to Brendan and said: 'Now, at last, you have found the land you have been seeking all these years. The Lord Jesus Christ did not allow you to find it immediately, because He wished to show you the richness of His wonders in the deep.'[9]

God is found in the journey with all its different experiences, not in standing still or remaining static. Faith is living with questions, not having neat answers. Faith is also travelling through the storms and wild seas, not immunity to suffering or difficulties nor in possessing certitudes. Faith is questioning and searching, an adventure at sea. For Brendan and his monks this was 'doing the will of God', and it is the spirituality that underpins our ethical commitment and the struggle in life to live ethically and faithfully.

Creativity and Imagination

Many of the recovered sources are in the form of poetry. The early Celtic people were wordsmiths or word artists. Poetry was an important way of expressing the deepest insights into life and God. Our modern world, the world of the Enlightenment, is heavily scientific, rational, verbal, analytical, scholastic. We are literalists and have been shaped as literalists. That is our biggest problem with reading and understanding the Bible. A word has only one meaning, a literal meaning. In the Celtic tradition poetry was often the medium. Early Irish Christians expressed their faith more in poetry than in propositional truths or doctrinal formulations. They produced more poetry and stories than scholastic theology. Metaphor, therefore, was prominent, and they knew the power of metaphorical language and symbols as well as profound myths to express the deepest realities and truths of God, life and the world. Art, such as the great High Crosses, was a highly visual expression of learning and prayer. A spirituality for the twenty-first century needs to recover creative imagination and the freedom of spirit that goes with it.

Art was especially significant for early Irish Christianity, and roots stretched far into other regions and earlier histories. Celtic artists had a love of pattern and their art was essentially imaginative. The La Tene period of 500 BCE to 100 CE, belonging to modern Switzerland, is believed to be the era of distinctively Celtic art.[10] There are:

fantastic combinations of animals and foliage, bizarre and unnatural images of natural objects, the flora and fauna of the East, lotuses, palms, lions, and the wild beasts of the desert, divorced from their realistic images and recombined in alien settings, sometimes wholly, sometimes only partially ... But how those Oriental elements came to the Northern Celts remains mysterious.[11]

The art forms did travel and there is evidence of this new art style as early as the third century BCE with decorated shields and sword scabbards found in Ulster. From the second century CE the decline of the Roman presence in Britain brought about closer relationships between Ireland and Scotland. This facilitated a 'common artistic development', and by the fifth century when an Irish kingdom was established in Argyll, Ireland and Scotland had a shared culture which produced metal work and jewellery of high artistic quality. An outstanding Irish example is the Tara Broach, a closed ring with a long pin, small but with highly decorative panels which include bird and beast heads.

Under the patronage of the church the eighth and ninth centuries produced splendid art work in Ireland:

> In particular, the church enriched its furnishings with objects which must have done worlds to arouse the imaginations of an illiterate congregation and to associate the church with beauty and splendour lacking in their homely domestic dwellings. Everything shone and gleamed.[12]

Chalices, croziers and gospel books were richly decorated. The most famous was the Ardagh Chalice, a large two-handled cup of beaten silver with dazzling decoration. The names of the apostles and animals are engraved.

This golden age of Irish religious culture saw the 'production of such extraordinary magnificent works as the *Book of Kells*, a masterpiece of European art ...'[13] The seventh and eighth centuries produced not only the *Book of Kells* but also the *Book of Durrow*. These were decorated gospels.

The *Book of Durrow* is probably the earlier of the two, perhaps from *c.*650 CE. The colours used are brown, yellow, red and green. There are influences in *Durrow* from the Syrian Christian tradition, reflecting close Irish connection with the eastern Christian faith traditions.

The *Book of Kells* is the great Irish treasure. It is not possible to be precise about its origin. It may have been begun on Iona and an early ninth-century date is probable. The Annals of Ulster do refer to it as being preserved in the church at Kells. In 1661 the manuscript was given to Trinity College, Dublin by Cromwell's son, and there it remains to the present. In *Kells* the beginning of each gospel has the symbol of the Evangelist. These symbol pages have borrowed from the Coptic tradition, another indication of the link between early Irish Christianity and the Egyptian desert tradition. Interlaced ribbon designs reflect Coptic influence while there are also spirals and fine twists.

The portraits of the four evangelists are iconic. An amusing but profound page depicts two rats eating a church wafer, watched by two cats. There are also two rats perched on the backs of the cats. It is humorous artwork but it also reflects the great vision from the Book of Isaiah, where the lion and lamb lie down together as the great symbol of God's peace. The margins of Kells often do show humorous and whimsical images:

The genius of Kells has the prodigal brilliance of easy mastery and unlimited resource. This profuse decoration, this prodigality of ornament, is scattered throughout the work, and is a perpetual delight as it appears, often with no apparent motive, in margins and inter-linear figures, bright, fantastic, graceful, throughout the text.[14]

Many have resorted to hyperbole when writing or speaking of the *Book of Kells*. There is much that is uncertain about it and much more that fascinates. Whatever Gerald of Wales was looking at in 1185 CE at Kildare, his words are appropriate for the *Book of Kells*, the book of the gospels prepared for use on the altar.

But if you take the trouble to look very closely, and penetrate with your eyes to the secrets of the artistry, you will notice such intricacies, so delicate and subtle, so close together, and well-knitted, so involved and bound together, and so fresh still in their colourings that you will not hesitate to declare that all these things must have been the result of the work, not of men, but of angels.[15]

Matching the splendour of the *Book of Kells* and the Ardagh Chalice are the Irish High Crosses. The Irish High Crosses are heavy stone sculptures mounted on a solid plinth: 'Remnants of well over two hundred crosses remain (an exact figure is hard to establish) and these probably represent less than half the number that once existed.'[16] They are rich in detail and were sculpted during two periods in medieval Irish history. Most belong to the ninth century, a time when Irish monastic learning was unparalleled in Europe. These were essentially scripture crosses rich in detail of biblical themes. The classic examples are to be found in Clonmacnoise, Monasterboice, Kells, Durrow, Armagh, Ardboe and the Moone cross in Co. Kildare. The other great period of High Cross sculpting was the twelfth century in places such as Roscrea, Cashel, Glendalough and Downpatrick. 'The idea of starting to create crosses again, after an interval of centuries, could even suggest an element of receiving past glories of the earlier groupings.'[17]

There is less emphasis in these later crosses on biblical themes. The triumphant rather than the suffering Christ is prominent, while the figure on the reverse side is probably the local monastic founder, suggesting popular pilgrimages. The presence of all these crosses on the sites of monasteries also suggests the involvement of church authorities. Scholarship and art were centred in the monasteries with 'the architectural glory of the monasteries being concentrated in the stone crosses, representatives in stone of the scriptural stories'.[18]

Who these stone masons were and how they were trained, or where they were based, are questions beyond our knowledge. It is thought that the same mason was at work on the Monasterboice, Clonmacnoise and Durrow crosses, given stylistic similarities. If so, he may have left his signature at Clonmacnoise, at least on a tomb slab. It is signed *Thuathal Saer* or Thuathal the craftsman.[19]

What we see today are large grey sculptures, but originally they were painted in bright colours, which must have been an impressive sight on approach. A painted replica stands in the interpretative centre at Clonmacnoise.

In a pre-literate age the crosses may have served as visual aids for Christian education. The crosses from the earlier era tell biblical stories often with stories from the Hebrew scriptures on the panels of one side with stories from the Christian gospels on the panels of the reverse side.

Clonmacnoise stands on a cross roads, or rather where rivers crossed, and with such a location it was one of the great cultural centres and schools of learning of early Celtic Ireland. The monastery was founded in 545 CE by Ciarán. Its most significant cross is the Cross of the Scriptures. Its first mention is in the Annals of the Four Masters in 957 CE, and a close examination of its panels reveals 'a rich biblical programme focussed on the Passion and post-Passion events'.[20] Intriguingly the plinth suggests from its incomplete inscription that the cross was erected by Colman when Flann was king, 879–916 CE. The panels of the west face depict: the seamless garment of Christ, the mocking scene at the trial, Christ in the tomb, the raised Christ, Christ entering Jerusalem, two women at the tomb and the resurrection. The crucifixion is in the ring or circle.

Monasterboice is one of the most important centres in Ireland for High Crosses. It was probably founded by Buite who died in 521 CE. The first cross one meets on entry to the site is Muiredach's Cross, so-called because of the inscription which tells that Muiredach erected the cross. On the head of the cross are Paul and Anthony, two Egyptian desert monks who mattered a great deal to early Irish Christians. At the top of the cross-piece Christ is portrayed in majesty, and one panel has the adoration of the Magi. On the west face there is the crucifix-ion and the ascension, Christ with Peter and Paul and the raised Christ. Towards the base is an inscription, with cats and animals present on the base itself.

The key theme appears to be Christ the King. The crucifixion scene portrays him as king of the

16.2 Muiredach's Cross, Monasterboice, Co. Louth.

16.3 The unique High Cross at Moone, Co. Kildare.

cosmos, the ring being supported by earth, ocean, sun and moon. Christ is Lord of the earth and cosmos through passion, death, resurrection and ascension, and a chalice at the feet of Paul and Anthony emphasises the Eucharist.

These crosses are not just splendid works of art in stone but also profound theology in stone, underlining the Christocentric theology and spirituality of the early Irish church. That monastery and king collaborated in the erection of these crosses, as seen in the inscription at Clonmacnoise, suggests not so much a church-state alliance, but a Christ above the king and an alternative model of power. The relationship between faith and politics was a critical one, and power was to be exercised as service not as domination.

One further significant cross is at Moone, Co. Kildare and probably on the site of a Columban monastery. It is a unique cross and the second tallest High Cross in Ireland. Biblical themes dominate the panels. On the base of the south side of the cross are the Flight into Egypt with Joseph pulling a 'reluctant, yet happy-looking, pony bearing the Virgin and Child'.[21] The other scene is the Miracle of the Loaves and Fishes. What is unique here are the two fishes which are not found in the Irish Sea but only in the River Nile. Along with Paul and Anthony, the Egyptian monks on the north side, there is the reminder of the roots of Celtic monasticism in the Egyptian desert tradition.

A key theme of the Moone Cross is the Help of God, especially through the stories of Isaac, Daniel, the Three Children, the Flight to Egypt, the hungry crowd and the placing of the Adam and Eve story back to back with the crucifixion: 'the latter was a consequence of the former'.[22] The theme recalls the Hebrew poet's experience. 'God is our refuge and strength, a very present help in trouble' (Psalm 46: 1). Or the eighth-century Celtic poet's insight in the *Breastplate*:

I bind unto myself today
The power of God to hold and lead …
I bind unto myself the name,
The strong name of the Trinity.

Beauty in Artwork

In the Tara Broach, Ardagh Chalice, *Book of Kells* and High Crosses, the creativity and imagination of Celtic Ireland comes to life and remains as a profound expression of its spirituality. There is a paradox in the rigorous asceticism of the penitentials on the one hand and the aesthetics of Celtic artwork on the other. The same spirit produced both. Perhaps the Celtic Christians saw no dichotomy between discipline and beauty. Spirituality and ethics require creativity and imagination to inspire and sustain. The spirituality of Celtic artwork lay in beauty and the profound appreciation of beauty. Early Irish Christians had the capacity for imagination and for thinking and creating through the imagination. Their artwork was produced to arouse the imaginations of the people, not just because they were pre-literate, but because imagination was and is an essential part of being human. These were people with a feeling for beauty.

It is an approach to spirituality and living, faith and ethics different from our Enlightenment rationalism, which is so verbal, logical and analytical. The Celts worked with an upside-down logic characteristic of other and older cultures. Angie Debo has written the definitive history of the Indians of the United States, definitive because it is from the Indian's point of view and from within their culture and worldview. Significantly she wrote: 'The Indian thought with his emotions instead of his mind. But his feelings were – and are – true. He had an integrity of spirit deeper than conscious reasoning.'[23]

Judging by Celtic artwork we may also say that Celtic Christians thought with their emotions and had an integrity of spirit deeper than rational thought or conscious reasoning. The feeling for beauty was an encounter with the divine. The experience of beauty was a disclosure moment when mystery came alive within and around them: 'Beauty does not linger, it only visits. Yet beauty's visitation affects us and invites us into its rhythm, it calls us to feel, think and act beautifully in the world: to create and live a life that awakens the Beautiful.'[24]

The encounter with beauty is transformative, we become more truly human and we feel, think and act differently. The spirituality of beauty 'quickly woven through our ordinary days'[25] arouses our imaginations to think with our feelings, go outside the box and respond more imaginatively to life's dilemmas and challenges. In other words, to live more ethically. Such is the call of beauty:

> I was with a friend out on Loch Corrib, the largest lake in the West of Ireland. It was a beautiful summer's day. Time had come to rest in the silence and stillness that presided there. The lake slept without a ripple. A grey-blue haze enfolded everything. There was no division any more between earth and sky. Reaching

16.4 The call of beauty at Glendalough, Co. Wicklow.

far into the distance, everything was suffused in a majestic blue light. The mountains of Connemara seemed like pile upon pile of delicate blue; you felt you could almost reach out your hand and pull them towards you. No object protruded anywhere. Trees, stones, fields and islands had forgotten themselves in the daze of blue. Then, suddenly, a harsh flutter as near us the lake surface split and a huge cormorant flew from inside the water and struck up into the air. Its ragged black wings and large awkward shape were like an eruption from the underworld. Against the finely woven blue everywhere its strange form fluttered and gleamed in absolute black. She had the place to herself. She was the one clear object to be seen. And as if to conceal the source as she soared, she left her shadow thistling the lake surface. This was an event of pure disclosure: a sudden epiphany from between the worlds. The strange beauty of the cormorant was a counterpoint to the dream-like delicacy of the lake and the landscape. Sometimes beauty is that unpredictable; a threshold we had never noticed opens, mystery comes alive around us and we realise how the earth is full of concealed beauty.[26]

Sustainable Justice

Without spirituality, living ethically is not sustainable. The passion for justice might damage our health. It is demanding and never-ending as well as often overwhelming. We may experience burn-out in the pursuit of justice. Motivational energy and an inner inspirational dynamic are essential so that our ethical vision and commitment can be renewed and sustained. The spirituality of early Irish Christianity offers such a dynamic energy – an inner presence and power. The vision of God enables us to live with our vulnerability and not to be dominated by the success syndrome or the pursuit and practice of dominating. We learn to experience vulnerability as gift.

Faith as a journey empowers us to live with life's tough questions and lures us to larger horizons of faith and integrity. We can even live beyond the boundaries of cultural convention and go well beyond the gatekeepers of identity and the *status quo* with its arrangements of élitist power. The metaphor of the sea voyage opens us up to constant discovery and encounter, ultimately with the unfathomable depths of God.

The encounter with beauty and the creation of beauty become for us the Invisible Embrace, and we learn to think with our feelings and imaginations, freeing us to find new solutions to both old and new problems. We are invited within the Invisible Embrace to new heights and depths of passion and creativity. Like the spirals of Celtic artwork, the journey between source and horizon never ends. We become alive and are intoxicated with a passion for justice.

Key Points from Chapter 16

❑ Spirituality is 'felt experience' and 'lived practice', in Christian terms our experience of God and our way of life in the social context.

❑ The primary early Celtic God-image, the high king of Heaven, was of the people, among the people and one of them.

❑ In the suffering of Jesus Celtic Christians encountered a suffering God who instilled a passion for justice.

❑ The primary metaphor for God in the Celtic Christian world was Trinity, a relational God, who revealed that authentic community is also relational. God vision was connected to social vision.

❑ The imagery of journey informs Celtic spirituality and missionary practice, reminding us that the faith journey is about movement, questing, pushing boundaries, going beyond horizons into the unknown in search of and in response to God's call to faith.

❑ The *Brendan Voyage*, possibly the work of a late eighth-century exiled Irish monk, is a myth about the faith journey.

❑ On mainland Europe Christians looked for heaven in the sky above, the Irish looked beyond the sea horizon. The former perspective revealed a transcendent idea of God, the latter an imminent vision, a God within all things, present in the world.

❑ The *Brendan Voyage* is about discovering and encountering God in the world, on the journey with all its different experiences, in the mix of suffering, uncertainty and moments of stillness.

❑ The early Celtic people expressed their deepest insights into life and God through poetry and art drawing on creativity and imagination.

❏ Art, such as the High Crosses, was a highly visual expression of learning and prayer.

❏ The *Book of Kells* (possibly early ninth century) and *Book of Durrow* (possibly 650 CE) are magnificent works of art that borrow symbols from the Egyptian desert tradition to decorate the gospels.

❏ The Irish High Crosses, which are heavy stone sculptures mounted on a solid plinth, belong mostly to the ninth century, when Irish monastic learning was unparalleled in Europe. They present biblical stories and themes in pictoral form.

❏ The crosses depict the theology and underline the spirituality of the early Irish church. Monastery and king collaborated in the erection of these crosses with political and religious power in the service of Christ, an alternative model of power.

❏ The same spirituality produced the rigorous asceticism of the Penitentials and the ascetics of Celtic artwork, revealing that Celtic Christians saw no division between discipline and beauty and that both created conditions for encounter with the divine.

❏ Like the Amerindians of the USA, Celtic Christians thought with their emotions and in the encounter with beauty became more truly human and lived more ethically.

❏ The Celts realised the importance of deep spirituality, of inner presence and power to live ethically and pursue justice.

❏ Thinking with our feelings and imaginations frees us to look outside the box and find real solutions to old and new problems.

Test Questions

❏ Discuss the importance of the journey metaphor for faith in the Celtic Christian tradition.

❏ Critically evaluate the view that a recovery of Celtic creativity and imagination is essential for ethical living in the contemporary world.

Bibliography

Books marked with an asterisk (*) indicate primary sources of material, or in some cases contain much direct use of primary Irish materials.

Amstutz, Mark R., *The Healing of the Nations: The Promise and Limits of Political Forgiveness* (Lanham, MD: Rowan & Littlefield, 2005).

Augsburger, David W., *Hate-Work: Working Through the Pain and Pleasures of Hate* (Louisville, KY: Westminster John Knox Press, 2004).

Bardsley, Warren, *Against the Tide: The Story of Adamnan of Iona* (Glasgow: Wild Goose Publications, 2006).

Bew, Paul, *Ireland: The Politics of Enmity 1789–2006* (Oxford: Oxford University Press, 2007).

*Bieler, Ludwig, *The Irish Penitentials* (Dublin: Institute for Advanced Studies, 1975).

Bitel, Lisa M., *Isle of the Saints: Monastic Settlement and Christian Community in Early Ireland* (Cork: Cork University Press, 1990).

_____, Land of Women: Tales of Sex and Gender from Early Ireland (New York: Cornell University Press, 1996).

Borg, Marcus J., (Pennsylvania: Trinity Press International, 1998).

_____, *Jesus: Uncovering the Life, Teachings and Relevance of a Religious Revolutionary* (San Francisco: HarperCollins, 2006).

Bradshaw, Brendan and Dáire Keogh (eds), *Christianity in Ireland: Revisiting the Story* (Dublin: Columba Press, 2002).

Brueggemann, Walter, *Reverberations of Faith: A Theological Handbook of Old Testament Themes* (Louisville, KY: Westminster John Knox Press, 2002).

_____, Peace (St Louis: Chalice Press, 2001).

Cahill, Thomas, *How the Irish Saved Civilization* (New York: Doubleday, 1995).

*Carey, John, *King of Mysteries: Early Irish Religious Writings* (Dublin: Four Courts Press, 2000).

Chadwick, Nora K., *The Age of the Saints in the Early Celtic Church* (London: Oxford University Press, 1961).

_____, *The Celts* (London: Penguin, 1971).

Cherici, Peter, *Celtic Sexuality: Power, Paradigms and Passion* (London, Duckworth, 1995).

Condren, Mary, *The Serpent and the Goddess: Women, Religion and Power in Celtic Ireland* (San Francisco: Harper & Row, 1989).

Conn, Eileen and James Stewart (eds), *Visions of Creation* (Alresford: Godsfield Press, 1995).

Crossan, John Dominic, *God and Empire: Jesus Against Rome Then and Now* (San Francisco: HarperCollins, 2007).

*Davies, Oliver (trans), *Celtic Spirituality: Classics of Western Spirituality* (New York: Paulist Press, 1999).

Debo, Angie, *A History of the Indians of the Und States* (London: The Folio Society, 2003).

Delaney, Frank, *The Celts* (London: Grafton Books, 1989).

De La Torre, Miguel A., *Doing Christian Ethics from the Margins* (Maryknoll, NY: Orbis Books, 2004).

*De Paor, Liam, *St Patrick's World* (Dublin: Four Courts Press, 1996).

*Dillon, Myles and Nora Chadwick, *The Celtic Realms: The History and Culture of the Celtic Peoples from Pre-History to the Norman Invasion* (London: Phoenix Press, 2000).

Donnelly, James (ed.), *Encyclopedia of Irish History and Culture*, vol. 1 (Farmington Hill, MI: Thompson Gale, 2004).

Duchrow, Ulrich and Gerhard Liedke, *Shalom: Biblical Perspectives on Creation, Justice and Peace* (Geneva: World Council of Churches Publications, 1987).

Ehrman, Bart D., *Peter, Paul and Mary Magdalene: The Followers of Jesus in History and Legend* (Oxford: Oxford University Press, 2006).

_____, *Whose Word Is It? The Story Behind Who Changed the New Testament and Why* (New York: Continuum, 2006).

Elliott, Marianne, *The Catholics of Ulster: A History* (London: Allen Lane The Penguin Press, 2000).

Ellis, Peter Berresford, *Celtic Women: Women in Celtic Society and Literature* (London: Constable, 1995).

English, Richard, *Irish Freedom: The History of Nationalism in Ireland* (London: Macmillan, 2006).

Farley, Margaret A. and Serene Jones (eds), *Liberating Eschatology: Essays in Honour of Letty M Russell* (Louisville, KY: Westminster John Knox Press, 1999).

Farmer, D. H. (ed.), *The Age of Bede* (London: Penguin, 1998).

Finlay, Ian, *Columba* (Glasgow: Richard Drew Publishing, 1990).

Freeman, Philip, *St Patrick of Ireland: A Biography* (New York: Simon & Schuster, 2005).

Friedman, Richard Elliott, *Who Wrote the Bible?* (San Francisco: HarperCollins, 1997 edn).

*Gantz, Jeffrey, *Early Irish Myths and Sagas* (London: Penguin, 1981).

Grassi, Joseph A., *Informing the Future: Social Justice in the New Testament* (New York: Paulist Press, 2003).

_____, *Peace on Earth: Roots and Practices from Luke's Gospel* (Minnesota: Liturgical Press, 2004).

Green, Miranda J. (ed.), *The Celtic World* (London: Routledge, 1995).

Hall, Douglas John, *The Stewardship of Life in the Kingdom of Death* (Grand Rapids: Eerdmans, 1985).

*Harbinson, Peter, *Irish High Crosses: With the Figure Sculptures Explained* (Drogheda: Boyne Valley Honey Co., 1994).

Harrington, Christina, *Women in a Celtic Church: Ireland 450–1150* (Oxford University Press, 2002).

Herbert, Marie, *Iona, Kells and Derry: The History and Hagiography of the Monastic Families of Columba* (Dublin: Four Courts Press, 1996).

Horsley, Richard A. and Neil Asher Silberman, *The Message and the Kingdom: How Jesus and Paul Ignited a Revolution and Transformed the Ancient World* (New York: Grosset/Putnam, 1997).

Kinealy, Christine, *A New History of Ireland* (Gloucestershire: Sutton Publishing, 2004).

*Kinsella, Thomas (trans.), *The Táin* (Oxford: Oxford University Press, 1970).

*Low, Mary, *Celtic Christianity and Nature: Early Irish and Hebridean Traditions*, (Edinburgh: Edinburgh University Press, 1996).

McDonagh, Seán, *Climate Change: The Challenge To Us All* (Dublin: Columba Press, 2007).

McEvoy, Kieran, *Making Peace with the Past: Options for Truth Recovery Regarding the Conflict In and About Northern Ireland* (Belfast: Healing Through Remembering, 2006).

McMaster, Johnston, *The Future Returns: A Journey with Columba and Augustine of Canterbury* (Belfast: Corrymeela Press, 1997).

_____, *We Believe In The Forgiveness of Sins: Cheap Rhetoric Or A Community Ethic For Healing* (unpublished paper, 2001).

*Meehan, Bernard, *The Book of Kells: An Illustrated Introduction to the Manuscript in Trinity College Dublin* (London: Thames & Hudson, 1994).

Menzies, Lucy, *St Columba of Iona* (Felinfach: J. M. F. Books Reprint, 1992).

Meyers, Carol L., Toni Craven and Ross Shepard Kraemer (eds), *Women in Scripture* (Michigan: Eerdmans, 2000).

Meyers, Chad, *Binding the Strong Man: A Political Reading of Mark's Story of Jesus* (New York: Orbis Books, 1995 edn).

Nardoni, Enrique, *Rise Up, O Judge: A Study of Justice in the Biblical World* (Peabody, MA: Hendrickson, 2004).

Ní Dhonnchadha, Máirín, *Adamnan at Birr* (Dublin: Four Courts Press, 2001).

Ó Cróinín, Dáibhí, *Early Medieval Ireland: 400–1200* (New York: Longman, 1995).

O'Donahue, John, *Divine Beauty: The Invisible Embrace* (London: Bantam Books, 2003).

O'Donoghue, Noel Dermot, *Aristocracy of Soul: Patrick of Ireland* (London: Darton, Longman & Todd, 1987).

_____, *The Angels Keep Their Ancient Places* (Edinburgh: T & T Clarke, 2001).

Ó Dunn, Seán, *The Rites of Brigid: Goddess and Saint* (Dublin: Columba Press, 2005).

*Ó hÓgáin, Dáithí, *The Lore of Ireland: An Encyclopaedia of Myth, Legend and Romance* (Woodbridge, Suffolk: Boydell Press, 2006).

O'Loughlin, Thomas, *Celtic Theology: Humanity, World and God in Early Irish Writings* (London: Continuum, 2000).

_____, *Journeys on the Edges* (London: Darton, Longman & Todd, 2000).

*_____, *Discovering Saint Patrick* (London: Darton, Longman & Todd, 2005).

*Ó Maidín, Uinseann, *The Celtic Monk: Rules and Writings of Early Irish Monks*, (Michigan: Cistercian Publications, 1996).

Onfray, Michel, *Atheist Manifesto: The Case Against Christianity, Judaism and Islam* (New York: Arcade Publishing, 2005).

Ó Riordáin, John J., *Early Irish Saints* (Dublin: Columba Press, 2001).

O'Toole, Fintan, *The Irish Times, Weekend Review* (3 February 2007).

Raymo, Chet, *Climbing Brandon: Science and Faith on Ireland's Holy Mountain* (Dingle: Brandon, 2004).

*Rees, B. R., *Pelagius: Life and Letters* (Woodbridge, Suffolk: Boydell Press, 1998).

Richter, Michael, *Medieval Ireland: The Enduring Tradition* (Dublin: Gill & Macmillan, 1988).

Sampson, Fay, *Visions and Voyages: The Story of Our Celtic Heritage* (London: Triangle Books, 1998).

Sellner, Edward C., *Wisdom of the Celtic Saints* (Notre Dame, IN: Ave Maria Press, 1993).

_____, *The Celtic Soul Friend* (Notre Dame, IN: Ave Maria Press, 2002).

_____, *Stories of the Celtic Soul Friends* (New York: Paulist Press, 2004)

*Sharpe, Richard (trans.), *Adamnan of Iona: Life of St Columba* (London: Penguin, 1995).

Shriver, Donald W., *An Ethic for Enemies: Forgiveness in Politics* (Oxford: Oxford University Press, 1995).

Simpson, Ray, *Soul Friendship: Celtic Insights into Spiritual Mentoring* (London: Hodder & Stoughton, 1999).

Stalley, Roger, *Irish High Crosses* (Dublin: Town House & Country House, 1996).

Stassen, Glen H. and David P. Gushee, *Kingdom Ethics: Following Jesus in Contemporary Context* (Downers Grove, IL: Inter-Varsity Press, 2003).

*Stokes, Whitley, *Lives of the Saints from the Book of Lismore* (Felinfach: Llanerch Publishers, 1995, facsimile).

Thompson, J. Milburn, *Justice and Peace: A Christian Primer* (Maryknoll, NY: Orbis Books, 2003).

Torjesen, Karen Jo, *When Women Were Priests: Women's Leadership in the Early Church and the Scandal of Their Subordination in the Rise of Christianity* (San Francisco: Harper, 1995).

Van de Weyer, Robert, *Celtic Fire: An Anthology of Celtic Christian Literature* (London: Longman & Todd, 1990).

_____, *The Letters of Pelagius: Celtic Soul Friend* (Evesham: Arthur James, 1995).

Walsh, J. R., *Religion: The Irish Experience* (Dublin: Veritas, 2003).

Watt, John, *The Church in Medieval Ireland* (Dublin: University College Dublin, 1998).

Welsh, Frank, *The Four Nations: A History of the United Kingdom* (London: HarperCollins, 2003).

Woods, Richard J., *The Spirituality of the Celtic Saints* (Maryknoll, NY: Orbis Books, 2000).

References

Chapter 1

1 Fintan O'Toole, *The Irish Times, Weekend Review*, 3 February 2007.
2 Frank Delaney, *The Celts* (London: Grafton Books, 1986), pp. 31–2.
3 Miranda J. Green (ed,), *The Celtic World* (London: Routledge, 1995), Introduction, p. 6.
4 Barry Raftery, "Ireland: A World Without Romans", in Green, op cit., p. 640.
5 O'Toole, op. cit.
6 Raftery, op. cit., pp. 640–1.
7 Michael Richter, *Medieval Ireland: The Enduring Tradition* (Dublin: Gill & Macmillan, 1988), p. 10.
8 Raftery, op. cit., p. 652.
9 Marianne Elliott, *The Catholics of Ulster: A History* (London: Allen Lane The Penguin Press, 2000), p. 4.
10 Richard English, *Irish Freedom: The History of Nationalism in Ireland* (London: Macmillan, 2006), p. 26.
11 Myles Dillon and Nora Chadwick, *The Celtic Realms: The History and Culture of the Celtic Peoples from Prehistory to the Norman Invasion* (London: Phoenix Press, 2000 edn), p. 30.
12 Ibid., p. 95.
13 Nora Chadwick, *The Celts* (London: Penguin, 1971), p. 85.
14 Richter, op. cit., p. 13.
15 The full story is told in Thomas Kinsella (trans.), *The Táin* (Oxford: Oxford University Press, 1970). An excellent summary version is related by Dáithí Ó hÓgáin, *The Lore of Ireland: An Encyclopaedia of Myth, Legend and Romance* (Woodbridge, Suffolk: Boydell Press, 2006), pp. 488–92.
16 Richter, op. cit., p. 17.
17 Helpful examples of the Irish legal system are found in Dillon and Chadwick, op. cit., pp. 98–102.
18 James Donnelly (ed.), *Encyclopaedia of Irish History and Culture* (USA: Thompson Gale, 2004), vol. 1, p. 59. There are comprehensive entries on political, social, legal and religious systems and life in Celtic Ireland in vol. 1.
19 Richter, op. cit., p. 22.
20 Lisa M. Bitel, *Isle of the Saints: Monastic Settlements and Christian Community in Early Ireland* (Cork: Cork University Press, 1990), p. 4.
21 Richter, op. cit., p. 23.
22 Bitel, op. cit., p. 6.

Chapter 2

1 Frank Delaney, *The Celts* (London: Grafton Books, 1989), pp. 78–9.
2 Dáithí Ó hÓgáin, *The Lore of Ireland: An Encyclopaedia of Myth, Legend and Romance* (Woodbridge, Suffolk: Boydell Press , 2006), pp. 366–70.
3 See the story on Danu, ibid., pp. 159–60.

4   Ibid., pp. 151–4.
5   Myles Dillon and Nora Chadwick, *The Celtic Realms: The History and Culture of the Celtic Peoples from Pre-History to the Norman Invasion* (London: Phoenix Press, 2000 edn), p. 145.
6   Nora Chadwick, *The Celts* (London: Penguin, 1971), p. 181.
7   Jeffrey Gantz, *Early Irish Myths and Sagas* (London: Penguin, 1981), p. 15.
8   Chadwick, op. cit., p. 182.
9   Nora Chadwick, *The Age of the Saints in the Early Celtic Church* (London: Oxford University Press, 1961), pp. 12–13.
10   Dáibhí Ó Cróinín, *Early Medieval Ireland, 400–1200* (London: Longman, 1995), pp. 2–3.
11   Ibid., p. 22.
12   For helpful summaries of the authentic Patrick and Patrick the legend see Ó Cróinín pp. 23–7. Also Michael Richter, *Medieval Ireland: The Enduring Tradition* (Dublin: Gill & Macmillan, 1988), pp. 43–9; Chadwick, op. cit., pp. 17–35; Brendan Bradshaw and Dáire Keogh (eds), *Christianity in Ireland: Revisiting the Story* (Dublin: Columba Press, 2002), pp. 11–20.
13   Philip Freeman, *St Patrick of Ireland: A Biography* (New York: Simon & Schuster, 2005), p. 155.
14   J. R. Walsh, *Religion: The Irish Experience* (Dublin: Veritas, 2003), p. 48.
15   Ibid., quoted from J. F. Kenny, p. 67.
16   Alfred P. Smyth, in Brendan Bradshaw and Daire Keogh (eds), *Christianity in Ireland: Revisiting the Story* (Dublin: Columba Press, 2002), p. 18. Smyth's article is on 'Bishop Patrick and the Earliest Christian Mission'.
17   Freeman, op. cit., p. 160.
18   Smyth, 'Bishop Patrick', in Bradshaw and Keogh (eds), op. cit., p. 19.
19   Smyth, 'Early Irish Monasticism', in Bradshaw and Keogh (eds), op. cit., p. 26.
20   Smyth, ibid., p. 25.
21   Ibid., p. 28.
22   John Watt, *The Church in Medieval Ireland* (Dublin: University College Dublin, 1998), p. 3.
23   Ibid., p. 7.
24   Ibid., p. 7.
25   Ibid., p. 11.
26   Ibid., p. 17.
27   Ibid., p. 17.
28   Ibid., p. 31.
29   John Watt, 'The Irish Church in the Middle Ages', in Bradshaw and Keogh (eds), op. cit., p. 48.

Chapter 3

1   Dáibhí Ó Cróinín, *Early Medieval Ireland 400–1200* (London: Longman, 1995), p. 23.
2   Ibid., p. 23.
3   Dáithí Ó hÓgáin, *The Lore of Ireland: An Encyclopaedia of Myth, Legend and Romance* (Woodbridge, Suffolk: Boydell Press, 2006), p. 418.
4   Paragraph 24 of the Confession. The text used and references throughout this chapter are from the translation in Thomas O'Loughlin, *Discovering Saint Patrick* (London: Darton, Longman & Todd, 2005), p. 155.
5   Noel Dermot O'Donoghue, *Aristocracy of Soul: Patrick of Ireland* (London: Darton, Longman & Todd, 1987), p. 25.
6   Ibid., p. 29.
7   O'Loughlin, op. cit., p. 51.
8   Ibid., see footnote biblical reference 13, p. 143.
9   Ibid., p. 53.
10   O'Loughlin, op. cit., see footnote 75, pp. 179–80.
11   Philip Freeman, *St Patrick of Ireland* (New York: Simon & Schuster, 2004), p. 120.

12   O'Loughlin, op. cit., p. 77.

13   Jurgen Moltmann, in Margaret A. Farley and Serene Jones (eds), *Liberating Eschatology: Essays in Honour of Letty M. Russell* (Louisville: Westminster John Knox Press, 1999), p. 203.

14   Ibid., p. 205.

Chapter 4

1   A helpful and more detailed explanation of the historical factors and sources of hagiographies is found in Edward Sellner, *The Celtic Soul Friend* (Notre Dame, IN: Ave Maria Press, 2002), pp. 151–62.

2   Ibid., p. 155.

3   Ibid., p. 157.

4   Michel Onfray, *Atheist Manifesto: The Case Against Christianity, Judaism and Islam* (New York: Arcade Publishing, 2005), p. 8.

5   Jeffrey Gantz, *Early Irish Myths and Sagas* (London: Penguin, 1981), p. 19.

6   Quoted in Sellner, op. cit., p. 159.

7   Ibid., p. 160.

8   Anne Ross, 'Ritual and the Druids', in Miranda J. Green (ed.), *The Celtic World* (London: Routledge, 1995), p. 436.

9   Daithí Ó hÓgáin, *The Lore of Ireland: An Encyclopaedia of Myth, Legend and Romann* (Woodbridge, Suffolk: Boydell Press, 2006), p. 50.

10   Mary Condren, *The Serpent and the Goddess: Women, Religion and Power in Celtic Ireland* (San Francisco: Harper & Row, 1989), p. 56.

11   Ó hÓgáin, op. cit., p. 51.

12   Condren, op. cit., p. 58.

13   Ibid., p. 61.

14   Ibid., p. 66.

15   The English text is found in Oliver Davies (trans.), *Celtic Spirituality: Classics of Western Spirituality* (New York: Paulist Press, 1999), p. 121.

16   Liam De Paor, *St Patrick's World* (Dublin: Four Courts Press, 1996), p. 208. The text of the Life is from this translation by De Paor.

17   The text is found in Oliver Davies (trans.), op. cit., pp. 140–54.

18   De Paor, op. cit., p. 211.

19   Ibid., p. 213.

20   Ibid., p. 223.

21   Ibid., p. 211.

22   Ibid., p. 212.

23   Ibid., p. 214.

24   Ibid., pp. 214–15.

25   Sellner, op. cit., p. 156.

26   Condren, op. cit., p. 75.

27   Oliver Davies (trans.), op. cit., p. 145. MacCaille giving Brigid the veil is also in ibid., p. 144 and De Paor, op. cit., p. 209.

28   Lisa M. Bitel, *Land of Women: Tales of Sex and Gender from Early Ireland* (New York: Cornell University Press, 1996), p. 192.

29   De Paor, op. cit., p. 208.

30   Edward C. Sellner, *Wisdom of the Celtic Saints* (Notre Dame, IN: Ave Maria Press, 1993), p. 73.

31   Ibid., p. 73.

Chapter 5

1   The contents of this chapter are mainly drawn from an earlier publication with permission. Johnston McMaster, *The Future Returns: A Journey with Columba and Augustine of Canterbury*

(Belfast: Corrymeela Press, 1997), pp. 16–25, 48–50.

2   Adamnan of Iona (Richard Sharpe, trans.), *Life of St Columba* (London: Penguin, 1995), pp. 205–6. Maire Herbert draws attention to the cautious opinion regarding the value of Adamnan's Life which is 'less for the history of Columba than for his own ideas, and for the circumstances of his own time'. She adds that 'like all hagiographical works, the VITE is a source of information about the period in which it was completed'; *Iona, Kells and Derry: The History and Hagiography of the Monastic Families of Columba* (Dublin: Four Courts Press, 1996), p. 13.

3   Ian Finlay, *Columba* (Glasgow: Richard Drew Publishing, 1990), p. 50.

4   Lucy Menzies, *St Columba of Iona* (Felinfach: J. M. F. Books Reprint, 1992), p. 3.

5   Finlay, op. cit., pp. 53–4.

6   Menzies, op. cit., p. 4.

7   Finlay, op. cit., p. 55.

8   Menzies, op. cit., p. 15.

9   Ibid., p. 25.

10 Ibid., p. 29.

11 Ibid., p. 135.

12 The Convention is dealt with by Menzies, pp. 134–41 and Finlay, pp. 152–63.

13 Menzies, op. cit., p. 139.

14 Finlay, op. cit., p. 160.

15 Menzies, op. cit., p. 145.

16 Ibid., p. 191. Menzies devotes a complete chapter to 'The Last Years', pp. 178–95. Finlay also writes of 'The Last Days of Columba', pp. 179–90. Adamnan ends his Life with 'How our patron St Columba passed to the Lord' in Sharpe's translation, pp. 225–34.

17 Ibid., p. 193.

Chapter 6

1   Myles Dillon and Nora Chadwick, *The Celtic Realms: The History and Culture of the Celtic Peoples from Pre-History to the Norman Invasion* (London: Phoenix Press, 2000), p. 189.

2   John J. Ó Riordáin, *Early Irish Saints* (Dublin: Columba Press, 2001), p. 81.

3   Dillon and Chadwick, op. cit., p. 189.

4   Edward C. Sellner, *Wisdom of the Celtic Saints* (Notre Dame, IN: Ave Maria Press, 1993) p. 23.

5   Ibid., p. 23.

6   Michael Richter, *Medieval Ireland: The Enduring Tradition* (Dublin: Gill & Macmillan, 1988), p. 57.

7   Richard J. Woods, *The Spirituality of the Celtic Saints* (New York: Orbis Books, 2000), p. 133.

8   Quoted in Richter, op. cit., p. 57.

9   Quoted in Woods, op. cit., pp. 132–3.

10 Ó Riordáin, op. cit., p. 85.

11 Ibid., p. 85.

12 Oliver Davies, *Celtic Spirituality* (New York: Paulist Press, 1999), p. 358. The full text of Sermon Eleven is on pp. 357–9. The texts of Sermon Five, Eight, Eleven and Thirteen are found on pp. 353–62.

13 Ibid., p. 358.

14 Ibid., p. 358.

15 Ibid., p. 358.

16 Ibid., pp. 358–9.

17 Ibid., p. 357.

18 Ibid., p. 359.

19 Ibid., p. 354.

20 Ibid., p. 354.

21   Ibid., p. 355.
22   Ibid., p. 355.
23   Ibid., pp. 355–6.
24   Ibid., p. 355.
25   James S. Donnelly (ed.), *Encyclopaedia of Irish History and Culture* (USA: Thompson Gale, 2004), p. 778. The translation of the Boatsong is by James Carney, 1967.
26   Richter, op. cit., p. 58.

Chapter 7
1   Richard Elliott Friedman, *Who Wrote the Bible?* (San Francisco: HarperCollins, 1997 edn). The sex of the authors is dealt with on pp. 85–6.
2   Ibid., p. 86.
3   Lisa M. Bitel, *Land of Women: Tales of Sex and Gender from Early Ireland* (New York: Cornell University Press, 1996), p. 103.
4   Lisa M. Bitel, *Isle of the Saints: Monastic Settlements and Christian Community in Early Ireland* (Cork: Cork University Press, 1990), p. 163.
5   Richard J. Woods, *The Spirituality of the Celtic Saints* (Maryknoll, NY: Orbis Books, 2000), p. 85.
6   Bitel, *Land of Women*, op. cit., p. 100.
7   Christina Harrington, *Women in a Celtic Church: Ireland 450–1150* (Oxford: Oxford University Press, 2002), p. 234.
8   Ibid., p. 100.
9   Ibid., p. 237.
10   Edward C. Sellner, *Wisdom of the Celtic Saint* (Notre Dame, IN: Ave Maria Press, 1993), p. 154.
11   Edward C. Sellner, *The Celtic Soul Friend* (Notre Dame, IN: Ave Maria Press, 2002), p. 202.
12   Ibid., p. 204.
13   Mary Condren, *The Serpent and the Goddess: Women, Religion and Power in Celtic Ireland* (New York: Harper & Row, 1989), p. 101.
14   Bitel, *Land of Women*, op. cit., p. 175.
15   Harrington, op. cit., p. 218.
16   Ibid., p. 218.
17   Ibid., p. 219.
18   Condren, op. cit., p. 101.
19   Ibid., p. 102.
20   Ibid., p. 102.
21   Sellner, *Wisdom*, op. cit., pp. 198–9.
22   Sellner, *Celtic Soul Friend*, op. cit., p. 166.
23   Sellner, *Wisdom*, op. cit., p. 198.
24   Condren, op. cit., p. 102.
25   Ibid., p. 102.
26   Ibid., p. 103.
27   The dialogue is found in The Life of Senan, in Whitley Stokes (trans.), *Lives of the Saints From the Book of Lismore* (Felinfach: Llanerch Publishers, 1995, facsimile), pp. 219–20. Also in Sellner, *Wisdom*, op. cit., pp. 77–8.
28   Harrington, op. cit., p. 243.
29   Ibid., pp. 243–4.
30   Bitel, *Land of Women*, op. cit., p. 176.

Chapter 8
1   Edward C. Sellner, *The Celtic Soul Friend* (Notre Dame, IN: Ave Maria Press, 2002), p. 107.
2   Dáibhí Ó Cróinín, *Early Medieval Ireland: 400–1200* (New York: Longman, 1995), pp.

208–9.

3   Ibid., p. 209.

4   Ibid., p. 209.

5   Bart D. Ehrman, *Peter, Paul and Mary Magdalene: The Followers of Jesus in History and Legend* (Oxford: Oxford University Press, 2006), p. xv.

6   Walter Brueggemann, *Reverberations of Faith: A Theological Handbook of Old Testament Themes* (Louisville, KY: Westminster John Knox Press, 2002), p. 98. Much of this section is based on Brueggemann's reflections on the theme of holiness in the Hebrew scriptures.

7   Marcus J. Borg, *Conflict, Holiness and Politics in the Teachings of Jesus* (Pennsylvania: Trinity Press International, 1998), p. 8. This perspective on compassion is central to Borg's book especially Chapters 4–7, pp. 88–212.

8   Ibid., p. 137.

9   Ibid., p. 137.

10   Ibid., p. 151.

11   Thomas O'Loughlin, *Discovering Saint Patrick* (London: Darton, Longman & Todd, 2005), p. 115.

12   Ibid., p. 192. Muirchú's Life is given in full by O'Loughlin, pp. 192–229.

13   Ibid., pp. 115–16.

14   Dáithí Ó hÓgáin, *The Lore of Ireland: An Encyclopaedia of Myth, Legend and Romance* (Woodbridge, Suffolk: Boydell Press, 2006), p. 43. The rich store of motifs with which hagiographers punctuate their texts are identified in this entry on 'saints', pp. 442–6.

15   Richard Sharpe (trans.), *Adamnan of Iona: The Life of St Columba* (London: Penguin, 1995), p. 110.

16   Ian Finlay, *Columba* (Glasgow: Richard Drew Publishing, 1990), p. 173.

17   Sharpe (trans.), op. cit., p. 59 from Introduction.

18   Ibid., p. 167.

19   Ó hÓgáin, op. cit., p. 443.

20   Mary Condren, *The Serpent and the Goddess: Women, Religion and Power in Celtic Ireland* (San Francisco: Harper & Row, 1989), p. 63.

21   Whitley Stokes, *Lives of the Saints from the Book of Lismore* (Felinfach: Llanerch Publishers, 1995, facsimile), p. 184.

22   Ibid., p. 199.

23   Ibid., p. 171.

24   Liam De Paor, *St Patrick's World* (Dublin: Four Courts Press, 1996), pp. 214–16.

25   Sharpe (trans.), op. cit., p. 227.

26   Ó hÓgáin, op. cit., p. 420.

27   Ibid., p. 421.

28   Sharpe (trans.), op. cit., p. 176.

Chapter 9

1   Lisa M. Bitel, *Isle of Saints: Monastic Settlement and Christian Community in Early Ireland* (Cork: Cork University Press, 1990), p. 196.

2   Ibid., p. 197.

3   Ibid., p. 201.

4   Ibid., p. 202.

5   Ludwig Bieler, *The Irish Penitentials* (Dublin: Institute for Advanced Studies, 1975 edn), pp. 173–5.

6   Seán Ó Duinn, *The Rites of Brigid: Goddess and Saint* (Dublin: Columba Press, 2005), p. 71.

7   Robert Van de Weyer, *Celtic Fire: An Anthology of Celtic Christian Literature* (London: Longman & Todd, 1990), p. 20.

8   Whitley Stokes, *Lives of the Saints from the Book of Lismore* (Felinfach: Llanerch Publishers, 1995, facsimile), pp. 187–8.

9   Ibid., p. 188.
10   John Carey, *King of Mysteries: Early Irish Religious Writings* (Dublin: Four Courts Press, 2000). The hymn with commentary is found on pp. 162–79.
11   Bitel, op cit. The references to Kevin, Maedoc and Ciarán are all found in Bitel, p. 198.
12   Uinseann Ó Maidín, *The Celtic Monk: Rules and Writings of Early Irish Monks* (Michigan: Cistercian Publications, 1996). The full text is on pp. 161–9.

Chapter 10

1   Kieran McEvoy, *Making Peace with the Past: Options for Truth Recovery Regarding the Conflict In and About Northern Ireland* (Belfast: Healing Through Remembering, 2006).
2   Mark R. Amstutz, *The Healing of the Nations: The Promise and Limits of Political Forgiveness* (Lanham, MD: Rowan & Littlefield, 2005), p. 65.
3   Pope John Paul II quoted in Amstutz, ibid., p. 65.
4   These two models are dealt with in Johnston McMaster, *We Believe in the Forgiveness of Sins: Cheap Rhetoric or a Community Ethic for Healing* (unpublished paper, 2001). 'The Jesus Model – Radical Love of Enemies' which is included here is from the same paper.
5   Ched Meyers, *Binding the Strong Man: A Political Reading of Mark's Story of Jesus* (New York: Orbis Books, 1995 edn), p. 39.
6   Richard A. Horsley and Neil Asher Silberman, *The Message and the Kingdom: How Jesus and Paul Ignited a Revolution and Transformed the Ancient World* (New York: Grosset/Putnam, 1997), p. 42.
7   Horsely quoted in Donald W. Shriver, *An Ethic of Forgiveness: Forgiveness in Politics* (Oxford: Oxford University Press, 1995), p. 36.
8   Hannah Arandt quoted in Shriver, ibid., p 55.
9   Ibid., p. 38.
10   Ludwig Bieler, *The Irish Penitentials* (Dublin: Institute for Advanced Studies, 1975), p. 129.
11   Ibid., p. 107.
12   Ibid., p. 85.
13   Ibid., p. 75.
14   Edward C. Sellner, *The Celtic Soul Friend* (Notre Dame, IN: Ave Maria Press, 2002), p. 183.
15   Ibid., p. 186.
16   Bieler, op. cit., p. 99.
17   Ibid., p. 99.
18   Ibid., p. 99.
19   Ray Simpson, *Soul Friendship: Celtic Insights into Spiritual Mentoring* (London: Hodder & Stoughton, 1999), p. 144.
20   Ibid., p. 142.
21   John Carey, *King of Mysteries: Early Irish Religious Writing* (Dublin: Four Courts Press, 2000), p. 139.
22   Ibid., p. 142.
23   Ibid., p. 142.
24   Ibid., p. 142.
25   Ibid., p. 241.

Chapter 11

1   Marcus J. Borg, *Jesus: Uncovering the Life, Teachings and Relevance of a Religious Revolutionary* (San Francisco: HarperCollins, 2006), p. 176.
2   Ibid., p. 176.
3   Joseph A. Grassi, *Informing the Future: Social Justice in the New Testament* (New York: Paulist Press, 2003), p. 265.
4   Ibid., p. 265.
5   Borg, op. cit., p. 175.

6   Joseph A. Grassi, *Peace on Earth: Roots and Practices from Luke's Gospel* (Minnesota: Liturgical Press, 2004), p. 147.
7   Ibid., p. 148.
8   Edward C. Sellner, *Wisdom of the Celtic Saints* (Notre Dame: Ave Maria Press, 1993), p. 163. The story is adapted from Sellner.
9   Richard Sharpe (trans.), *Adamnan of Iona: Life of St Columba* (London: Penguin, 1995), p. 194.
10   Ibid., pp. 178–80.
11   Ibid., p. 181.
12   Ibid., p. 175.
13   Edward C. Sellner, *Stories of the Celtic Soul Friends* (New York: Paulist Press, 2004), p. 103.
14   Liam De Paor, *St Patrick's World* (Dublin: Four Courts Press, 1993), p. 212, from Cogitosus's Life of St Brigid.
15   Sellner, op. cit., pp. 104–5.
16   John Carey, *King of Mysteries: Early Irish Religious Writings* (Dublin: Four Courts Press, 2000), p. 231.
17   Ibid., p. 239.
18   Uinseann Ó Máidín, *The Celtic Monk: Rules and Writings of Early Irish Monks* (Michigan: Cistercian Publications, 1996), p. 21.
19   Robert Van de Weyer, *Celtic Fire: An Anthology of Celtic Christian Literature* (London: Darton, Longman & Todd, 1990), p. 99.
20   Ibid., p. 100.
21   Ibid., p. 101.
22   B. R. Rees, *Pelagius: Life and Letters* (Woodbridge, Suffolk: Boydell Press, 1998), pp. 130–1.
23   Ibid., p. 119.
24   Robert Van de Weyer, *The Letters of Pelagius: Celtic Soul Friend* (Evesham: Arthur James, 1995), p. 19.
25   Ibid., p. 19.

Chapter 12
1   Bart D. Ehrman, *Whose Word Is It? The Story Behind Who Changed the New Testament and Why* (New York: Continuum, 2006), p. 178.
2   Ibid., p. 180.
3   Carol L. Meyers, Toni Craven and Ross Shepard Kraemer (eds), *Women in Scripture* (Michigan: Eerdmans, 2000), p. 135.
4   Karen Jo Torjesen, *When Women Were Priests: Women's Leadership in the Early Church and the Scandal of Their Subordination in the Rise of Christianity* (San Francisco: Harper, 1995), p. 33.
5   Ibid., p. 33.
6   John Dominic Crossan, *God and Empire: Jesus Against Rome Then and Now* (San Francisco: HarperCollins, 2007), p. 173.
7   Ehrman, op. cit., p. 181.
8   Crossan, op. cit., p. 174.
9   Ehrman, op. cit., p. 181.
10   Ibid., p. 182.
11   Crossan, op. cit., pp. 176–7.
12   Lisa M. Bitel, *Land of Women: Tales of Sex and Gender from Early Ireland* (New York: Cornell University Press, 1996), p. 1.
13   Peter Berresford Ellis, *Celtic Women: Women in Celtic Society and Literature* (London: Constable, 1995), p. 13.
14   Bitel, op. cit., p. 82.
15   Ibid., p. 82.

16   Ibid., p. 82.
17   Mary Condren, *The Serpent and the Goddess: Women, Religion and Power in Celtic Ireland* (San Francisco: Harper & Row, 1989), p. 54.
18   Ibid., p. 54.
19   Warren Bardsley, *Against the Tide: The Story of Adamnan of Iona* (Glasgow: Wild Goose Publications, 2006), pp. 108–9. The quotation is from Ní Dhonnchadha, Máirín from her chapter in *Adamnan at Birr* (Four Courts Press, 2001).
20   Peter Cherici, *Celtic Sexuality: Power, Paradigms and Passion* (London: Duckworth, 1995), p. 139.
21   Ibid., p. 139.
22   Michael Richter, *Medieval Ireland: The Enduring Tradition* (Dublin: Gill & Macmillan, 1988), p. 92.
23   Christina Harrington, *Women in a Celtic Church: Ireland 450–1150* (Oxford University Press, 2002), p. 272. What follows in this section owes much to Harrington's writing on Eve in Irish literature.
24   Ibid., p. 274.
25   Ibid., p. 275.
26   Ibid., p. 276.
27   See Chapter 7, 'Marginalised Women: The Struggle for Justice'.

Chapter 13

1   Seán McDonagh, *Climate Change: The Challenge To Us All* (Dublin: Columba Press, 2007), p. 11.
2   Ibid., p. 7.
3   Ibid., p. 8.
4   Ibid., pp. 10–11.
5   Douglas John Hall, *The Stewardship of Life in the Kingdom of Death* (Grand Rapids: Eerdmans, 1985), p. 68.
6   Oliver Davies (trans.), *Celtic Spirituality* (New York: Paulist Press, 1999), p. 40.
7   Mary Low, *Celtic Christianity and Nature: Early Irish and Hebridean Traditions* (Edinburgh: Edinburgh University Press, 1996), p. 10.
8   Ibid., p. 11.
9   Ibid., pp. 11–12.
10   Thomas Kinsella (trans.), *The Táin* (Oxford: Oxford University Press, 1970), p. 101.
11   Ibid., p. 111.
12   Low, op. cit., p. 18.
13   Eileen Conn and James Stewart (eds), *Visions of Creation* (Alresford: Godsfield Press, 1995), p. 23.
14   Davies, op. cit., p. 427. The text of the homily on John's Prologue is found on pp. 411–32.
15   Ibid., p. 420.
16   Conn and Stewart, op. cit., p. 29.
17   Ibid., p. 29.
18   Ibid., p. 30.
19   Davies, op. cit., p. 58.
20   Low, op. cit., p. 170. The quotation is from Meyer's translation of the Law of Adamnan.
21   Ibid., p. 171.
22   Ibid., p 180.
23   Ibid., p 181.
24   Ibid., p 181.
25   Ibid., p 181.
26   Ibid., p 182.

Chapter 14

1   J. Milburn Thompson, *Justice and Peace: A Christian Primer* (Maryknoll, NY: Orbis Books, 2003), p. 29.

2   Miguel A. De La Torre, *Doing Christian Ethics from the Margins* (Maryknoll, NY: Orbis Books, 2004), p. 32.

3   Ibid., p. 56.

4   David W. Augsburger, *Hate-Work: Working Through the Pain and Pleasures of Hate* (Louisville, KY: Westminster John Knox Press, 2004), p.203. The various forms of justice have been adapted from Augsburger, pp. 201–3.

5   De La Torre, op. cit., p. 263.

6   Enrique Nardoni. *Rise Up, O Judge: A Study of Justice in the Biblical World* (Peabody, MA: Hendrickson, 2004), p. 57.

7   Ibid., p. 105.

8   Glen H. Stassen and Donna P. Gushee, *Kingdom Ethics: Following Jesus in Contemporary Context* (Downers Grove, IL: Inter-Varsity Press, 2003), p. 25. This work provides a comprehensive treatment of the basis for the Reign of God in the book of Isaiah. The key texts from Isaiah are: 9: 1–7, 11; 24: 14 to 25: 12; 26; 31: 1 to 32: 20; 33; 40: 1–11; 42: 1 to 44: 8; 49; 51: 1 to 52: 12; 52: 13 to 53: 12; 54; 56; 60; 61–2.

9   Ibid., p. 349.

10   Ibid., p. 349.

11   Ibid., p. 357.

12   Ibid., p. 362.

13   Richard J. Woods, *The Spirituality of the Celtic Saints* (Maryknoll, NY: Orbis Books, 2000), pp. 163–4.

14   Thomas O'Loughlin. *Discovering Saint Patrick* (London: Darton, Longman & Todd, 2005). Quotations from the Letter are from the version in O'Loughlin, pp. 173–83. The paragraphs are in parenthesis and referenced in the text of this chapter.

15   Woods, op. cit., p. 164. The quote is from Thomas Cahill, *How the Irish Saved Civilization* (New York: Doubleday, 1995), p. 114. Cahill's book is generally an overstatement of Irish Celtic Christians' contribution to Europe and there is some exaggeration in his claim for Patrick.

16   Ibid., This story is alluded to on p. 164.

17   Thomas O'Loughlin. *Celtic Theology: Humanity, World and God in Early Irish Writings* (London: Continuum, 2000), p. 70.

18   Ibid., p. 72.

19   Richard Sharpe (trans.), *Adamnan of Iona: Life of St Columba* (London: Penguin, 1995), p. 152.

20   Oliver Davies (trans.), *Celtic Spirituality* (New York: Paulist Press, 1999), p. 357.

21   Ibid., p. 357.

22   Ibid., pp. 357–8.

23   Ibid., p. 357.

24   Ibid., p. 39.

25   Ibid., p. 235.

26   Ibid., p. 236.

27   Ibid., p. 236.

28   Woods, op. cit., p. 30.

29   Davies, op. cit., p. 391.

30   Ibid., p. 393.

31   Ibid., p. 396.

32   Ibid., p. 402.

33   Ibid., p. 402.

34   Ibid., p. 387.

Chapter 15

1   Paul Bew, *Ireland: The Politics of Enmity 1789-2006* (Oxford: Oxford University Press, 2007), p. 521.
2   Ibid., p. 537.
3   Ibid., p. 541.
4   Ibid., pp. 548–9.
5   Ulrich Duchrow and Gerhard Liedke, *Shalom: Biblical Perspectives on Creation, Justice and Peace* (Geneva: World Council of Churches Publications, 1987), p. 54.
6   Walter Brueggemann, *Peace* (St Louis: Chalice Press, 2001), p. 14.
7   Ibid., p. 15.
8   Ibid., p. 15.
9   Ibid., p. 16.
10   Ibid., p. 19.
11   John Dominic Crossan, *God and Empire: Jesus Against Rome, Then and Now* (San Francisco: HarperCollins, 2007), pp. 24–5.
12   Ibid., p. 141; see also p. 29 for the alternative programmatic themes.
13   Ibid., p. 141.
14   Thomas O'Loughlin, *Celtic Theology: Humanity, World and God in Early Irish Writing* (London: Continuum, 2000), p. 70.
15   Dáithí Ó hÓgáin, *The Lore of Ireland: An Encyclopaedia of Myth, Legend and Romance* (Cork: Collins Press, 2006), p. 137.
16   Ibid., pp. 137–8.
17   Thomas Kinsella (trans.), *The Táin* (Oxford: Oxford University Press, 2002 edn), pp. 62–3.
18   Ó hÓgáin, op. cit., p. 238.
19   Ibid., p. 240. The Fionn cycle of stories is dealt with on pp. 238–49, showing the extent of the development of Fionn stories over 1,000 years, and portraying much ferocity and violence, reflecting the violent culture of Ireland from medieval times.
20   Lisa M. Bitel, *Isle of the Saints: Monastic Settlement and Christian Community in Early Ireland* (Cork: Cork University Press, 1993), p. 147.
21   Ibid., p. 148.
22   Ibid., p. 149.
23   Ibid., p. 149.
24   Ibid., p. 150.
25   Ibid., p. 150.
26   Ibid., p. 150.
27   Ibid., p. 151.
28   Ó hÓgáin, op. cit., p. 82.
29   Ibid., p. 83.
30   Richard Sharpe (trans.), *Adamnan of Iona: Life of Columba* (London: Penguin, 1995), p. 176.
31   Oliver Davies (trans.), *Celtic Spirituality* (New York: Paulist Press, 1999), p. 57.
32   Ibid., p. 406.
33   Ibid., p. 410.
34   Bitel, op. cit., pp. 155–6.

Chapter 16

1   D. H. Farmer (ed.), *The Age of Bede* (London: Penguin, 1998), p. 11.
2   Ibid., pp. 11–12.
3   Fay Sampson, *Visions and Voyages: The Story of Our Celtic Heritage* (London: Triangle Books, 1998), p. 75.
4   Chet Raymo, *Climbing Brandon: Science and Faith on Ireland's Holy Mountain* (Dingle: Brandon, 2004), p. 7.

5   Ibid., p. 8.

6   Farmer, op. cit., p. 235. The complete text of the Voyage of St Brendan can be read in Farmer, pp. 233–67.

7   Ibid., p. 265.

8   Ibid., p. 266.

9   Ibid., p. 267.

10   Myles Dillon and Nora Chadwick, *The Celtic Realms: The History and Culture of the Celtic Peoples from Pre-History to the Norman Invasion* (London: Phoenix Press, 1967), p. 288.

11   Ibid., pp. 289–90.

12   Ibid., p. 307.

13   Frank Welsh, *The Four Nations: A History of the Und Kingdom* (London: HarperCollins, 2003), p. 34.

14   Dillan and Chadwick, op. cit., p. 312.

15   Bernard Meehan, *The Book of Kells: An Illustrated Introduction to the Manuscript in Trinity College Dublin* (London: Thames & Hudson, 1994), p. 89.

16   Roger Stalley, *Irish High Crosses* (Dublin: Town House & Country House, 1996), p. 5.

17   Peter Harbinson, *Irish High Crosses: With the Figure Sculptures Explained* (Drogheda: Boyne Valley Honey Co., 1994), p. 13.

18   Welsh, op. cit., p. 35.

19   Stalley, op. cit., p. 13.

20   Harbinson, op. cit., p. 38.

21   Ibid., p. 96.

22   Ibid., p. 98.

23   Angie Debo, *A History of the Indians of the Und States* (London: The Folio Society, 2003), p. 2. The book was originally published by the University of Oklahoma Press, USA in 1970, has gone through various printings and remains the definitive history.

24   John O'Donahue, *Divine Beauty: The Invisible Embrace* (London: Bantam Books, 2003), p. 23.

25   Ibid., p. 22.

26   Ibid., pp. 21–2.

Glossary

Anthropocentric
- A human-centred approach to life and existence.
- Life, values and needs are measured from an exclusively human point of view.
- The human as the most important and central life form in the universe.

Archetypal
- The most typical example of a particular kind of person or the original model for all that follows.
- Brigid is the archetypal Celtic saint.

Chalcedon/Chalcedonian
- The Council of Chalcedon met in 452 ce in response to controversies and specific historical problems that were raised in the historical contexts of the fourth and fifth centuries.
- The Chalcedonian Creed is one of the classical doctrinal summaries of who Jesus is, seeking to balance an exaggerated emphasis on the divinity of Jesus.
- Chalcedon proposed that Jesus was one person with two natures, truly divine and truly human, of the same nature as God and of the same nature as human beings.

Celtic Seasons
- The seasons were celebrated at eight points in the year.
- The solar festivals were:
  - ✤ winter solstice – 20–23 December;
  - ✤ summer solstice – 20–23 June;
  - ✤ spring equinox – 20–23 March;
  - ✤ autumn equinox – 20–23 September.
- Solstice is Latin for *'the standing of the sun'*.
- The lunar festivals were:
  - ✤ samhain – 31 October or 1 November;
  - ✤ imbolc – 1 February;
  - ✤ beltane – 1 May;
  - ✤ lughnasadh – 1 August (or Lammas).
- These were often known as fire festivals.

Cosmology
- The science of the origin and development of the universe.
- A theory of the origin of the universe.
- The ninth-century Irish theologian John Eruigena articulated a cosmology in which God is the supreme cause of all things, therefore the created world is a disclosure of God, who is also unknowable in the essence of Godself.
- Contemporary cosmology is often articulated as a scientific story or evolutionary approach,

which does not rule out God-talk, though it does change the way we talk about God and image God.

Constantinian Era
○ With the Edict of Milan in 313 CE, Constantine the emperor Christianised the empire, more for reasons of political stability than spirituality.
○ Faith became identified with politics, religion with politicised power and throne and altar became inseparable.
○ The constitutional collusion between church and state became the dominant norm for western faith and politics creating state churches which in turn legitimised the state, blessed its armies and wars and structured itself after models of political power.
○ The Constantinian era or Christendom dominated Europe until the mid-twentieth century when it began to collapse leading to the death of Christendom and a major challenge to institutional churches increasingly at the edge of society rather than the centre.

Double Predestination
○ A theology taught by Augustine of Hippo in north Africa in which God had predestined or elected some to salvation and predestined or elected others to damnation.
○ The Reformed theologian John Calvin also taught this theology, both wanted to emphasise the greatness of God's sovereign grace and glory.
○ Others like Pelagius had moral difficulty with this theology and its view of God.

Doxology
○ *Doxa* is Greek for glory and *logos* is Greek for word.
○ The word of glory or praise to God.
○ The act of giving glory, worship and praise to God for God's gracious activity in all of life.
○ Many of the Psalms of Israel are poetic expressions of such praise, e.g. Psalm 95.

Eight Capital Sins of Cassian
○ John Cassian was a European greatly influenced by the monastic movement which began in the Egyptian desert.
○ Eight capital or principal sins feature often in his writings, though the last probably originated in Egyptian desert spirituality.
○ The capital sins were:
  ✤ gluttony;
  ✤ lust;
  ✤ covetousness;
  ✤ sorrow;
  ✤ anger;
  ✤ slackness;
  ✤ vainglory;
  ✤ pride.
○ There are variations on the list but these capital sins are found in many of the Irish penitentials. e.g. Columbanus.

Eschatology
○ Traditionally the Christian doctrine of the end or last things.
○ There is eschatology in St Patrick's confession where he appears to believe that he belonged to the last days, and when the gospel was preached to the ends of the Earth, i.e. Ireland, the end would be imminent.
○ Patrick may not have been so literal but rather interpreted the collapse of Roman Britain as the end of an era opening up possibilities for the kingdom or reign of God.

○ Today eschatology is understood as God's ultimate vision of things, e.g. kingdom or a new heaven and earth.

○ Eschatology is something of this kingdom or newness breaking into the present and is the vision and motivation for people of faith to co-operate with God in making the ultimate vision or purpose real in the here and now.

Eulogists

○ People who make a speech or write a piece in which they praise someone or something highly.

○ The Celtic hagiographers wrote their Lives in praise of particular saints, highlighting their virtues and actions as models of faith and holiness, e.g. Cogitosus on Brigid.

Excommunication

○ When a person is officially banned from the sacraments and services of the Christian Church.

○ Patrick's Letter to the soldiers of Coroticus was a public letter of excommunication.

○ Coroticus could not murder and enslave the innocent with impunity or without consequences.

○ Patrick believed that his actions excluded him from Christian worship and he declared it as official.

Hagiography

○ A genre of writing in the Celtic Christian tradition which produced Lives of saints.

○ The literature is not biographical or historical but mythical and legendary.

○ Healing and nature miracles abound, which are primarily intended to model the saint on Jesus or in imitation of Jesus.

○ The point of the Lives is to present saints as models of holiness to inspire later Christians and encourage them to imitate the saint in holiness of life.

○ Hagiography is creative and imaginative storytelling for the faithful.

Hebrew Scriptures

○ The preferred description for what used to be called the Old Testament.

○ Reference to Old and New Testaments tended to suggest that the latter had superseded the former, that the New was superior to the Old and that Christianity had superseded and was better than Judaism.

○ This was often a form of anti-Judaism and fed into anti-Semitism which contributed to the horror of the twentieth-century Jewish Holocaust.

○ Hebrew scriptures and Christian scriptures or testament is an attempt to be less insensitive and offensive to Jews.

Honour-Shame Culture

○ At the heart of the legal institutions of early Irish society.

○ The culture underpinned that fast for justice where the victim fasted outside the privileged offender's home from sunset to sunrise.

○ If the offender disregarded the fast and refused to pay, he lost his honour.

○ Compensation for a wrong was estimated according to damage suffered, and according to the rank of the injured party, the victim, which was known as the honour-price.

○ The most important aspect of the legal status of every freeman in Celtic society was his honour-price.

○ The culture was also part of the practice of hospitality, and was perceived as a code for honourable behaviour.

○ Inhospitality was described by the 'six sons of Dishonour' and included niggardliness, refusal and denial.

Jubilee

○ The name for a radical ethical-economic practice called for by Israel's Torah or Way of Life in Leviticus 25.

○ Every forty-nine years there was the year of release when land was returned to its original owners.

○ Other practice was in the release of debts and setting free of slaves.

○ The Jubilee underlined the redistribution of land and wealth as a radical economic alternative to the élitist-based economics surrounding Israel.

○ To live in covenant relationship with God was to live in a radical, ethically based, economic and political society.

○ Jubilee teaching is found in Deuteronomy, Nehemiah, especially in Isaiah 61: 1–4, Luke 4: 18–19 and in the essence of the Lord's Prayer in Matthew 6.

○ Jubilee was essentially about the practice of social justice.

Myth

○ Often misunderstood as fictitious, false belief, untrue or 'fairy tale'.

○ A profound and creative story attempting to explain the way things are, a why question, and expressing the deepest meaning of creation, life or history.

○ Not historically or literally true but profoundly true in a metaphoric or symbolic way.

○ Examples of myths are creation stories which almost every culture possesses. These are the Babylonian Enuma Elish and Genesis 1, the Galgamish Epic, a flood story, and modelled on it with a faith perspective the Noah story in Genesis 6–9.

○ We may not know whether a myth happened this way or not but it is true in a much deeper sense of being true.

○ Myths help us to appreciate that truth does not depend on being historical or literal, but that some of the deepest truth and meaning are expressed in the telling of creative and imaginary stories or through poetry as in Genesis 1.

○ See variations below on the connections between myth and theology, poetry and ethics.

Mythological Cycle

○ This is a collective term for stories in Irish literature that describe the activities of characters from the underworld.

○ The cycle consists of ancient Celtic myth and the characters met are Irish manifestations of the pantheon of Celtic gods.

○ The core story is about a battle between two supernatural groups, a theme also found in Norse and Greek myths.

○ The Irish conflict myth is between the divine Tuatha Dé Danann and the underworld Fomhóire and was written down in the eighth century.

○ The Surviving text is eleventh century and is known as the *Second Battle of Moytirra*, a furious battle between divine races or Celtic deities for the possession of Ireland.

○ The cycle is a myth about power and control and like many Irish myths portrays violence as a legitimate path to power over or domination.

○ It encapsulates the myth of redemptive violence that violence pays, achieves, defends or brings peace, a myth at the heart of modern Irish history.

Nicaea/Nicene

○ The Council of Nicaea met in 325 CE and affirmed that what we encounter in Jesus, God's Word or Son, is not less than God the Father.

○ The incarnate one is of the very same stuff as God.

○ The stress on the divinity of Jesus was so strong that his humanity was often lost.

○ Controversies continued and eventually led to the Council of Chalcedon in 451 CE.

○ The Council of Nicaea produced the Nicene Creed, still used by many churches today, though expressed in Greek thought-forms and language reflecting specific historical problems from a particular historical context.

○ Today many feel that the classical formulations require reinterpretation and that key to this is an imaginative, historical construction of Jesus, i.e. Jesus in his Jewishness and humanity.

○ Whatever Nicaea and Chalcedon were trying to say in their own historical particularity, twenty-first century people will find God through the humanity of Jesus

Orthopraxis

○ The word has connection with orthodoxy which means correct or right belief, or traditionally accepted beliefs.

○ Who determines what is traditional or which interpretation of traditional is norm are burning questions, complex and not easily answered.

○ Others hold that more important than orthodoxy is orthopraxis, which means correct practice or right action.

○ What we do is more important than what we believe, though the two are not unconnected.

○ Celtic Christians were not primarily concerned with correct doctrine or right beliefs, but were committed to the practice of faith, the doing of justice, building of peace and offering of hospitality.

Panentheism

○ Early Celtic theologians, such as John Eriugena, are often suspected of being pantheists which suggests that God is everything and everything is God, e.g. the wooden chair or table is God or the large deposit of ice-age rock is God.

○ Celtic theologians and even their pre-Christian druidic priests were more subtle.

○ The subtle difference is that God is in everything and everything is in God, hence the more modern word to describe their position, pan-en-theism.

○ Panentheism in the theology of Eriugena and other Celtic thinkers and poets perceives God in everything and at the same time believes that God is other than creation, and is both above and within all things.

○ In panentheism God is both transcendent and immanent, beyond and within all creation.

○ It is the 'withinness' of God, God in all things and all things in God, that makes practical sense for twenty-first-century people of faith and makes Celtic creation theologians so relevant.

Parousia

○ The Greek word used in the Christian scriptures was borrowed from the world of the Roman Empire and was the metaphor to describe the arrival of the emperor as supreme and in power to some part of his empire.

○ Early Christians borrowed this word and used it as an eschatological metaphor, a colourful and subversive way of speaking of God's end-coming in Jesus to bring all things into peace and harmony

○ The word is used metaphorically and not literally, and is a subversive metaphor announcing the truth that the Roman emperor does not have the last word in human history.

○ At the same time the power of the God who will come in Christ is not military, coercive or dominating power, but giving, serving power with, in contrast to power over.

○ Parousia power and empire, kingdom or reign are radically and ethically different and suggest a very different style of leadership and faithful social living in the present.

○ Patrick may or may not have had a parousia theology believing that the literal end of the world would take place in his lifetime.

○ If he did believe this then he and a literalistic Paul were wrong, but they too may have been more subtle and metaphoric in their belief.

Penitentials

○ The leading Celtic saints and founders of monasteries produced penitentials, each of which differed and was unique to the particular community.

○ The Irish penitentials were handbooks of Celtic confessors and were developed in Ireland in the sixth century and later brought to Europe.

○ Irish monks engaged in a rigorous quest for holiness, therefore they had need for a penitential system if penance was to provide a way to holiness of life.

○ The penitentials are heavily characterised by sexual anxiety and a mistrust or dislike of the body, which also expresses itself in misogyny or hatred of women.

○ At the same time the penitentials are strong on the role of the soul-friend or anamchara, a person to whom one opened one's heart in trust and honesty and who was a wounded healer.

○ The Irish penitentials were, in contrast to the practice of mainland Europe, used in private and saw sin as disease or the breaking of relationships and were therefore a form of healing dialogue and reconciliation.

○ Not only were Cassian's eight capital sins taken seriously, Cassian's 'principle of contraries' or cure by contraries enabled an approach to penance which was curative and medicinal.

○ The key Irish penitentials are those of Cummean, Finnian, Columba and Columbanus.

○ The penitentials have rich affiliations with scripture and drew deep from its well of spiritual direction and penance.

Praxis

○ It is practice as distinguished from theory, the action rather than what we believe as doctrine or theory.

○ It is also more in that praxis is reflection on practice and practice that leads to reflection.

○ In this sense Celtic monks, contemporary clergy, peacebuilders and activists for justice are reflective practitioners.

○ They reflect on their experience and action and allow theory to emerge from their reflective practice.

○ Early Celtic Christians produced very few theological propositions or doctrinal theories; rather they were active people who prayed and reflected on their action and then expressed a practical, earthy theology.

○ Reflective practitioners produce practical ethics of peacebuilding, environmental care, social justice, hospitality and gender equality.

Psalms of Lament

○ These poems are central to the faith and prayer of ancient Israel, comprising of one-third of the book of Psalms.

○ It comes as a surprise that there are more Psalms of lament than Psalms of praise in Israel's song or prayer book.

○ Laments are prayers of protest or complaint often offered in a context of public crisis.

○ They are deeply honest, raw, at times savage and brutal, urgent and often desperate outbursts to God.

○ Lament is not an expression of polite faith but an angry outburst, even a cry for vengeance on some hated enemy, e.g. Psalm 137.

○ Psalms 39 and 88 are angry, demanding prayers with no hope of resolution and reflect an experience of the absence or silence of God.

○ Though such lament has almost disappeared from Christian worship with negative consequences, it was a natural and normal part of Israel's worship.

○ Lament is itself an act of faith and reflects Israel's understanding of faith as an ongoing argument with God, e.g. Book of Job.

○ Ultimately all the anger and longing for vengeance in real life experiences is for Israel, a cry for justice.

○ Lament is known in the Celtic tradition and the women in Celtic society were keeners or those who expressed public lament and so voiced the longing in Celtic society for justice.

Sacrilege

○ The treating of something sacred or highly valued with great disrespect, e.g. desecration of a grave, insulting Mohammed the prophet for Muslims and mocking the death of Jesus for Christians.

○ Patrick's strong language to Coroticus following his murder and enslavement of innocent Irish Christians suggested an act of sacrilege against the image of God in human life.

Synoptic Gospels

○ The Gospels of Matthew, Mark and Luke suggesting a synopsis of shared material.

○ The consensus is that Mark is the primary source and that Matthew and Luke borrowed from Mark, though each arranged the material according to their own distinctive theological emphases.

○ Matthew and Luke each had material exclusive to themselves known as Special M and Special L.

○ The description of John's Gospel as a more spiritual gospel is misleading in that it suggests that the Synoptics are much less or not at all spiritual.

○ The Synoptic Gospels are not biographies or historical accounts but profoundly theological interpretations of Jesus, each with their distinctive theological themes, which also means that they cannot be harmonised.

Theoethical

○ Ethics as a way of living with a theological basis and perspective.

○ The Celtic stories and Lives are often theoethical in that they express a practical way of living in relation to the poor, creation or making peace.

○ Israel's foundational story of the Exodus from Egypt is theoethical and became the basis for Israel's response to the injustices and oppression of its own leaders and to the superpowers or empires which dominated its existence.

Theopoetic

○ The imaginative use of poetry to express theology or God-talk.

○ Recognises that when we attempt to talk about God we can only use poetic language or speak in metaphors because God is incomprehensible mystery and human experience, and language is always limited.

○ Israel's creation theology was expressed in imaginative poetry such as Genesis 1 and Psalms 96 and 104.

Theomythical

○ Recognises the powerful use of myth to express theological insights and articulate God-talk. (See myth above.)

○ Acknowledges that God-talk goes far beyond a literal use of language and historical events.

○ Israel's foundational story is the Exodus from Egypt and as told in the Bible is not literal history but a theological interpretation of something which happened, but is told in a theomythical way.

○ As with all myth there is an attempt to express liberating truth for living, a truthful norm which can be retold and reinterpreted in different situations of oppression and injustice.

○ The theomythical Exodus story goes through this process in different parts of the Bible itself, and the Book of Revelation is yet another theomythical telling of the Exodus story.

Theophany

○ Refers to a disclosure or manifestation of God to humans.

○ The story of God's disclosure to Moses in the burning bush in the book of Exodus is a theophany.

○ Moses realises that God will empower him to share in the divine purpose of liberating justice.
○ Patrick's dream in which he hears the voice of the Irish calling him back to Ireland with the humanising story of God in Christ is a theophany, a disclosure of God.

Via dolorosa
○ Refers to the way through Jerusalem taken by Jesus as he journeyed to his public execution on a cross.
○ Used metaphorically to describe the painful journey experienced by a person who offers forgiveness to a perpetrator of crime or harm against them
○ The way of the cross, often spiritual and emotional suffering, when one denies or loses oneself for the sake of a higher good.

Index

Note: page numbers in italics denote maps, illustrations or figures